MISFITS AND MISSIONARIES

A School for Black Dropouts

The City
& Society

a series of books edited by **GERALD D. SUTTLES**
University of Chicago

MISFITS and MISSIONARIES

Jon Wagner

 SAGE Publications   Beverly Hills / London

For information address:

SAGE PUBLICATIONS, INC.
275 South Beverly Drive
Beverly Hills, California 90212

SAGE PUBLICATIONS LTD
28 Banner Street
London EC1Y 8QE

Printed in the United States of America

Library of Congress Cataloging in Publication Data

Wagner, Jon.
    Misfits and missionaries.

    (The City and society ; 2)
    1. Problem children—Education—Illinois—Chicago.
2. Afro-American dropouts—Illinois—Chicago.
3. Juvenile deliquency—Illinois—Chicago.
4. Mission Academy.   I. Title.   II. Series.
LC4801.W3   371.9'3'0977311   77-22316
    ISBN 0-8039-0722-2
    ISBN 0-8039-0723-0 pbk.

FIRST PRINTING

Contents

Foreword

Since the 1950s, America has experienced progressive disenchantment with the potentials of the school as an instrument of social reform. The school systems of the great cities, many of them once centers for professional practice, increasingly came to be seen as primitive bureaucracies incapable of adapting to a great growth in the numbers of poor and minority students. During a dramatic period of innovative activity in the 1960s, it seemed possible that the schools might be fundamentally altered so as to improve the situation of the disadvantaged. This hope died, however, as innovations proved ephemeral, attempts at integration failed, resources problems became more acute, and the middle masses continued to leave the cities. Moreover, even where incremental improvements could be made in the city schools, the socioeconomic payoff of improved schooling was not what had been anticipated. The "action" had gone elsewhere—to higher levels of education in a vastly expanded college system and to the jobs that had also moved to the suburbs.

To some unknown degree, social scientists have contributed to the disenchantment with education, not only in the city, but at large. They have done so—if unhappily—by demonstrating that across large samples of American public schools, much more of the variation in how pupils perform academically is explained by their social backgrounds than by variations in the quality of the schools they attend. In retrospect, one should expect such a finding, given the high degree of standardization (and randomization of teacher assignment and performance) in the public education system and recognizing the overlap of school quality and pupil socioeconomic status. Dialogue over this finding is healthy when it shows the limits to the mythology that education could single-handedly eliminate poverty or break the nexus of social class advantage. Reaction to the finding is destructive if it leads to a tacit assumption that variations in the character of the school cannot have effects worth the bother to study.

What is deeply needed is study of schools serving the disadvantaged that differ in some radical ways from the conventional school. And we need study that is excellent both technically and theoretically—avoiding both the superficiality of reliance on handy quantitative measures seen in most educational research and the unassimilated anecdotage of the self-confessional "I taught in the ghetto and it was groovy (or it was awful)" genre. Jon Wagner's study of Mission Academy meets this need, and many others, in extraordinary fashion. The Academy was an exciting place to work and study, a radical effort to provide a second chance for high school dropouts in Chicago's West Side ghetto. The school's experience makes it a prime object of study because, at the minimum of the reality principle, it *did* operate in radically different ways from the public schools, it *did* take the "worst kind" of students and enable many of them to get into college, and, as Wagner shows, many of its staff participants *were* true reformers.

The book itself is a multifaceted event. The volume is extremely rich and in no way shall I attempt to encapsulate its points comprehensively. Wagner writes as a full participant turned observer and analyst, struggling with the greatest seriousness to be as honest and realistic about the Academy as possible. In his view, there is no way to avoid the realities of the role of education in sorting and selecting the young into the stratification order. The academy starts with losers and creates its own further winners and losers. But this reality is not to be allowed to disillusion the reform in the name of dismantling capitalism, nor to demean the modest successes that can be achieved. As Wagner shows, both the students and the teachers are misfits who to a greater or lesser degree can come to help each other on with life.

Similarly, there is no "formula for innovation," no honest and realistic way to solve once and for all the dilemmas of the enterprise—the cultural, organizational, political, and moral dilemmas that arise again and again. Thus, it can never be fully settled how radical versus conventional the school is to be, either in terms of its curriculum, pedagogy, and order-keeping or in terms of its image in a suspicious community. Nor can it be settled once and for all how to balance an ideology sharing power with students against staff peroga-tives, how "Black" the curriculum and staff need to be, or how teachers are to win the esteem of their colleagues and their students both. These and other matters produce recurrent ambiguity, confusion, and cycles of trust (at "normal" times) and rampant mistrust (in "crises"). The attention of the actors cycles from issue to issue in a process Wagner captures beautifully as "serial advocacy." Yet in all this Wagner finds a creative tension; the idea seems to be that were there to be solutions, there would no longer be an experiment.

It follows that Wagner's organization theory is complex and subtle. He starts with an assumption that there are multiple realities and sees the central problem as the social construction of the school. He partakes of the tradition of analyzing organizational structure and mission, but the organization is never reified except when the actors so treat it. Action is voluntaristic, and activity is not necessarily integrated or consistent. The organization can live with contradictory goals. What others often treat as variables of organiza-tional structure Wagner tends to treat as problems that may or may not be salient. It follows that processes are more important than structures, but such processes (e.g., routinization) are in no sense inevitable. Wagner's refusal to force his data into natural history phases is as productive as it is honest.

The volume then stands as a model for research on the social psychology of organizations that resists the unwarranted imposition of macrosociological categories. This does not inhibit Wagner from addressing broad questions of theory and practice, however, and the volume has strong implications for those who would set up experiments for similar student populations. Thinking of the Mission Academy as a relative success, the reader will find it possible to extract attributes of the school that seem necessary for this to be the case. A brief initial list can be suggested:

(1) *Voluntarism.* Enrollment, attendance, and the amount of student work done were not coerced. This, of course, had an essential effect of self-selection; it also made the school attractive to the students when compared with the conventional school, and it gave the teachers immediate feedback as their enrollments fluctuated.

(2) *Pluralism of pedagogy.* A variety of teaching techniques was used, and while many students were engaged in political and socio-emotional discussions, others studied individual programs in English and mathematics. It was critical that several of the learning alternatives gave specific success experiences (diplomas, passing high-school equivalency examinations, admission to college, positive feedback) to both students and teachers.

(3) *High staff commitment.* The staff members came from a variety of backgrounds, they worked together to learn to teach in an open way more professionalized teachers would not have, and they thereby reinforced their commitments to reform. An extremely high level of energy and commitment was necessary to live with the ambiguities and conflicts of the school.

(4) *View of the student.* How one constructs the student, Wagner suggests, shapes how one constructs the school. The students may be seen as pained or revolutionary young people in need of therapy or forum, when in reality they are ready to be self-disclosing only when the instructor carefully negotiates trust. Or the students may be seen as ready to respond only to materials that are "culturally relevant." As Wagner sees it, a key to the Academy was for the faculty to learn to construct the students as young people to whose intelligence one should appeal.

Such attributes stand in marked contrast to those of the conventional school. Thus to understand the Academy is to learn as well about the whole of American education. And to understand the relationship between the Academy and conventional schools is to learn about social reform.

— David Street
University of Illinois at Chicago Circle

Acknowledgments

I owe my greatest debt to the subjects of my study, the characters described in this book. They took me places I had never been before, and the world we shared stands as an intellectual, moral, and experiential watershed in my own life. I feel quite lucky to have known them all.

In addition, I would like to thank those who guided my dissertation research—which led to this book—at the University of Chicago: Jim Fenessey and Robert Dreeben were generous and thoughtful in commenting on my work; Morris Janowitz asked the right questions at the right time and has been a continuing source of assistance and encouragement; and Dave Street took the time to help me understand what I was doing, insuring that I would do it better. During my graduate training at Chicago, I was fortunate to receive a Special Humanities Fellowship. This provided me with financial support independent of the existing departmental research centers, for which I continue to be grateful.

Several people read earlier drafts of the manuscript and give me useful comments, for which I am thankful to John Schultz, Ruth Brandon, Paul Pekin, Jane Tuleja, and Barbara Graves. Others have helped in ways too numerous to mention, but I want to acknowledge the assistance given by Jerry Suttles, University of Chicago, and Rhoda Blecker, of Sage Publications, in preparing the manuscript, and that given by Doris Perry, Lynne Hollingsworth, the Conference, and my students in preparing myself to write it. I dedicate this book to my parents, Marge and Carl.

The passages dealing with "cultural relevance" (Chapter 7) have appeared previously as "Education and 'Black' Education: Some Remarks on Cultural Relevance," *School Review* 80 (August): 591-602. I thank the *School Review* and the University of Chicago Press for allowing it to be reprinted here.

—*J.W.*

Preface

This book describes the business and spirit of a school which was started in the late 1960s in order to provide a "second chance" for black high school dropouts. This was an "inner-city" school, and much of what happened there bears on the problems of urban schooling and the design of other institutions of urban social welfare. In addition, the school was designed not only to assist local dropouts, but to serve as a model for reform of conventional public schools. As a result, an account of the school is necessarily an account of an effort at social reform.

I ask the reader to keep these more general concerns in mind. My narrative recounts particulars in the lives of those involved with the school I studied. The larger story, of which these particulars are an important part, is the continuing drama of the American social order and deliberate attempts to change it.

–J.W.

Part I
Introduction

1

Missionaries, Misfits, and Social Reform

It is the summer of 1967, and it is Chicago. A young black man whom I shall call Lamont has just returned to his parents' house on the West Side after an eight-month stay at St. Charles reformatory.[1] This is neither the first time Lamont has been incarcerated nor the first time he has returned home. For the last four or five years he has spent roughly a third of his time in similar institutions of rehabilitative or punitive custody. A dropout of Derrick High School—his transcript shows less than two years' worth of courses completed —Lamont has just passed his eighteenth birthday.

Eighteen months later, we find Lamont not only in possession of a high school diploma, but also enrolled in a large western university, a predominantly white college where he has been elected freshman class delegate to the campus council.

In the same summer of 1967, Pud, another young black man, is on trial for first-degree murder. Another dropout from another high school in Chicago, by summer's end he is acquitted of the charge. While evidence in court shows that the victim died of knife wounds inflicted by Pud, it also shows that Pud acted only to defend himself after the victim viciously attacked him with a tire iron. Pud's school record shows even fewer credits than Lamont's. More important, tests show that his skills in math and reading are below the sixth grade level.

A year later we can find Pud on the street in the same hangouts he frequented in the summer of 1967. In between, however, he has learned to read, write, and do arithmetic equivalent to the ninth grade level.

If we look farther along the streets of Chicago in the summer of 1967, we find other high school dropouts. There is Sarah, a bright young black woman who has been dismissed from public school for reasons unknown to us. She becomes the "problem" student in an Upward Bound program at Northwestern University. There is Mose, pushed out of school with the label of "educable but mentally handicapped" (EMH). His language and arithmetic skills well below the fourth grade level, Mose spends his time hanging out with his friend Darnell and trying to repair broken radios he finds in the trash. There are also Pud's friends, a group of young black men whom Yablonsky might call a "near gang." Though lacking an official name, they have identified with a distinctive territorial area on the West Side, walking its streets and frequenting its pool halls, barbeque joints, and taverns.

And there are many others who have been kicked, pushed, eased, taken, cooled, helped, or pulled out of the city's high schools, both public and parochial. For some of these, our look into the future shows that something has happened. Like Lamont and Pud, they have "got more education." Mose and Darnell are both enrolled in colleges, a surprise not only to them, but also to their families and friends. Sarah has become an asset to Upward Bound rather than a problem. About a hundred other young blacks—both male and female, who have become acquainted with those mentioned above—have seen their skills in reading, writing, and arithmetic rise several grade levels, and a group of thirty has been fortunate enough to see these increased skills result in a high school equivalency diploma. We might well ask how this happened, for there is nothing usual about it.

The achievements of these students were notable; their failure in school was not. In the innards of large American cities, we find a large number of such "misfits," those for whom the urban high school does not work. In 1967, we would find these high school dropouts so numerous on the West Side of Chicago as to constitute a "misfit majority."[2] In contrast to the minority of students who were actually finishing high school at that time, these former students found their way into unskilled work, other social institutions, or the street, there to reinvent the fortunes of their mothers and fathers.

In some cases, these dropout students have passed through more schooling than did their parents, many of whom did not complete elementary school. But this is not a manifestation of successful upward mobility, for the additional schooling these young people receive only allows them to stand still relative to those from more socially and economically advantaged families. While high school dropouts make it through the elementary school their parents never completed, other students make it through the high schools their parents began but never finished. Others will even go on to colleges or graduate schools. They may all complete more schooling than did their parents, but when everyone takes one step up, relative positions stay the same.

Within the reality of increased levels of schooling completed and a relatively unchanging class structure, high school dropouts are "normal." The

American equality of opportunity ideal is so powerful, however, that failed or failing students are seen as a problem. Whether the crisis is formulated in terms of education, urban life, crime, or confidence, this misfit majority is seen to play a major role.

It should come as no surprise that these young people are frequently the targets of efforts at social reform. Old enough to be physical, moral, and electoral threats, high school dropouts are also seen by many as young enough to be saved. Our cultural definitions of adolescence encourage this "treatment" orientation. As a time between childhood and adulthood, adolescence is seen as a point of inflection in a person's life, a long moment where things can go either way.

With all this in mind, let us answer the question.

For Lamont, Pud, Sarah, and other young black men and women, life chances and social opportunity were given an extra boost by an attempt at educational reform that picked them as appropriate targets. In contrast to most high school dropouts—who end their formal education when they leave high school—these students made additional academic progress. What they shared, in doing this, was participation in an appropriately missionary effort at social reform, an alternative high school.

The school was called Mission Academy, and it was founded by an ecumenical organization of churches on Chicago's West Side.[3] While the leaders and members of these churches were responsible for starting the school and providing for its financial support, the missionary characteristics of the Academy were not overtly sectarian or even religious. The school was designed primarily to deal with the problem of high school dropouts in the West Park area. The ministers and church members who founded the Academy hoped that its success would encourage other communities to develop similar schools and provide conventional educational systems—the Chicago public school system in particular—with a model for reform.

Those who started the Academy viewed it as an "alternative school," one in which the stereotypes and procedures of conventional schooling would not apply. They rejected the practices of tracking, age grading, codes for student behavior, letter grades, and the sovereign powers of the school principal. They proposed instead a school in which there would be no rules other than those decided upon by students and faculty, one in which power and responsibility would be shared. The principal of Mission Academy told students and teachers, "This school belongs to the students, because it exists for them."

It might have been more appropriate for her to state that the school could not exist without them. The school did serve the students whose needs it was ostensibly designed to meet, but, as we shall see, it also served the missionaries who were there to meet them.

In 1967, while Lamont is doing time in the reformatory, Rider is putting in long hours at his small candy store. He spends one evening a week at "Story Workshop," an experience that nurtures his ambitions and skills as a writer. Eighteen months later, after working as a workshop director at the Academy, Rider has secured a position at a small private college in Chicago. He leaves the candy store business and makes his living teaching college English.

Cockey is another kind of dropout, one different from the students at the Academy, but a dropout all the same. He has left this seminary before graduation, and now he, too, takes his turn at the Academy as an English teacher. In the space of a year and a half he has become skilled at this trade and is in demand to teach and speak at schools around the city.

Judith, Hal, and I are also dropouts turned missionaries. Judith comes to the Academy because she has no desire to use her MAT (Master of Arts in Teaching) in history in the Chicago public schools. Hal arrives in mid-year; he was asked to leave the public school where he had been practice teaching—as part of his MAT program—and finds a new (if temporary) home at the Academy. I leave my graduate classrooms behind with hopes of "doing something productive in the real world."

All of us take our places within a school founded by those whose intentions are equally missionary. Nancy Sheen, after returning from a Peace Corps term in Africa, works to design, realize, and administer the Academy. She is the school's first principal, as well as Program Coordinator for the Mission churches. Rev. Keen, whose church is one of those active in Mission, is appointed by the Mission Council to be chairman of the advisory committee for the Academy. What begins for these two as meetings about how to improve a Mission tutoring program leads to the solicitation and administration of a $100,000 budget for the school and its program for educational reform. These activities take them around the country as well as to the offices of the influential, powerful, and interested.

Those who have taught and worked at the Academy clearly have done something for the school and the students who have attended it, but just as clearly the school and students have done something for them.

These reciprocal dynamics are a powerful feature of the Academy, and they are characteristic of other service activities as well. Our cultural ethos is such, however, that attention is usually focused on the impact of the staff or institution on the clients, patients, or students who are seen to be served by them. What this more limited view ignores is that staff and clients cooperate in creating order in these institutions, an order that has an impact on those "above" as well as on those "below." While the official resources of hospitals, schools, prisons, clinics, and other service establishments are extensive, these places depend on the patronage of clients for survival and stability. We have no schools without students, no prisons without prisoners, and no service staff without clients to be served. Served and server are reciprocal roles; participation in one of them demands that we find a partner willing to take on the other.

The Academy was designed, developed, and funded within this dominant cultural assumption about service. As a result, "success" for the school would mean that its students were helped several steps up the educational ladder, and this did indeed happen. The Academy encouraged and enabled black high school dropouts to increase their skills, achieve high school diplomas, and, in some cases, attend college. The school's history is a strong confirmation of institutional and systemic theories of the origins and persistence of educational inequalities.

As a result of the reciprocal dynamics of service, however, there are other Academy stories that parallel the "success story" mentioned above. There is the story of how moral order was created in a school started from scratch—a school that was unaccredited, noncompulsory, and founded on critiques of the existing moral order. There is the story of how the school survived in the surrounding community, how an organization of churches managed to bring in a predominantly white staff to work with black youth in a predominantly black community. There is the story of how these dynamics of race, educational aspirations, and community involvement temporarily upset the Academy's equilibrium—a crisis in which responsibility for the school's direction and design changed (or seemed to change) hands. And finally, there is the story of the school as a cultural event, a matrix of work, learning, and social reform in which people came together to make a change, bringing what they had and leaving with something other than what they brought.

Within the particulars of these stories can be seen more general images of urban dynamics, the social processes by which city residents build meaning into their lives. While the period covered here (1967-1969) was characterized by dramatic events, the concerns that these events reflected have not vanished. The crises of the Sixties are not necessarily the crises of the Seventies, but the conditions from which these earlier crises emerged have not ceased to exist, with the singular exception of the Vietnam war. Blacks and other minorities have neither disappeared nor found all the equal opportunities they fought for in the late Sixties, and students have not quit dropping out of school. In more general terms, the crises of social welfare programs have moved from acute to chronic, and there remains a profound lack of consensus about what is to be done with them.

The important context for this book, then, is a world with which we have become familiar rather than a world that no longer exists. The central ingredients which that world offers to this study are twofold: First is a conventional ideology about education, a set of beliefs about individual responsibility, academic achievement, and social status which focuses on the situations of schooling. It is an ideology in which education is seen as salvation. This being the case, we can expect to find missionaries working among those far from the cathedrals of learning. Second is an "all or nothing" romance about social change, the context in which the work of these missionaries is continually questioned and assessed by outsiders. With this romance comes a general reluctance to value social reforms of short duration or limited impact. Given this absolutist climate, and the criticisms it implies, it should come as no surprise that missionaries frequently adopt a defensive posture about the value of their work. While they know the impact to be more complex than "all or nothing," the support they get from those outside frequently depends on demonstrating that their program is indeed *the* answer to any of a number of social problems.

To understand Mission Academy, we need to move beyond these romances and examine schooling and social reform in alternative perspectives. We should keep in mind, for example, the dialectical sense in which experiments in social reform will always be incomplete, for they are inextricably tied to the conditions they try to change. In addition, most experiments will flourish only briefly; ambiguities between their internal dynamics and relations to the conventional order are usually too powerful to make survival anything but precarious. In addition, some may "fail" by the very terms in which they "succeed."

At Mission Academy, for example, an initial success with hard-core dropouts attracted students to the Academy who were already doing well in conventional schools, and these students made the school less attractive to the hard-core dropouts for whom it was intended (see pp. 18,19).

The compromise and complexity of reform practice which these dynamics suggest, however, justify neither conservatism nor pessimism. Social experiments can make fundamental changes in the lives of individuals, even if they do not deliver on the implicit promise of a new social order. They may also generate the energy and wisdom required to make certain as yet undefined adjustments in our path of cultural evolution.

Fatalism, naive surprise, or agony about the "failure" of past reforms—or the transient quality of present innovation—distracts us from whatever possibilities are present in this historical moment. We can hang onto efforts once made, or we can remain alert to the forms which subsequent generations of experiments might take. If we pursue this latter course, we may be able to create the resources and space needed for essential reforms yet to come. None of these will be the "last step," but one of them may well be an important "next step."

STUDYING MISSION ACADEMY

This book is based upon information I gathered during the eighteen months I was directly involved with Mission Academy as a teacher, researcher, and curriculum coordinator.[4] From September 1967 until February 1969 I took notes, completed formal and informal interviews, recorded the academic progress of students, and lived through that time in the school's history with other members of the Academy.

The chapters that follow describe the social dynamics that characterized the school, but there are certain features of its operation that ought to be clarified at the outset. During its first full academic year, the Academy served about eighty students for a total cost of $72,000, or about $900 per pupil. This was comparable to the cost per pupil in Chicago public high schools at the time, and Mission administrators saw this as proof that the Academy was a feasible solution to many of the ills besetting the public schools.[5]

Students attended the school to learn and to get credit for their learning. Although it was not accredited by the state and local superintendents of education, the Academy offered courses to prepare students for the test of General Educational Development (G.E.D.). Those who did well enough on this exam—it was administered by the state board of education—received an accredited high school equivalency diploma. In addition, Mission offered three diplomas of its own, each based on a student's cumulative performance, and most student work was directed toward these certificates.[6]

In addition to this incremental academic program, those at the Academy sought to develop a new approach to education, one that both emphasized students' abilities to design their own program of study and used elements of inner-city culture as curriculum material. This orientation, which at conventional schools would be considered "extracurricular," was central to offerings at the Academy. The school also experimented with programmed instructional materials, democratized classrooms, cooperative administration, mixed-media performances (designed to aid students in developing collective spirit), and organizational advocacy of programs for change in the immediate community.

The Academy began its operation in February 1967 on a "pilot phase." The school recessed for the summer months and reopened again the following September for a year that might be entitled its "experimental phase." The experimental phase lasted until June 1968, when once again the Academy recessed for the summer. During this recess, however, a program was offered to help community residents prepare for the G.E.D. exam. The building was open four nights a week as a school, and recent Academy graduates served as teachers. Beginning in September 1968, the Academy began its "demonstration phase," a stage of development that has continued to the present date.[7]

Currently, the school offers a "fully recognized" curriculum for 200 full-time students a year. Mission publications indicate that as many as 65% of the Academy's graduates now go on to college and that students continue to make the dramatic achievements they did some ten years ago, improving their reading and math levels an average of one grade per month. What began in 1967 as a "pilot program" has become much more than that. As a place to learn, Mission Academy seems to work; as an organization, it seems to survive.

I hope that this book will be of use to all students of schooling and educational reform, whether they be professional sociologists and educators or less "trained" but equally curious lay readers. In particular, I want the professionally inspired elements of my social analysis and theory to be accessible to those uncultivated and/or unfettered by professional training. As a result, I have kept methodological discussions to a minimum within the narrative of the book. I refer those who wish to explore these issues, or my understanding of them, to the appendix: "Field Research as a Full Participant." I trust that the discussion and references to be found there will be adequate to the task of placing my work within the major traditions of sociological research.

In studying the Academy, I have tried first and foremost to be forceful in my commitment to analysis. I feel I have a great stake in schools and issues about schools. At this time, it is a stake that I hope to further by the careful analysis not only of conventional schools, but also of the alternatives they have inspired. My commitment to political and social change is informed by my contention that "good" change is not achieved through increased mystification. In order to make schools better, those who spend time in them must be encouraged to use their imagination, dignity, and strength to see them for what they are.

TABLE 1

Dramatis Personae: Academy Members

	Age in 1967	Race	Sex	Position
			Administrators	
Nancy Sheen	28	White	Female	Academy Principal 2-67 to 9-68
				Mission Program Coordinator 9-66 to 6-69
				Strategy for Change Director 9-68 to 6-69
				Member, Mission Council and Steering Committee

cont'd.

TABLE 1 (cont'd.)

	Age in 1967	Race	Sex	Position
				Administrators (cont'd.)
Rev. Keen	35	White	Male	Academy Advisory Committee Chairman 2-67 to 4-69 Mission Building Committee Chairman 10-67 to 4-69 Pastor, West Park Church Member, Mission Council and Steering Committee
Call Strow	30	Black	Male	Academy Principal: 9-68 to 2-69
				Teachers
Betsy	19	White	Female	Teaching Aide—Swahili and Crafts: 9-67 to 1-68
Candy	19	White	Female	Teaching Aide—English: 9-67 to 1-68
Cookie	21	Black	Male	Music teacher, disciplinarian, "student organizer": 9-67 to 2-68
Cockey	22	White	Male	English and Drama teacher: 9-67 to 2-69
Hal	24	Black	Male	Science teacher: 2-68 to 6-68
Jon	23	White	Male	Math, Science, Art teacher: 9-67 to 6-68 Coordinator: Summer school 6-68 to 8-68 Research and Curriculum Coordinator: 9-68 to 2-69
Judith	23	White	Female	History teacher: 9-67 to 6-68
Theodore	52	White	Male	Afro-American history teacher: 2-67 to 6-69
Rider	42	White	Male	Story Workshop director: 2-67 to 6-69
Martha	61	White	Female	Librarian: 9-67 to 6-68
Suzanne	31	Black	Female	Home Economics teacher: 9-67 to 6-68
Marcel	28	Black	Male	Science teacher, Speech teacher: 9-68 to present time

cont'd.

TABLE 1 (cont'd.)

	Age in 1967	Race	Sex	Position
Additional Staff				
Ruth	24	Black	Female	Social Worker: 9-67 to 9-68
Lenny	31	Black	Male	Social Worker: 9-67 to 9-68 Member, Academy Advisory Board: 2-67 to 9-68
Students				
Cassiona	20	Black	Female	Attended 2-68 to 6-68; received Level Two Diploma; began training program for bank during summer 1968
Darnell	18	Black	Male	Attended 9-67 to 6-68; received Level Two Diploma; began college in California in 9-68
Doreen	18	Black	Female	Attended 2-67 to 6-68; received Level Three Diploma; G.E.D. exam certificate; began training program as hospital staff worker in summer 1968
Fester	19	Black	Male	Attended 2-67 to 6-68; received Level One Diploma, began work as social-psychiatric trainee 8-68
Twister	19	Black	Male	Attended 2-67 to 6-68; did not receive diploma because of being held in jail; began work for community action political organization 11-68
Lamont	19	Black	Male	Attended 10-67 to 6-68; worked as teacher in summer program 6-68 to 8-68; began college in west in 9-68; returned to Chicago 4-70; received Level Three Diploma and G.E.D.
Mose	19	Black	Male	Attended 9-67 to 6-68; worked in Academy summer program 6-69 to 9-69; began attending Columbia College in Chicago 9-69; received Level Two Diploma
Pud	19	Black	Male	Attended 2-67 to 4-68; received no diploma; worked at various odd jobs after leaving Academy

cont'd.

TABLE 1 (cont'd.)

	Age in 1967	Race	Sex	Position
			Students (cont'd.)	
Sarah	17	Black	Female	Attended 2-67 to 6-68; received Level Two Diploma; married, summer of 1968
Slinky	19	Black	Male	Attended 2-67 to 6-68; received no diploma; boy friend of Sarah from 2-68 to 5-68

Part II
Organization

2

The Illusion of
Shared Authority

Our most common images of the educational process are full of teachers, students, and administrators. While individuals certainly learn a great deal on their own and with peers, "official" learning is seen to involve "teaching" and "schools." When we see an organization devoted to teaching, we expect its social structure to contain the roles of teacher, student, and administrator, in one form or another.

The desirability and necessity of maintaining these roles in schools has been questioned from time to time, and efforts have been made to practice "official" learning in alternative social structures. Although criticism of these conventional roles is varied, most of it focuses upon the threat to free learning posed by the potentially oppressive authority of the teacher. As a result, the most common reforms call for redefining this authority, usually through sensitizing teachers to student concerns. Sometimes this is carried further; attempts are made to change legal or bureaucratic definitions of power and responsibility so that the student activity in school is noncompulsory, nondirected, or institutionally franchised. Similar reforms have been suggested of the relationship between teachers and administrators. In these, free teaching is to be protected in much the same way that free learning is defended for students. Thus we have three identifiable roles—student, teacher, and administrator—and liberal reform has called for those on the bottom to be protected from abuses of power by those immediately above.

Mission Academy was conceived, in part, out of this reform ideology, and efforts were made to insure that teachers would be sensitive to student concerns. In addition, there was administration advocacy of a redefinition of institutional authority such that students and teachers would participate significantly in what can broadly be called, "running the school."

The Academy was thus designed to be a cooperative service organization.

It was hoped by its founders that a cooperative administrative format would emerge from the efforts of students, teachers, and administrators. Commitment to this ideal, however, was never realized in the formal organization of the school. In spite of efforts to think of the school as a group of equals, it was clear that the authority at the Academy was organized, that certain individuals or positions had responsibilities and powers they did not share with others.

This will come as no surprise to those familiar with the sociological characteristics of organizations, but the members of the Academy found it confusing. They wanted very much to think of the school as an alternative, not just to the conventional schools from which the students had dropped out, but also to a whole range of social behavior they characterized as exploitative and destructive within the larger social order. And, as it turned out, the difficulties Academy members experienced in coping with differentials of authority in the school were not mitigated by an openness in discussing them. Instead, those involved with the Academy supported a complicated normative system that, on the one hand, maintained their ideals as descriptive of behavior in the school and, on the other, allowed for at least half that behavior to be considered as an exception to the ideals.

A STORY ABOUT THE SCHOOL
AND THOSE WHO RAN IT

Two individuals played central roles in the creation and later development of the Academy: Nancy Sheen, the Mission Program Coordinator, and Rev. Keen, pastor of a Baptist church in the West Park area. Both Sheen and Keen were young, energetic, and tireless in their advocacy of the school. Nancy Sheen was referred to with some affection by other members of Mission and by the young children who participated in its programs as "Mother Mission." Hanging in her office was a drawing made by some of these children. This pencil and crayon sketch showed her in caricature, her large head tapering down into a body half its size, gigantic glasses with round lenses, and a cap of dark hair. Though an exaggeration of her physical appearance, the drawing captured some of her self-presentation in the Mission organization, most conspicuously that of her broad, ubiquitous smile. A large sun shining down from over her shoulder would not have been an inappropriate addition to this naïve drawing.

Rev. Keen, on the other hand, was known not for his sunny disposition but for his energy, persistence, and practicality. He had come to the area from a small town in Indiana—an environment that was simply too quiet and "out of it" for his tastes. He was often seen in the Mission buildings wearing a black suit, sometimes in clerical collar and sometimes not (occasionally in a light blue sport coat), always on the go, politicking with visitors, replacing blown fuses, "rapping" with students and others, or making his strong voice heard in numerous meetings for the many Mission programs.

Had the artist of "Mother Mission" drawn a likeness of Rev. Keen we would have seen his glasses with their dark frame, his blond combed hair and goatee, and perhaps a cigarette smouldering in his hand. This last detail, however, was no doubt more conspicuous to the Academy staff from whom Rev. Keen, in a kind but relentless way, "bummed" the better portion of the cigarettes he smoked. Instead of a blazing sun over his shoulder, an appropriate motif for Rev. Keen would be a large shiny key ring, jammed to bursting with brass and steel keys for all the locks on the doors in the building.

Collaboration between "practical" Rev. Keen and "idealistic" Nancy Sheen characterized most important decisions made about the Academy. Before the school itself began, these two put together an Advisory Board that included educators, publishers, social scientists and other professionals from Chicago, and a few individuals from the West Park community. Their goal was to coordinate (and through the Academy to implement) all of the most recent information available about schools: curriculum, financing, community organizing, and so on. Initially, Rev. Keen and Nancy Sheen took the responsibility for bringing such information to bear on the growth of the school.

A large part of the power and authority they exercised in the operation of the school stemmed from official positions within the Mission organization, the controlling body of which was the Mission Council (see Figure 1). The Council was composed of the pastor and five lay representatives from each of the Mission churches. It was to this body that all of the individual Mission programs were accountable, and the Council appointed one of its members to be the immediate supervisor of each individual program. Rev. Keen, for example, was the Mission Council appointee as Academy Program Supervisor. Each program supervisor, in turn, appointed members of an "advisory committee" to assist in supervising the operation of the program. Mission Council program supervisors were automatically designated as chairmen of these advisory committees, and in this position they exercised their authority to set agendas and schedule meetings. For example, Rev. Keen appointed members of an Academy Advisory Committee of which he was chairman; he also determined when the committee would meet and what it would discuss.

In addition to the program supervisors, the Mission Council established the position of Mission Program Coordinator to which Nancy Sheen was appointed. The responsibilities of this position were to coordinate the efforts of the various Mission programs, a process that usually took the form of

Figure 1a: MISSION ACADEMY AND "THE MISSION"

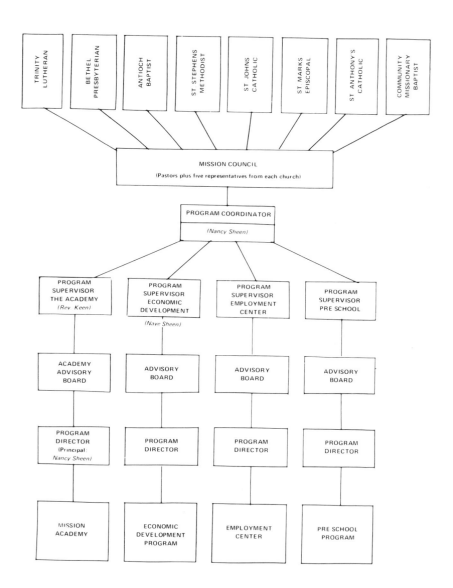

meetings of the program supervisors. During the experimental phase of the Academy's development, Nancy Sheen was Mission Program Coordinator as well as Program Director (Principal) of the Academy. During the demonstration phase, she was Strategy for Change Director and Mission Program Coordinator (see Figure 2). The authority and responsibilities incumbent upon these positions gave her a unique presence in the Mission organization. In addition to acting as coordinator for all Mission programs, she was director of one of the programs: the Academy.

The initial intention of the Mission Council was that the advisory committees appointed by program supervisors would monitor and direct the efforts of the individual programs; the actions of these committees, as reported by the committee chairmen (program supervisors) would then be subject to review by the Council. However, in some instances, the attendance at advisory committee meetings was so irregular and members of such little assistance in making decisions about the programs that policy was established largely through the direct cooperation and negotiation of the program supervisor and the program director.

This was particularly true of the Academy. The individuals appointed to the Academy Advisory Committee were selected on the basis of the potential contribution they might make to the operation of the school. However, once the school was in operation, committee members were far more inclined to

Figure 1b: MISSION ACADEMY—DEMONSTRATION PHASE

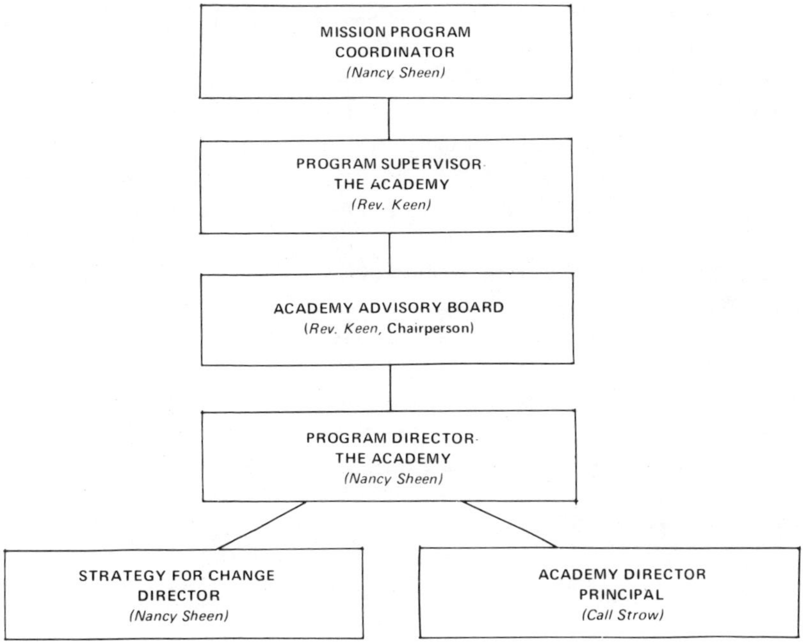

ask for help in solving problems than they were to offer it. This became increasingly the case once Academy teachers were given a place on the committee, an event that occurred at the beginning of the experimental phase. Meetings of the Academy Advisory Committee typically found committee members asking questions about how the Academy was doing, and responses (from Nancy Sheen, Rev. Keen, or an Academy teacher) were given that indicated that it was doing all right. There were very few meetings when policy or "problems" of the school were actually discussed.

With other Mission programs, cooperation was not always present between the program director and the program supervisor, and the Council arbitrated disagreements. Because of the close and friendly relationship between Rev. Keen and Nancy Sheen, such arbitration was never called for with respect to the Academy. Invariably, they settled their disagreements by themselves rather than taking them to the Mission Council. This process became somewhat institutionalized, and the predictably laudatory and harmonious "Reports from the Academy" became an integrative element of Mission Council meetings. Nancy Sheen once told me, "When the Council hears how well things work out here, they pick up, regardless of how messed up things are with some other program."

Because of the superimposition of Nancy Sheen's administrative positions and the close relationship she had with Rev. Keen, these two individuals assumed a great deal of authority in directing the development of the Academy. Most decisions of general policy were made by them—although often after consultation with other members of the Mission Council, the Academy staff, or friends. Their authority was not open to challenge by students or faculty of the Academy. Although students and faculty were invited to Council meetings, they had no vote and no "right" to be heard. The extent to which Nancy Sheen and Rev. Keen were entrenched in the total Mission organization made it very unlikely that such a challenge could take place without their approval. Through a powerful combination of official positions and personal relations, Nancy Sheen and Rev. Keen were effectively "in charge" of the Academy.

An example of the free hand which these two had in running the school occurred in the Spring of 1968. Hal and I had been working well together in developing a curriculum for science and mathematics, and Nancy Sheen and Rev. Keen were very impressed. After a particularly trying week of school— in which Nancy had been robbed, a number of small fights took place, and funding for the coming year looked implausible—Nancy and Rev. Keen walked through the science room in which Hal and I were talking. Rev. Keen said, "Listen, I have a proposition for you two guys . . ." at which point Nancy cut him short by saying, "No, not yet. . . . I want to talk to you for a moment first."

They left the room and went to Nancy's office where they talked for an hour or so. When they returned to the science room, Rev. Keen continued: "What would the two of you think about closing down the school and setting up a consulting firm? If you two could promise to stay on, we would do it. I think we can get more done in terms of changing education if we just have a couple of bright people who really know what's happening, than if we have a whole school full of kids that don't even know if they want to be here. We'd be willing to pay you whatever it would take. Twelve thousand, fifteen thousand dollars. How about it?"

Both Hal and I were caught totally off guard by this remark. Hal mumbled something about already having another job for the coming year, and I said I'd have to think about it. But the importance of the encounter was that this proposal had not been raised by the Council, nor had it been raised by Nancy and Rev. Keen before the Council. It had not been discussed seriously at faculty meetings, and the students had never heard of it. Rev. Keen and Nancy Sheen were in a position to make decisions about the Academy and count on the Council to endorse their recommendations, even if they involved closing the school itself.

What this meant for those who worked and studied at the Academy was that the administration of the school—that is, the "administration" they experienced in all their dealings with the school—was Nancy Sheen and Rev. Keen. In fact, there had been no liberalizing of the distribution of authority in the school, for the ultimate responsibility for governing the Academy rested with the Mission Council, whose membership included neither students nor teachers. In appearance, however, there were indications that the school operated, at times, on a consensual basis. When interpersonal relationships between and among Sheen, Keen, teachers, and students were going well, it almost looked as if we were really running the school—and running it together.

By the following year, things had greatly changed for there was a new principal, a black man who was committed to the Academy but not necessarily to the larger Mission organization. For the first time, the Mission Council was troubled by the principal of the school. For the first time, for students and teachers, the administration became the Mission Council. The line between administration and staff was drawn above the position of principal rather than below it, and interpersonal informality gave way to formal channels of authority. The process by which all this occurred deserves more attention.

At their last meeting before summer recess in 1968, the staff had recommended that a black principal be found to replace Nancy Sheen. This recommendation was not made out of criticism of her performance as principal, but out of the conviction that black students needed a black principal as a model for their own growth and development. We were informed by Rev. Keen, however, that this would not happen—that Nancy would continue as principal for the foreseeable future. In this case, the foreseeable future was not very long, for less than a week later Rev. Keen and Nancy Sheen announced their intention to find a black principal for the school for the coming year.

It is difficult to reconstruct the events, encounters, and deliberation behind this change in plans, but two items appear to have had some importance. The first was that Lenny, director of a social-psychiatric research and family center on the West Side, recounted to Nancy Sheen how his office had been invaded and "occupied" by a group of angry community residents. When Nancy asked him how he dealt with the situation, he said, "Well, I was just really glad I was black, and I told them all to get out."

In addition to this encounter, which Lenny later reported as a situation in which he "encouraged" Nancy to rethink her role as principal of the school, a great deal of pressure was put on the Mission administration to raise bail funds for Twister, a former student of the Academy. Along with five others, he had been arrested on suspicion of conspiracy to commit arson during the turmoil following the assassination of Dr. Martin Luther King, Jr. Bail for these six men was initially set at the astounding figure of $125,000 each; this was later reduced to $75,000 each, a sum which, although smaller than the first, was only a little less difficult to raise.[1] It was clear to the Mission administration that these six West Park residents were being subjected to direct political repression. The Academy had shortly before been awarded a sizeable grant from the Carnegie Foundation, and friends of those held in jail demanded that the Academy "get off" some of its recently awarded funds to free them on bail.

During that week, I made a trip to Cook County jail with Nancy Sheen to see the accused conspirators, and they demanded in threatening but calm terms that the Academy raise money for Twister's bail.[2] While riding back to the Academy with Nancy, I suggested once again that it was impossible for the Academy to continue under the leadership of a white principal, and she agreed. Four days later, Rev. Keen told me that Mission Academy was looking for a black principal and that this had been part of their plans all along. A number of people were interviewed and one of them, Call Strow, was hired after having been unanimously recommended for the position by the Personnel Committee.

The apparent commitment to "Black Power" that this change in plans indicated should not be exaggerated. Six months later, in the middle of the school year, the same Mission administrators who had hired the new black principal met and fired him, effective the next day.

This firing was the outgrowth of intense and unremitting conflict between

Nancy Sheen and Rev. Keen on one side and Call Strow on the other. By and large, the students and staff in the Academy were sympathetic to Call. Sympathy did not amount to much, however, for the ultimate authority rested with the Mission Council—of which Nancy Sheen, her brother Nave Sheen, and Rev. Keen were members.

The conflict was expressed through a number of issues: the staff teaching night school -a responsibility the Personnel Committee had not stipulated but one that was insisted on by Nancy Sheen and Rev. Keen; efforts by Rev. Keen to ask for the personal cooperation of staff members before handing them their pay checks; whether or not the Academy was "collapsing"; and, finally, the extent to which students, teachers, and parents would have control over the operation of the Academy itself.

Call Strow was upset by what he saw as attempts by Sheen and Keen to sabotage his leadership of the Academy and to restrict the formal powers of his position. In citing their refusal to grant needed funds and their efforts to intimidate the staff, Strow was suggesting that they were trying to maintain— through informal and subversive means—the power they once held over the Academy by virtue of their official positions. Rev. Keen and Nancy Sheen, on the other hand, saw Call Strow as the problem, and they explained their actions as attempts to insure responsible leadership for the Academy.

By November 1968, the conflict had heated up to the point where Nancy Sheen and Rev. Keen reported to the Mission Council that the Academy was going "downhill" and was on the verge of collapse. As proof of their claims, they cited the presence of students in the halls between periods, irregular attendance of most students, and the limited amount of work being done by those who did attend.

Strow and the staff were insulted by Sheen and Keen's report, and they responded with one of their own. All aspects of the Academy were documented, accounted for, and evaluated. As Research Coordinator, I prepared a report on selected items that compared the operation of the school to what it had been the year before (see Table 2). In addition, a host of supporters from around the city showed up to express their solidarity (with Call Strow) in the conflict. Persuaded by the evidence and testimony, the Mission Council gave a full vote of confidence to Call Strow and the staff of the Academy, commending them on their efforts to make the school a success.

But the move to fire the principal was hardly over. Two months later, a group sympathetic to the point of view expressed by Sheen and Keen and in favor of Strow's dismissal marshaled their forces for a routine Council meeting where they would call for a vote on his principalship. They were successful in keeping their plans secret, and Council members who supported Strow had no idea that his performance would even be considered at the meeting. The official agenda was set by the Steering Committee on the

TABLE 2

A Comparison Between the Academy at November 1, 1967
and the Academy at November 1, 1968

Category	1967	1968
Total enrollment	72	170
Day school	58	113
Night school	14	57
Sex in the day school		
Percentage of males	79	69
Percentage of females	21	31
Average age in day school	18.4	18.1
Students in English I	33	59
Completed English I by Nov. 1	0	10
Students in Math I	31	42
Completed Math I by Nov. 1	3	7
Average grade level of CTB diagnostic test[a] for entering students		
Reading	6.37	7.75
Math	6.20	7.29
Language	5.95	7.40

[a]California Test Bureau, Test of Adult Basic Education (TABE)

Saturday prior to the Tuesday night Council meeting. When the official agenda appeared, Call Strow was not on it. As a result, it came as a complete surprise to Strow, the staff, students, and his other supporters when a Council vote was taken that Tuesday and he was fired. The secrecy and organization had paid off; a generally low turnout for the meeting allowed those hoping to terminate his appointment to achieve their goal.

The Mission administrators and Council members who had organized the move to get rid of Strow anticipated the surprise of his supporters and prepared for it. Expecting hostile reactions from the students and staff of the Academy, they declared the school closed the following day. However, when Cockey and I arrived at the front door, we protested strongly and forced Nave Sheen to open the building. As we made our way to our classrooms in order to meet with and teach the students, he called the police, "just to make sure nothing happened."

The lack of confidence and trust between the Mission administrators and the staff and students set off unproductive mass meetings and a flurry of accusations. Taking action on some of the charges made by the administrators, a newly formed Personnel Committee fired Cockey and me, and this led Rider to resign and Theodore (the Afro-American history teacher) to "wind down" his involvement with the school. In anticipation of student reaction to these new firings, Nancy Sheen produced a series of field trips, complete with buses and drivers. During the next week of "school," students found themselves whizzing around to Chicago's major museums, the Brookfield Zoo, and even to a neighboring state.

The whole series of events, culminating in the firing of the principal and two staff members and the resignation of a third, provided a clear indication of the structure of ultimate authority in the Academy. That authority might plan for Black Power, responsiveness to students and teachers, and a cooperative administration, but it did little to guarantee them.

INSTITUTIONALIZING PERSONAL POWER

Other efforts had been made to reform the organization of authority at the school, but these had concentrated on "higher-ups," ignoring the potential for participation by staff and students. Members of Mission churches and the Mission Council itself were aware of the exceptional power and authority of Nancy Sheen and Rev. Keen. While they were appreciative of all that these two had done, they were also dissatisfied with relying on them to get things done. Partly out of criticism of the influential roles these two played in the Mission organization, and partly as an effort to "streamline" the organization, the Mission administrative structure was changed during the summer of 1968 (before Call Strow began his term as principal). The new structure called for the establishment of a Steering Committee of the Mission Council; it would be subject to review by the Council but would effectively act as the decision-making board of the organization. It was the purpose of the Steering Committee to recommend actions to the Council for endorsement. In addition, the Steering Committee was to appoint various subcommittees to deal with the business of administering and reviewing Mission programs.

These provisions effectively dissolved the previous advisory committees and constituted new advisory boards composed exclusively of Mission members, a process that "tightened up" Mission control of the programs it sponsored. They also established a number of committees (e.g., personnel, budget, building) that were to act in their areas of authorization for all Mission programs. Thus, the Personnel Committee was responsible for hiring and firing all employees in all Mission programs.

The situation created by this administrative change was one in which personnel had been hired by committees that no longer existed, and this was true for five of the Academy staff. The following year, when Call Strow, Cockey, and I were fired, we attempted to appeal our cases to the Academy Advisory Committee, but we were informed that that committee no longer existed. As a result, the only body to which we might appeal was the new

Personnel Committee, the one which had just fired us. Clearly there was a new order, and—just as clearly—it did not include us.

The development of the administrative organization of Mission can be seen in part as a familiar process of institutionalization. The extent to which operating procedures were formalized and legitimated within visible administrative bodies increased over time. However, the new administrative organization did not effectively curtail the exceptional power and authority of individual persons—most notably. Nancy Sheen and Rev. Keen. In the new scheme, Nancy Sheen was still Program Coordinator and Strategy for Change Director. Rev. Keen was a member of the Personnel Committee and Chairman of the Building Committee. Both served on the Steering Committee, the Mission Council, and the new Academy Advisory Committee.[3] Their cooperation in bringing about the administrative reorganization of Mission should be viewed from this perspective; the new structure, in that it was less open to criticism as an arbitrary order, gave their persistently exceptional powers new legitimacy. By creating an organization that appeared to function on the basis of more universalistic criteria, one in which they maintained a great deal of power, Nancy Sheen and Rev. Keen legitimated their authority. No fundamental change occurred in the manner in which decisions were made about the Academy; "business" proceeded as before.

It is important to note that neither students nor teachers participated in restructuring the Mission administration. The organization of ultimate and tertiary authority for the school had been changed without consultation with those who were actively learning and teaching there. Students and teachers were upset about this, but they were not outraged. There was some cognitive mechanism that allowed them to maintain their involvement with the Academy as a "free school"—an "experimental school" in which power and responsibility were shared. This was done in spite of the fact that the Council fired the principal and two of the eight staff members, re-constituted the Academy Advisory Committee, and reorganized the governance of the school itself. The cooperative ideal was essential to participating in the school, so essential that it was not to be diminished by assessing the extent to which it was realized in actual practice.

3

Academy Behavior

A cloth appliqué organizational chart was hung prominently in the conference room of the Mission building. On it, yellow circles of felt were stitched, each labeled as one of the various Mission programs. In addition, mimeographed copies of the organizational structure were handed out to visitors and included in reports and proposals. On paper, it was clear that the Mission Council, composed of representatives of the eight churches, was in charge.

Even though this body was legally identified with ultimate authority, it did not control all behavior in the Academy or other Mission programs. In that decisions could be made by teachers and students without consulting the ultimate authority, the school could operate on a daily basis that was somewhat independent of the Council.

The preceding chapter has described both the organization of authority in the Academy and the extent to which it contradicted the initial ideal of a cooperative administration. In one respect this structure was static, the ultimate source of authority remaining unchanged throughout all the machinations of internal reorganization, changes of personnel, and crises of confidence. It should be no surprise, however, to see that this static and rigorous hierarchy of authority was for the most part dormant. It served as a set of symbolic and legal resources that could be called upon when necessary, but it was not the crucial system within which people acted.

Sociologists have long been fascinated with the relationship between the formal structures of organizations and the informal patterns of behavior that people initiate and that exist beside or in spite of the formal structures. Usually, this informal infrastructure is considered incidental or supplemental to the core of the formal structure. At the Academy, however, it was officially denied that this was the case. Rather, administrators, teachers, and students stressed the importance of their informal process and practical consensus over and above that of the official organizational chart. Even though the Mission Council, on the books, had absolute power, members of the school took every opportunity to ignore that fact and to claim the school as their own.

For its part, the Council usually cooperated, though at times only after encouragement from Nancy Sheen and Rev. Keen. As a result, the formal structure served as an ultimate weapon, a final process for judging otherwise unresolved disputes. It was law, but a law accessible only to those in control, to be used to defend against threats to that control. It had little to do with daily events at the school.

In fact, this inclination of Academy members to play down the authority of the Council discouraged the establishment of any other formal structure. If the school's organization had been explicitly codified, it would have been all too clear that everything was under the rule of the Council, and formal reform would have been a hot issue. By leaving everything ambiguous and casual, it was possible to maintain the belief that this was, indeed, a school run in a cooperative manner with shared power and responsibility.

Thus, the static organizational chart was totally inadequate to explain the way the Academy operated. Rules, roles, and principles were always changing, and no one insisted that they be established once and for all. The organization of activity in the school was a product of the immediate, continuing, and existential concerns of those who were involved with it. There was a consensus that the school would have students and teachers and a principal—and so there were, in one form or another. These cultural identities, more than the official charts, provided the basis for an order of authority.

The fact that this structure was dynamic needs to be emphasized. In resisting official recognition of a division of authority in the school, Academy members allowed the development of indirect and ambiguous institutions of differential power. A half-hidden structure of authority developed—a system of power and privilege worked into the walls of the building itself.

THE BUILDING AS MEDIUM: A SOURCE OF NORMS

As the common meeting place for all those involved with the Academy, the building acted as a powerful medium in structuring the way individuals spent their time there together.[1] This medium was more fully developed in a new building into which the Academy moved in November 1967 than it had been in the old church where the Academy had been housed during the pilot phase. The old church contained only five designated areas: classrooms, the library, Nancy's office, the assembly hall, and a dark basement. Classrooms had been undifferentiated by subjects taught in them; any empty classroom was occupied by any class. In the new building, however, there were separate classrooms for different subjects: history, writing workshop, English, home economics, math and science, and art. In addition, there was a greater variety of kinds of building space in the new building than there had been in the old church; as a medium, it contained greater potential for conveying information. For example, the new building contained a lobby, an independently operated employment center, the offices of the Mission administration, a teacher's office, three sets of washrooms, a number of large storage closets, a cafeteria and lunchroom, a student lounge, a conference room, and a roof onto which students clambered on occasion to take advantage of pleasant weather.

The physical layout of the building was an important factor in the creation of order at the Academy. Because it contained a variety of kinds of space, it was useful in segregating various functions of the school (as well as those of the larger Mission organization) and in suggesting priorities, statuses, and procedures. In this respect it represented a distinct resource in the hands of those who held the keys, a resource which was of great assistance in ordering social interaction and encouraging some forms of reliable behavior.

That this two-story, concrete, glass, and steel structure was indeed an important resource—capable of prescribing behavior through its doors, halls, rooms, and furniture—was not lost on those spending time at the Academy. The interior space was the object of continuous conflict among students, teachers, and Mission administrators. Nancy Sheen reported this conflict in January of 1968 in the following manner:

> The first week in the building was a difficult one because students wanted full control of the building and resented the locks on some of the doors, even though the Academy was sharing the building with the [Mission] headquarters. It became almost a matter of gang-like idea of turf and control. With time, this settled into some kind of understanding.

The issue was somewhat different, however, than her report would indicate. Students did not so much want control of the building as they wanted access to all parts of it. In contrast, the Mission administrators did want control of all the space within the building. Some students resented the locks on many of the doors and were often successful in rendering them ineffective with small wads of paper or stolen keys. This collapsed the status differentials symbolized by restricted possession of the keys and often literally gave the administrators severe attacks of indigestion. The students did want control of one of the carpeted, furnished front offices that they thought should be officially theirs, but the administrators refused this demand, stating that these offices were reserved for use by Mission alone. They offered the students a small, uncarpeted, unfurnished, windowless office at the back of the building. The students maintained their preference for the front office but occupied the rear alternative on a temporary basis "under protest."

The official designation of function per space in the new building was made by Nancy Sheen, Rev. Keen, and the other Mission administrators; neither teachers nor students participated in this process. When the move to the new building was made, however, the physical work was done by the students and teachers. Then Nancy and Rev. Keen spent long hours straightening and organizing so that Nancy could accurately report that "not a single class was missed." After moving all the furnishings and supplies belonging to the Academy, students and teachers felt they should have some say about how building space was to be used. The feeling that this was their "right" was the basis for the continuing conflict throughout the year. As the use of space in the building served as a map of functional priorities, teachers and students wanted to participate in this indirect description of the Academy's policies.

Without engaging in a complete reexamination of the mechanisms of authority responsible for initial decisions about building use, the Mission administration could not secure the full cooperation of teachers and students. The fact that the building was in use made such reexamination appear to be impractical and dangerous to the administrators as it would threaten the continued performance of a number of Mission activities. As a consequence, conflict about the building took the form of a series of small skirmishes over the use of particular rooms; the more fundamental question of authorizing building space for various functions never fully surfaced.

To the Mission administration, the building was "theirs"; legal ownership of the building was reflected in their sense of control over it. Although few of these individuals were ever present at any time, they wanted space reserved for them to use when they wished. For example, the main conference room was not supposed to be used by Academy members, except for teacher's meetings, because Mission administrators might want to use it. This meant that it was used only five or six hours out of the twenty-five hours of Academy classes each week. And when their use of the room coincided with a scheduled teachers' meeting, the teachers' meeting was held elsewhere. The use of the room for teachers' meetings was articulated as a "special" or "exceptional" function by the Mission administration, and when I held a seminar in the conference room, I was advised not to do so again. When I did hold class in the room again, I was told that this would have to stop because some of the pastors or administrators might need the room while I was using it. I replied that if that was the case they could ask me to leave and I would. To this there was no further response, a strategy that preserved the illegitimate status of my use of the room while at the same time avoiding a significant confrontation about building space in general.

Because of their lack of direct contact with the students and teachers in the Academy, these administrators also interpreted the respect shown for the building as an indirect expression of respect shown to them as Mission administrators. They saw the building as an extension of themselves. Thus, when "disrespect" was shown for the building (e.g., it was messy, halls were dirty and scuffed, or a great deal of noise was being made), the administrators took this as an indication of a lack of respect for Mission itself.

For example, one day the students were angered by some remarks Nancy made and called a meeting for the history room. Theodore, who was teaching a class in the room at the time, left at the students' urgent request. As students began filing into the room, Nave Sheen (Nancy's brother and a Mission pastor), who happened to be in the building at the time, tried to block their way by standing in the open doorway and insisting in a very excited voice that they could not meet there. The students hardly broke stride as they pushed by him into the room to conduct their meeting. Nave became so disturbed that he ran down the hall to the phone in the front office and called the police, much to the embarrassment of his sister and the rest of the staff, to whom such behavior by the students was an everyday occurrence.

In explaining why he called the police, Nave Sheen said that it was his considered opinion there was absolutely no order in the school and that the total chaos he observed was a threat to the safety of the entire building and everyone in it. The staff of the Academy, as well as Nancy, criticized Nave for acting hastily in the face of a situation with which he was unfamiliar. His behavior was symptomatic of the Mission administration's experience with the building as an area of their responsibility—an area they believed they should control—and their lack of interpersonal information about students and teachers. With such little contact with the members of the Academy, it was perfectly understandable that these administrators responded to the most conventionally stereotypical clues in assessing the order and functioning of the school.

The concern of Mission administrators over maintaining order in their building grew as the school developed. One of the clearest manifestations of this growing concern was the increasing restriction that the Council placed on the number of people to whom keys to the building might be given—another example of the institutionalization of authority in the school. During the experimental phase, Cockey, Judith, Hal, and I all had keys to the building, but we were each forced to relinquish them as the months passed. In November 1968, during the principalship of Call Strow, the Mission Council passed a resolution that stipulated that the only member of the Academy who could have a key to the building (as opposed to individual classrooms) was the principal. The importance of the Council's action is that it was not a direct response to thefts and misuse but to more general fears about the building being out of their control, a fear that paralleled their feelings about the Academy under the principalship of Call Strow.

The building was both the strength and the vulnerability of the Mission organization. The building gave the organization a real presence in the community; it housed their offices and duplicating equipment; and it was a place where guests and visitors could be taken to "get a sense of what Mission was all about." In that it was visible, however, it was also a focus for community resentment against Mission, and it was something that needed to be properly maintained in the face of its use by a large number of "strangers" (i.e., Academy students).

The apparently vulnerable characteristics of the building were important to some aspects of social control that developed among the people inside it. In asserting that "if the building is closed, there will be no more Academy," Mission administrators found a rationale for reducing their previous commitment to a "student run" school and suggesting a number of rules for conduct within the Academy. Nancy was responsible for articulating these building rules, and she did so by making reference to the "precarious survival" of the school as an experiment in the face of great opposition from the Board of Education, the police, social work agencies, building inspectors, and "jealous nihilists who wished to see Mission fail." Because of these various forces, she would argue, it was necessary that there be no marihuana smoking in the building, no drugs, no weapons, and no fighting.[2]

This "survival" rationale was only partly successful in legitimating the administration-sponsored rules. To some extent this reflected the lack of significant involvement and responsibility that students experienced in the operation of the school. For example, the prohibition against smoking marihuana was violated frequently but with discretion. Although students were told that they could not go to an initial orientation session at Happy Hills Retreat if they brought marihuana with them, this did not act as an effective deterrent. About ten of the twenty-six students were smoking during one of these trips, although always in the casual privacy of their dormitory-like rooms. This rule was also violated at Academy functions such as parties and dances, and it was almost totally ignored on field trips. But when the students organized and produced a talent show at a local school gymnasium, they took the marihuana prohibition very seriously. Several hundred people from the surrounding community attended the performance, and the Academy students policed the audience, quickly ejecting anyone they found smoking marihuana. Students commented that they could not afford to have the police arrest anyone for smoking at their talent show as they would not then be able to put on another show.[3]

Thus, the building was involved in a number of important symbolic systems at the Academy. Through its physical structure, the kinds and varieties of encounters that individuals had in the school were regulated. It also provided a medium for specifying in spatial terms the relationships among various functions the school sought to perform. As an area of collective vulnerability, it also legitimated a number of behavioral prohibitions by identifying them as necessary to the survival of the Academy. The importance the building achieved in terms of these complicated functions was transferred to other activities.

One of the more interesting sets of such building-related experiences involved the attempts by Mission administrators to use the labor of students and teachers to maintain and improve the building. When the experimental phase began in September 1967, Rev. Keen and Nancy Sheen stipulated that students would pay $5.00 a week tuition to attend the school or they would receive a "work scholarship." A work scholarship entitled the student to attend the school in exchange for four or five hours of work a week. Neither the collection of $5.00 tuition nor the work scholarship equivalent was successfully pursued. As no other provisions had been made for maintaining the building, it was often in a state of disorder and ill-repair. Nancy Sheen and Rev. Keen handled this condition by enlisting the participation of individual staff members to do particular jobs. However, a great deal of work had to be done in the new building before it was serviceable as a school: cleaning, painting, removing the furnishings that remained from the previous tenant (a bank), erecting a number of partitions, and dismantling some electrical circuits. Having only limited financial resources, the Mission administration wanted the Academy staff to do this work. Rev. Keen set aside Saturdays as work days for the staff in the new building, and several of us participated.

The rationale by which the staff were directed into this work was that the Academy and Mission represented one large family—often referred to as the "Mission Family"—in which everyone shared in all the work. However, as the year progressed it became more and more apparent to the staff that they shared in the physical maintenance of the building more than did the students or the Mission administrators (other than Rev. Keen and Nancy Sheen). Nancy assigned each teacher a work group of students who were to help the teacher clean, mop, and wax a particular area of the building, but irregular attendance patterns and a plethora of "un-work" excuses rendered these groups inoperable. Teachers still found themselves cleaning and mopping the floors. Dissatisfaction with this situation grew as it became clear to the staff that the Mission administrators set standards for the cleanliness and orderliness of the building that were far more rigorous than their own. The administrators were enlisting them to perform tasks that the staff felt were unnecessary. The staff applied themselves less and less to their duties as maintenance workers, and in the spring of 1968 Mission hired a part-time janitor to insure that the building would be presentable to guests. It was clear that if there were a Mission Family, it was one in which some people were expected to share more than others.

Nancy Sheen and Rev. Keen experienced some ambivalence in asking teachers to do this maintenance and construction work. To some extent, this was lessened by the extraordinary amount of such work that they did themselves, a factor that allowed them to be somewhat righteous in their requests. The ambivalence showed up, however, when they were confronted with staff members who were working but not in a way that they would have liked. In such situations, they found it very difficult, if not impossible, to act in a normal supervisory capacity and ask the teacher to do the job differently. For example, Cockey and I had been given the task of scrubbing a line of asphalt off the floor of the English room. This asphalt had been left from the base of a partition that had previously divided the room. After numerous experiments with scrub brushes and cleanser, we discovered that we were most effective by pouring some cleanser on the floor and then pushing the brush back and forth with the weight of our foot. This method, of course, allowed us to work standing upright and freed both of our hands, in which we were soon holding cigarettes and cold cans of beer. When Rev. Keen and Nancy Sheen came into the room they were rather miffed by the casual and apparently ineffectual way in which we were working. The fact that we were working late in the afternoon at tasks that were still conceived of as rather exceptional (even though they took place every day) kept them from complaining, however, and they eventually even shared a sip of beer.

This ambivalence did not keep them from asking the staff to perform arduous and sometimes dangerous jobs. For example, Rev. Keen was unable to locate the switches necessary to cut off the current of the electrical circuits that needed to be dismantled in the new building, but he told Rider and me, "Just be careful, and don't get shocked." Although we attempted to be careful, on four occasions live wires crossed and set off substantial shocks, destroying two screwdrivers and several outlet boxes and scaring us silly. Rev. Keen thanked us for the job we had done, but Rider and I left the building feeling that we were fools for having gone along with him.

As these examples should indicate, students, teachers, and administrators each had their own ideas about what kind of order should exist in the building and how it should be maintained. In terms of images and sensibilities, the students wanted the building to be somewhat like the street, uncontrolled but understandable to the street person; the staff wanted the building to be like a lounge, also uncontrolled but less problematic than the affairs of the street; and the administrators wanted the building to be like a well-organized business establishment or factory—controlled, predictable, and well maintained. In these fantasies as well as in their everyday experience of it, the building was a manipulable structure through which individuals could promote their own ideal for interaction within it.

All groups working in the school competed to get others to accept their definition of the building situation and oriented their own actions as if their definition was indeed accepted by all. Neither teachers nor students wanted norms in the building to be too clearly formalized, and they sought to define the situation so that there was a great deal of latitude for individual behavior. In contrast, Mission administrators, who had very little interpersonal contact with either students or teachers, sought to impose rather explicit rules for conduct in the building. The competition between students, teachers, and administrators eventually took the form of name-calling. While the administrators called the teachers and students "sloppy and irresponsible," the staff and students referred to the administrators as "tight-assed businessmen."[4]

In both cases, the building became the intervening medium between the parties involved. The staff and students resisted explicit and direct rules for their conduct handed down by Mission administrators, but they would frequently honor situational proprieties corresponding to the uses and vulnerability of the building. The Mission administrators, for their part, wanted to control the behavior of those in the school, no doubt a consequence of their feeling of responsibility for the building and their ignorance—both interpersonal and cognitive—of what was going on inside it. However, they recognized both the educational and morale dysfunctions of attempting to directly control the staff and students. By stipulating rules and schedules for the use of the building rather than for individuals, they managed to describe a code of conduct for members of the Academy without appearing to do so, and they thus preserved the Academy's identity as an "alternative school." By defining the situation of the building, they went a long way toward defining the kind of behavior that would occur within it.

The success of their efforts, though frequently sabotaged, was apparent. The resource of the building, controlled largely through the agency of keys and the legality of ownership, was important in communicating to actors what was expected of them. In acting in accord with these expectations, students, teachers, administrators, and others tended toward reliability in their social behavior.

EXTINGUISHING STUDENT POWER

Statements about the reform of conventional authority at the Academy were not limited to the relatively neutral expression of "cooperative administration." Even stronger claims were made in an effort to describe the school as student oriented, the most extreme of which Nancy Sheen would utter from time to time: "This school belongs to the students."

Although the Academy's members conceived of it as student oriented, there was no effective student organization. The development of such an organization suffered greatly, as is often the case, from cooptation by faculty and administrative programs. The greatest obstacles to "student power" at the Academy came not from an authoritarian administration but from efforts by the staff and administrators to encourage "representative" student leaders, from the academic structure, and from the exaggerated responsiveness of the staff to incipent student demands.

During the pilot phase, student-selected officers and representatives operated with some efficacy within the predominantly gang-type social structure that then existed. And, at the beginning of the experimental phase, Pud and Twister, two officers from the pilot phase, assumed informal leadership during the week-long orientation session at Happy Hills Farm. In this capacity, they chaired meetings and represented the students to the faculty, Mission administrators, and the Happy Hills maintenance staff. They appeared to act fairly and moderately as spokesmen for the students; all students who wished to speak were allowed to do so, and Pud and Twister took the will of the majority as binding on their behavior.

In their efforts to help the students organize themselves, however, the staff recommended that official student elections be held so that "representative" student leaders could be elected, and they called a meeting for that purpose. At Nancy's suggestion, this election meeting was chaired by Cookie, the one black male on the Academy staff, and it was clear from his behavior that he wanted the students to officially elect Pud and Twister. Pud and Twister, however, declined every office for which they were nominated, angering Cookie, who complained, "You guys just don't care about this, do you? You just don't care about the Academy."

In the midst of this strained encounter between Cookie, Pud, and Twister, a vote was taken and four students were elected as a governing board. But as soon as the results of the election were announced, Nancy Sheen rose from her seat at the back of the room, walked forward to the stage of the small assembly hall from which Cookie was chairing the meeting, and accused the students of not taking the elections seriously. She said, "Because you didn't take this election seriously enough, I think we need to have another one. You can't *really* intend for this vote to count. Let's have another vote."

Nancy's remarks brought forth a barrage of cries from students who were indignant that she would not accept the election results and moans from others who were tired of sitting for two hours without apparently accomplishing anything and who had no inclination to sit there for two more hours for the same result. Cookie tried to quell the outburst by loudly repeating over and over, "Let's just have one more vote for officers. Let's just have one more vote. One more vote for officers. Let's just have one more vote for officers."

At one point Pud held everyone's attention when he remarked, rather pointedly, "We already had a vote. Now you say *that* one was no good. So now we're supposed to have *another* vote, but how do we know you won't tell us that *this* one's no good either?" Pud's remarks were effective in convincing students, as well as some staff, of the absurdity of this particular form of electoral process, and no further vote was taken that day. The meeting lasted another half hour, ending only after a list of Academy "rules" was drawn up by the students, an act that the staff and administration took as an expression of good faith.

It is not surprising that Pud and Twister did not accept nominations for elective offices in an election called by the faculty and administration. The students had already accepted them as leaders, even if the staff had not. As students, with a student constituency, they had nothing to gain by such a vote and a great deal to lose. If they won, they would not really increase their authority and status among their fellow students, and there was always the chance that they might, by some turn of events, lose. Or, even if they did not lose, if they were voted against, it would undermine the trusting and consensual manner in which they acted as leaders. Further, if they won they might find themselves saddled with a set of unwanted and, to them, unwarranted responsibilities.

In attempting to help the students organize, the staff tried to impose their own standards of legitimacy on student leaders. Had the students been total strangers without any informal organization, such standards would have been far more appropriate. Under those conditions, an election could have initiated some form of interaction among strangers. As it was, the election only called into question the work and process with which the students had already become involved.

The staff felt a commitment to encourage students to engage in democratic processes. There was a general feeling among teachers that the tyranny of gang oppression that they imagined operating on the street should not be reconstructed within the walls of the Academy. In their efforts to protect against such objectionable social forms, the staff overemphasized democratic forms of election, ignoring the democratic process of assembly the students had evolved with their informally selected leaders. Blindness to this existing democratic process was not incidental, for it reflected the staff's conception of developing social control in the school. Teachers and administrators wished not only that students should be organized, but also that their organization should be one that could be held accountable for student behavior. Having no desire to be responsible for disciplining students, they saw a "legitimately" constituted student government as an easy solution.

An additional inhibiting factor in the development of a student organization was the academic structure of the Academy. The emphasis on individualized, programmed instructional materials reduced the amount of contact students might otherwise have had with each other and made it difficult for students to perceive their common condition. The heterogeneous school population (with respect to age, sex, neighborhood, occupation, and educational achievement level) presented another obstacle to be overcome if students were to develop an organization. Further, provisions for allowing irregular attendance patterns augmented the individualized experiences that students reported having at the Academy.

Not only were there impediments to collective student activities in the academic structure of the Academy, there were no structural rewards for the development of student organization. The only visible inducements to students to involve themselves in organizing other students were the use of the small student office and the promise of a phone, a promise that was never fulfilled. "Student power" did not lead to a degree, nor was student government given the status of conventional academic work. In spite of rhetoric that stressed the development of the student as a civic individual through experiences in self-government, student involvement in the administration of the Academy was considered incidental to academic achievement.

Perhaps the most inhibiting influence on student power at Mission Academy was the effort by the staff and administration to anticipate student demands and criticism. Rather than assuming control of the Academy and providing the students with a confrontable presence, the staff attempted to determine points of student resistance before these were clear to the students themselves. In trying to "predict" what would happen next, the staff consistently took the initiative for critical action away from the students. If an instructor noticed one or two students complaining about the lack of a particular course, he would report it at a regularly scheduled faculty meeting. In many cases, a decision was made to offer the course in order to "keep in touch with student goals." As was often the case, the course would be offered before students had the opportunity to realize their collective desire to have it offered. The staff felt they were doing the students a big favor by being sensitive to their opinions of the school when in fact they were cutting off one of the few opportunities for students to develop a collective enterprise.

On a couple of occasions the students caught the staff by surprise. In October 1967 they demanded that the school be renamed "Malcolm X Academy" and put up signs to that effect. Nancy commented on this action at the next faculty meeting by saying, "It's nothing serious. Don't be worried about it." The point is that it was something "serious," if the staff was going to take the collective development of students as a serious objective. If the staff had wished to foster that development they could have resisted the student demands or they could have embraced the demands and worked for the change before the Mission Council. But the staff chose to ignore the demands, and the students were deprived of a potential rallying point.

An additional manner in which the staff and administration subverted student organization was through invidious ideological comparisons with students. Teachers would remark to one another or to students: "The faculty here are a lot more revolutionary than the students." Statements such as this were quite misleading. The faculty were well versed and literate in the ideology of student power and Black Power, perhaps more so than most of the students. However, the faculty could afford the luxury of behaving as student power or Black Power advocates because such behavior did not directly affect their position in the school. It is significant that the faculty did not act to organize themselves within an ideology of "teacher power" or as a union collective. Thus, teachers were quick to point out how far students deviated from a radical student ideology, yet they offered no explanation (nor felt any was necessary) for their own conservative and status quo behavior. For a teacher at the Academy, it was far easier to be a "radical student" than it was to be a "radical teacher."

While students at the Academy had no control over the operation of the school, they could be effective in sabotaging and subverting programs initiated by the faculty or administration. They were not, however, in a position to initiate programs of their own. Students were never effective in boycotting, striking, or collectively bargaining to achieve their objectives. In fact, the lack of a well-developed student culture made the collective nature of any student objectives very problematic. When objectives did have the potential for mobilizing collective student support, they were usually endorsed or advocated by the staff before such support could fully materialize. Students were left with a situation in which they were more likely to get what they wanted by acting as individuals and getting the ear of a sympathetic teacher than by talking to other students about their collective needs, anxieties, and ambitions.

The fact that they had no control over the operation of the school does not mean that students had no influence. In some respect, they had more influence as individuals than they wanted, for the staff scurried off to transform student opinions into programs overnight, often under unwarranted circumstances.

There was among the staff a deep respect for individual student imagination and experience, and this provided part of the motivation for assessing and reacting quickly to real student concerns in the school. But another factor in this dynamic was the staff's naive assumptions about the creation of interest group organization. Teachers and administrators at the Academy felt that their good intentions and concern could be effective in gracefully and politely encouraging students to develop collective organizations. But this assumption limited the staff's ability to respond creatively to students, for it ignored or denied the constructive potential of student-teacher conflict. The notion that such conflict might give expression to underlying structural dimensions of the Academy was a frightening one for these "radical" educators who were working in an "alternative" school. Ultimately, the staff found it easier to change the curriculum to meet projected student criticism than to openly confront the student body about an explicit conflict of interest.

The building, cultural roles of students and teachers, official and unofficial rhetoric, and organizational charts all served as parts of a symbolic system through which people came together at the school. But these were only elements of the system and lacked any meaning of their own. Individuals picked or chose among them as situation or personal inclination indicated.

In this respect, the organization of the school was no more and no less than a language shared by those who went there—be they students, teachers, or administrators. And, as with other languages, the organization was claimed by people as their own through distinctive jargon, dialect, and voice. As elements of the language were used by members of the school, they took on meaning to others and became part of their phenomenal world. The organizational chart, which was hung in the front office day in and day out, only became real for those at the school in times of crisis. Student power, however, was real for everyone even though it was never provided with an institutional guarantee.

The organization I studied, then, was less a lifeless chart than it was the lives of those who participated in the cultural event called Mission Academy.[5] And this organization, I contend, both emerged from and influenced the engagement of individuals in a distinctive configuration of behavior, beliefs, process, and identity. To the social scientist, these elements might indeed appear as a kind of language.[6] For those whose lives were engaged with the Academy, this language was no less than literature.

4

Ambiguities
of School Design

One of the difficulties encountered by social reformers lies in convincing people that a newly reformed institution deserves the same legitimacy as it was accorded in its former, unreformed state. When alternative institutions are designed, the problem is to have them respected as much as conventional ones without having to make modifications that would cripple their alternative essence. The ambiguities of the situation are apparent, and reform rhetoric is full of them, calling upon the public to endorse "real learning," "real education," "real therapy," or "real community." Efforts to diminish the credit of conventional practices complement this advocacy, and we are asked by reformers to turn away from "so-called learning," "so-called education," or "so-called community."

On the one hand, social reform is essential; institutions live on long after they have ceased to meet the human needs for which they were designed. As a result, there is some truth to statements that alternative schools engage in "real" education while conventional ones process students through "so-called education." It was certainly true at the Academy with respect to academic achievement. Students at Mission did learn more—and more quickly—than they had in public school classrooms.

On the other hand, reform is impossible without a complex adversary identity. It is not enough to be *for* something under conditions of scarce resources, yet the social reformer must be careful about what he or she is against. Efforts to start new schools cannot be founded on a rejection of education in general, but rather must be presented as a response to specific kinds of education. A constant effort must be made by social reformers to identify the evils of the conventional order without having these criticisms be so general that they apply to the reformed order as well.

The expression of these ambiguities was a common feature of Mission

Academy. Members of the school wanted to identify with the respect given to education in this culture, but they wanted to underline the distinctions between an Academy education and one offered by the Chicago public school system. We wanted outsiders to take the Academy seriously, more seriously even than the surrounding high schools whose dropout students we were teaching. Our efforts to convince others of the school's worth represented competition for popular legitimacy with these more conventional schools.

The fact that many people outside the Academy did not take it seriously as a school was brought home in a number of ways. Students would report that when they were attending one of the high schools in the area, previous to enrolling at Mission, their teachers and counselors would refer to the Academy variously as "a bunch of crazy people," "a really screwed-up place," or in more general terms as a sort of sub-cellar catchall for educational rejects; one student had been told: "All their students are dope-addicts, tough gang members, and revolutionaries. You don't want to go there."

Other students reported to me that their parents did not think the school really existed until they attended the graduation ceremony in which their children received one of the three levels of Mission diplomas. The description of the school these students had shared with their parents previous to this—a place where you could say what you wanted and wear what you wanted, and where you could smoke in class and study what you wanted—led the parents to think that this was just a "crazy outfit of wierdos," as one student recounted, not a "school." When the educational product of this "outfit" became visible—this student not only received a diploma but was accepted to attend college the following September—her parents took the Academy more seriously. They decided that it was indeed a school.

On two occasions local police officers gave me large doses of derogatory comment about the school and its students, stressing the fact that "it's not a real school." Although they showed some familiarity with our curriculum, their remarks made me very angry, for they treated the school I took seriously as a joke: "Oh, I know that place. They teach dumb niggers there how to read," and, "No, they don't; they teach them A-f-r-o American history, but it's a short class; it only meets once a year. There isn't very much to teach." I was similarly furious when a bus driver for one of the Academy's field trips asked me if I taught "these people." When I answered that I did, he replied, "What a waste of fuckin' time. What a fuckin' waste of time."

It was hard for Mission personnel to defend against some of these criticisms, for the school was not an unqualified success, and what appeared as an exaggeration in a critique (e.g., the teachers are "weird") might be true in part. In other cases, criticism might single out items that were explicit in the design of the Academy. Nancy Sheen wrote an early statement of this design as part of a progress report (it described the school as of February 1967), and her account contained a number of elements that were criticized by those outside the school.

> [Mission] was excited by the combination of features that was to make the Academy unique—(1) programmed learning as a tool to individualize instruction, and allow for a non-graded, non-semester plan; (2) a student oriented school, which sought to involve students in all decisions; (3) a strong emphasis on Negro History; (4) inclusions of new, but proven, imaginal [sic] techniques in theater games and writing workshop; and (5) part-time job possibilities.

As the school developed, some of these design principles changed, but not radically. The basic posture of the school remained much the same as that expressed in Nancy's very early statement, but these principles of operation became more elaborate and more extensive. This development represented an attempt to design a school for black high school dropouts, a school that would be attractive enough to this student population so that they would attend without pay, and a school that was effective enough in educating them that it would continue to be supported by outside financial sources. The school's reputation was at stake to two significant populations: the dropouts (potential and actual) in the surrounding community and the educators and parents who would ultimately endorse or dismiss the Academy's efforts.

DESIGNING A SUCCESSFUL SCHOOL: STUDENTS AS CLIENTS

The first months of the school's operation, from February to June 1967, were considered to be a success by Academy members. This meant that students had shown that they liked the school; enrollment was increasing rather than decreasing; students had made a great deal of conventional academic progress; the Academy had become acceptable in the community; and other communities and community organizations were beginning to direct their attention toward the Academy as a real alternative to conventional school systems. Thus the recommendations that were based on this "pilot phase" were largely concerned with insuring that the Academy would continue in the "successful" direction it had taken the previous academic year. Organized around these recommendations, the design for the following year's operation—drafted at a meeting of the staff just prior to the opening of the school in the fall of 1967—appeared as follows:

"Students should be treated as individuals."

This was seen to involve, among other things, the use of individualized instructional materials—particularly in English, foreign languages, mathematics, and science. Some materials were already available in these areas, and it was suggested that additional materials of this type be constructed by teachers in U.S. History, Afro-American history, home economics, and sex education. An additional provision inspired by the "student as individual" recommendation called for the staff to offer courses that students asked for and to allow them to work in whichever courses they desired.

"Power and responsibility in the school should be shared."

In order to insure a student voice in Academy affairs, the staff decided that the students, at their earliest convenience, should elect representatives to meet with the staff and the Advisory Board of the Academy. In addition to this formal mechanism of shared power, each teacher was to be the counselor and advocate of a certain group of students. This meant that he or she was to represent the interests of these students in courts, before prospective employers, in the Academy itself, and so on; in general, the teacher was to interact with the students as much as possible—outside the Academy as well as inside. Both this interpersonal process and the more direct process of soliciting student participation in the design of the Academy were intended to make the school responsive to the needs and desires of the students. Other than these general guidelines, no specification of responsibilities or limitations of authority were made. The notion of "shared power" that was to characterize the Academy was informal, flexible, and subject to endless interpretation, as subsequent events would indicate.

"Collective experiences should be encouraged."

The staff wanted the students to "get themselves together," and a number of vehicles for creating this "togetherness" were suggested: involving the students in musical productions, talent shows, and the like; offering classes in Afro-American history and forming an Afro-American history club; engaging the students in group counseling; and working with the students to develop economic enterprises, several of which were suggested (e.g., packaging plastic spoons and forks for United Airlines; forming a maintenance and janitorial service; operating a bookstore and cafeteria in a new building into which the Academy would soon move, and the like).

"The Academy should be a continuous experiment."

Liaison was established between the Academy and nearby universities, several of which had expressed an interest in the Academy as a "field laboratory," and regular contact with representatives of these universities was attempted by appointing them to the Advisory Board of the school. The staff felt that this arrangement would provide a constant influx of new ideas from the universities to the Academy and that it would aid the Academy staff in critically evaluating their own activities. In addition, Nancy Sheen, as principal of the school, explained that a number of in-service training and education activities would be held through the year, consisting of consultation sessions with members of the Urban Training Center, the Church Federation, well-known educators, and others.

The major tenets of this design are quite general, but they should be seen as having been derived from the assessment Mission administrators made of their potential student body, many of whom they were familiar with through their operation of a tutoring program in the community. In order to work with dropouts—many of whom had taken part-time jobs, some of whom had children of their own to care for, and still others who might be expected to be in and out of jails, hospitals, and reformatories—the Academy had to operate in terms of individual scheduling. The lockstep class structure of most schools would insure that students who had such complicated demands on moments of their time would be at a real disadvantage. Programmed instruction seemed logical: students could miss school for a few days, weeks, or even months and not be set back in their work; they could begin anew where they had left off.

Dropouts, as well as those who manage to stay in school, are not equally prepared in academic matters, and this was clearly shown by the diagnostic tests given to entering Academy students. In order to deal with achievement levels that varied not only between students, but also for each student between subjects, it was necessary for each student to be allowed to work at his or her own rate. Other instructional formats would be woefully ineffi-cient, but once again programmed instruction made sense.

Similar reasoning lay behind provisions for teaching students what they wanted to learn and for allowing students to study what they wanted. Once it was assumed that anything Academy students might learn was a credit to them and an encouragement to learn more, it made sense to grant them this freedom. Although slightly inclined to wonder, "what would happen if . . . ," the designers of the Academy realized they were playing an extremely consequential game, one in which they wanted a particular outcome, not just a record of their effort. This was not just an experiment—which might easily have been conceived in terms that would indicate the lack of viability of certain schooling practices—but a dedicated attempt to find alternatives to what were thought to be the unsuccessful efforts of conventional schools.

The other dimensions of the Academy's design were derived in a similar manner. If the cooperation of students in the school was to be insured without coercion and without payment—two inducements to "cooperation" that are exercised by more conventional schools with debatable success—then it made sense for the staff and administration of the school to involve the students in its operation. To insure their support and continued participation, students were told that the school was "for them" and that they would participate in decisions made about it. Once the decision was made to educate a dropout population whose academic potential was largely unknown, the design of a school responsive to their needs and ambitions appeared to be a sensible way to get information about how to teach them. If the Academy's efforts could be informed by experience, then it made sense to continue to experiment with different teaching techniques as the effectiveness of some efforts seemed diminished or were reevaluated in terms of more successful endeavors.

The emphasis on how "sensible" these decisions were, given the general intent of the school, is not just my own; it illustrates the orientation of those involved with designing the school. Although alternatives to some of the Academy's operating principles were considered, these were rejected not because they failed to conform to a general ideological position, and not because they complicated what was otherwise a well-designed educational experiment, but because they appeared unhelpful to efforts to educate dropouts in the West Park area. It is true that the designers of the Academy were committed to educational reform, not experimentation, but their understanding of what needed to be reformed and what would constitute a successful reform was derived from their everyday experience with students, parents, and others in this community.

This is not to suggest that the school's administrators and staff did not bring their own prejudices and predispositions to the endeavor. It seems clear that such personal contributions of imagination and ideology were important to the Academy's operation. But none of the individuals influential in the founding of the school and its later development had clearly identified his or her own educational posture with respect to historically important educational issues or models for schools. Although the Academy was seen by its members (as well as others) as part of a general movement toward educational reform, it was not a Montessori school, another Summerhill, a Dewey school, a Pestolazzi school, or a Bruner school; the Academy was not a socialist school, a communist school, or a capitalist school; nor was it a school designed to promote any other particular set of ideas, principles, beliefs, or practices. The particular configuration of ideas and activity that the Academy developed was a direct product of the experience of individuals who were involved with it, their ambitions, fears, ideals, and energy, and the community in which they sought to design, construct, and operate this thing they called a school.

Actually, to call this a direct product may be slightly misleading. I do wish to distinguish, however, between a school whose design is inspired by a utopian philosophy and a school like the Academy, which expressed its members' concern first and foremost with a particular group of students at a specific point in time. The product was indirect in other ways. Features that were considered in designing the school were elements of a set of cultural objects, some of them familiar mainly to those concerned with schools and schooling. Thus, there was specific input from the educational profession in addition to that derived from our American heritage. Input also came from two other sources: the personalities and imagination of individual members of the school, and the collective interaction process in which we participated. The design process this describes may be of general applicability and descriptive of the way in which architects, artists, city planners, novelists, and legislators produce their distinctive products.

This is not the end of the line, however, for a product designed in this manner becomes a new element for the next generation of designers to choose from. The novel, painting, building, or theory becomes a new cultural object for the individuals involved, the profession, or the culture as a whole, depending on its distribution and renown. A complete model of the design process must take this circular and cumulative impact into account. It was certainly much in the minds of Mission personnel, for they hoped that their product—the Academy—would be a source of ideas and inspiration for those who would design or redesign schools in the future.

THE ACADEMY IN THE COMMUNITY: SERVICE FOR PROTECTION

The Academy was a point of contact for diverse elements of the community in which it was located, as well as for other communities, cities, states, and even countries that took an interest in its growth and development. When controversies existed among these elements, the Academy (and the larger Mission organization) frequently found itself to be a focal point of the conflict. To some extent this was encouraged by the paternal attitude that many Mission administrators took toward the West Park community; they interpreted their religious roles to include many political and social functions, and they were both praised and damned for doing so by community residents.

It was the Academy, however, that created and maintained the contact among conflicting groups and that acted as a catalyst for many of these controversies. The Academy brought together the church members and administrators of Mission; the teaching staff, many of whom were white and from outside the community; the students, who otherwise would have little contact with the churches; parents of students; political and social clubs or organizations that were interested in the welfare of the community's young men and women; charitable foundations; conventional institutions of social control—the police, schools, and social workers—that wanted to keep an eye on students they thought to be troublemakers; the Chicago "Red Squad," that thought the school was a revolutionary training camp; local businessmen, some of whom did not like the idea of a school for dropouts on their commercial front; the FBI, who associated the school with a black community leader (who had been tried for treason in 1966 and acquitted); representatives from national religious denominations who were intrigued by the ecumenical nature of Mission; and members of Chicago's black community who were interested in just what those white missionaries were doing out there on the West Side.

In the late 1960s, there was indeed a lot of conflict among these elements, and the Academy showed great resiliency as it was pressured by the pushing and pulling of these interest groups. Nevertheless it did not survive unmarked; the racial, economic, and political dynamics of the surrounding community were too forceful, pervasive, and violent to leave it unchanged.

One crucial factor in these community dynamics was that West Park was not in any formal sense a "community." Rather, it was a "community area," the residents of which were, in 1967, newly arrived, jammed together, poor, and politically disenfranchised. Ten years earlier this had been a pleasant residential area with well-cared for lawns and healthy trees. By 1967 the trees, especially along the main boulevard, were dying. Curbs and gutters were cracked and fractured into chunks, and the lawns were bare, brown earth spotted with the garbage of convenience consumption—cans, bottles, paper wrappers. It was a slum and a ghetto, the home of a disadvantaged and disenchanted population.

This decade-long transformation was associated with the movement of middle-class whites from the area and the influx of poor blacks, a transition that took place in a predictable manner. Large dwellings were split into flats so that the same building that had previously housed a single white family became the home of three, four, or five black families. And with this racial change—some argue because of it—city services diminished: curbs and gutters had always cracked, but now they were no longer repaired; trash had always existed, but now it was no longer collected.

The area draws its name from West Park, which lies just to the east, one of the large pleasure garden parks forming an almost completed semicircle around Chicago, part of the famous Burnham plan. To the south, the area is marked off by an expressway, with ten lanes of traffic and a rapid transit line down the middle. On the north boundary a line of the elevated subway—the "L"—parallels the expressway and extends rapid transit service from Lake Michigan westward to Oak Park, a suburb noted for its numerous Frank Lloyd Wright houses.

City engineering has constructed a powerful geometry here as it has elsewhere: lines connect points with each other, and they separate areas. The residents of West Park are effectively cut off from the blacks to the south and the whites and Puerto Ricans to the north. The park itself provides a buffer between residents and the blacks living to the east, leaving only the western boundary unmarked. As a result, a "battle line" formed, a transition zone between the blacks of West Park and the whites to the west, a zone two or three blocks wide and the scene of vicious real estate "block busting" and scare tactics throughout the summer of 1967. The movement of this frontier was rapid; I noticed the leading edge of the blacks (or, if you will, the trailing edge of the whites) move westward at a rate of up to one block every two months during the time I lived here.[1]

Although transportation facilities link the area to the rest of Chicago (buses on major arteries, rapid transit on both the north and south boundaries), they are used primarily for traveling to and from work. Other everyday social and economic transactions of most residents are carried out where they live, and, with the exception of businessmen, residents of other communities do not spend time in the West Park area. There are enough services and attractions to provide for local residents, but there is none of the commercial specialization, historical significance, or distinctive "character" necessary to attract outsiders as visitors or consumers.

In 1967, the state and local political representatives for this black population were absentee whites, two of whom lived in prestigious luxury high-rises on Lake Shore Drive. The only focus for political energies in the area was the group of churches in Mission and a community action project developed by Mission itself. The pastors sometimes referred to it as "a child of Mission, but a bastard child."

Mission itself had begun to form after a serious riot in 1965 called attention to some of the more pressing problems of the community. This "outbreak," the so-called "firehouse riot," was precipitated when a fire truck ran over and killed an elderly female resident, but it took nourishment from the poverty, disease, and disenfranchisement characteristic of the area.

There was real racial tension in West Park, and expressions of it often singled out the white shopowners, white aldermen, white doctors, white teachers, white school principals, white policemen, white congressmen, and others. As five of the eight churches in Mission had white ministers and pastors, and as most of the Academy teachers were white,[2] and as the school's principal Nancy Sheen was white, Mission exhibited structural vulnerability to attacks stemming from this tension. As a result, various efforts were taken by Mission administrators to shore up their organization so that it could deflect such attacks or simply outlast them.

At the orientation sessions just prior to the opening of school in the fall of 1967, the new staff expressed some anxiety over the prospect of working as whites in the black community. This anxiety had its historical antecedents, for the summer of 1967 had been marked by great urban unrest; both the Newark and Detroit insurrections had taken place, and "integration" was not an exciting notion to most people—black or white. The black community was reacting to the deaths of their fellow black men and women at the hand of "trigger-happy" and poorly prepared National Guard or police patrols, and the prevailing climate on the West Side (among community organizers, "militant" blacks, and others) was becoming separatist. In the face of this, the Mission explicitly promoted integration; it espoused the notion of blacks and whites living together in "Christian harmony."

There were at this time three black members of the staff, and Ruth and Suzanne, the two black women, told the rest of us that they would like to see the Academy students have extensive contact with black adults and professionals. If these were not to be found on the staff, they suggested that they be brought in as advisors to the school. The one black male on the staff, Cookie, a sharp and lively young man of 21, set the tone for discussions of this issue. Speaking quickly and with great animation, he remarked:

> I don't have any fear at all, any fear at all, about relating to these guys. I *know* these guys; I know where they come from, what they've been through, what they like, what they don't like. I know these guys because, well . . . I came from the same place, *I've* been through what they've been through, and I'm confident that things will work out just fine. Not that there won't be any problems . . . I might have to wire someone up about this or that . . . but I just think that a person is a person, white, black, or whatever, and if you treat someone as a real person, they will respect you. I mean, that's been *my* experience.

It was comforting to the white members of the staff to hear such humanistic comments from a black person, but it was not completely convincing. We did not doubt Cookie's honesty or his sincerity, but we wondered about how representative his position on this matter was. What about all those people we saw on the street? When Judith and I raised the issue again, we did so explicitly. How was it that in a school that promoted black culture, community development, and student power, most of the staff were white? Was this the will of the black students and community residents?

The returning staff and Mission administrators tried to assure the new staff that this was not a problem, in part by describing examples of the personal relationships they had with the students and other residents and in part by suggesting the important service that the Academy and Mission performed for the students and larger community. According to them, this service was not only important in our terms, but also greatly appreciated by those "served."

For example, Theodore, the white Afro-American history teacher, recounted his rewarding experiences in teaching the Academy students black history and cited numerous examples of the students' appreciation of his efforts to teach them about their own culture. Nancy Sheen corroborated this with a report she made of the pilot phase:

> Negro history became one of the most stimulating subjects. Students said, "I didn't know anything about Negro history until I came here." "Everybody looked down at our race and so did we. I used to think Negroes were a big flop, but now I know to be proud of my race and not ashamed." This emerging self-image and pride began to have visible effects. By May, none of the boys were wearing "process" hair-do's and students began to wear African skull caps, spreading their knowledge of Negro history around the community to younger teens and in their own parties.

Other assertions were made: that the community was glad the school was doing something constructive for the young men and women who attended it, the dropouts and delinquents they had all but given up on; that Mission was all the community had in the way of an organization through which to effect beneficial social change; that the local "Deacons for Defense" appreciated the Academy's efforts, as did Vin Hascot, a black political candidate, Hu-Hu Howell of the Cobras street gang, "Mellow" of the Vice-Lords, and numerous other important, tough, and influential blacks in the community. In short, we were told—and there was some truth to it—that the most militant, the most politically active, and the most significant blacks in the community were in favor of the school and what it was doing. Our confidence increased as some of these individuals were brought in and openly welcomed the staff; it seemed that they would protect us while we served the community.

WITH BLACK POWER ON OUR SIDE

There was another dimension to the kind of emotional "insurance policy" that the veteran missionaries sold to the new recruits, and that relied on the seriousness with which students and residents regarded "Black Power." Rev. Keen, pulling lightly on the corners of his goatee and speaking in very even tones described to the group the following incident:

> Let me tell you something about Black Power. The other day I saw Twister, one of our students, bothering one of the female students . . . they were standing over there on the steps. She was telling him to leave her alone, but he kept . . . molesting her. I saw this and I yelled, "Black Power, Twister!"
>
> Twister stopped and turned around: "Black Power? Just what do you mean Black Power?"
>
> I said, "Black Power means economic freedom, political freedom,

and cultural respect for all black people. If you respect black people you won't treat that young lady that way." This, he understood. Twister understood what I meant and apologized to the girl.

The anecdote indicates that the white ministers and staff members of the Academy could use "Black Power" and "Black Consciousness" to make the students take themselves seriously, seriously that is in staff and administration terms. And, rather consistently, these terms were not personal. It was a great comfort to the staff to be able to discuss specific behavior in ideological and political terms, thus avoiding what might otherwise have been rather difficult face-to-face interpersonal exchanges. The rhetoric was used to demonstrate that students were responsible to "Blacks," Black Power, and their professed political ideals, not just to Academy staff and administrators. It was more convenient, and safer, to be able to say to a disruptive student, "Stop, for the sake of Black Power" than to say, "Stop, for *my* sake."

In some instances, students expressed suspicion about such efforts at avoiding the personal basis of judgments about their behavior. They would remark, for example, "Don't jive me. . . . Don't give me any of that bullshit! What's the *real* reason for ['you working here,' 'you saying that,' 'you acting that way,'] ?" It seems that this suspicion was cumulative, contributing to the general distrust that students showed for staff motives at the Academy. However, this distrust was still less than that they had showed for other teachers and administrators with whom they had come in contact.

Even more than making them suspicious, I suspect that this gambit by the staff confused the students. The constant denial of personal motives or a personal frame of reference for interaction in the school no doubt encouraged the mystification of this aspect of the students' experience.

Rev. Keen's anecdote also indicates that conditions were such that influential whites (i.e., teachers, pastors, and others) could assist young blacks in defining the terms of their own identity.[3] The Academy staff and administration were instrumental in defining the phrase Black Power for the students, and, of course, the phrase was defined so that it would allow for the continued presence of the Academy in the black community.[4] This process depended, of course, on some positive affect toward these whites by the students. Without feelings of respect, admiration, or affection, those who worked at the school would have had little influence on the students.

The Academy was perhaps most important to Black Power in an indirect way. By simply providing a place where young blacks could come—regardless of their academic credentials, police records, family circumstances, poverty, wealth, or neighborhood (which often implied gang membership)—and be rewarded for discussing the vicissitudes of their individual lives, the school served to refine and sophisticate the political climate in the community. Young blacks became articulate, not just in the provincial jargon of their street, block, and neighborhood, but also in a more general language of social, political, and economic criticism. As a result, Academy students were well known throughout the community for their political sophistication, a quality in evidence not only at meetings and in their writings, but also at demonstrations, "incidents," and during the major outbreak of burning, looting, and violence set off by the assassination of Dr. Martin Luther King and nurtured by Mayor Richard J. Daley's orders to "shoot to kill all arsonists, and shoot to maim all looters."

That the Academy reaped some rewards for the welcome and encouragement it showed its students was clear, as events following Dr. King's death indicate. The day after Dr. King was assassinated, students from Sherrif High School stormed through their school (after an attempted memorial assembly) setting numerous small fires, smashing some windows, and making a lot of noise, and then gathered a few blocks away in West Park for a large rally. Speakers at this rally encouraged those present (a crowd estimated by participating Academy students at two thousand) to "keep the cool," to take Dr. King's death as a lesson in what to expect from whites and, more importantly, in what to expect from America. Not only was Dr. King shot down, they argued, but also Malcolm X and John F. Kennedy. Among the speakers were two Academy students and others from the community or the crowd who simply wanted to make their voices heard. Although the speakers at this meeting exhorted their audience to end white control of black communities, to demand better jobs and better schools, and in general to put an end to racial oppression, they did not tell people to go out and burn and loot. In fact, some speakers explicitly told the crowd that they would only be hurting themselves by rioting.

As the speeches dragged on, however, a movement began from around the periphery of the crowd to march to Meadows High School, fourteen blocks to the west and predominantly white. As this notion gained attention and momentum, the crowd swelled and buckled and began moving west toward the high school. When they reached the school, numerous fights broke out between Sherrif and Meadows students, fights that reflected the racial split between the two schools. And as the unorganized and leaderless mob pushed its way back down the sidewalks toward the park—spilling into the street, walking and jogging five, six, and seven abreast—some of the more daring young men and women began smashing windows. Others, following them both in the line of march and in daring, plucked items from shop windows, and still others shamed them for doing this.

At one point the crowd surged thickly in front of the Academy, which had two large plate glass windows on its storefront facade, and Pud took brief command by waving his arms, yelling, and threatening individuals who refused to listen to him. The swell in the mob receded and the marchers moved down the block. Pud, who was one of the students most critical of the school, had saved the Academy from certain acts of destruction.

At other times the Academy's image did not fare so well. The firing of Call Strow was met with great hostility from numerous black professionals around Chicago. The school's reputation as a sensitive and responsive community school was damaged by these events. To advocate Black Power in public speeches and yet fire a popular black principal of the Academy did not sit well with some of the school's supporters.

But even in this case, a strange irony emerged, for the strongest advocates of Call Strow and the students in this conflict were the veteran white staff teachers. When they were fired or resigned, it was black and not white replacements that were found for them. Slowly, the Academy increased the proportion of blacks on the staff. At some point, Black Power became a very confused issue, an incompletely formed ideology complicated by the lack of an institutional target. Structural vulnerability had been alleviated: the Academy had teachers who were black. The issues raised with the energy of demands for "black control," issues which were general in their implications (e.g., questions of student, parent, and community control; questions of the political focus of the school), were required to find another source of sustenance. In some ways, Mission could stand pat.

During the two years of its operation with which I am most familiar, the Academy represented the institutional racism that characterizes the whole of American society. In spite of the fact that the proportion of blacks involved with the school showed a general (but not continuous) increase, the "educational experiment" was largely administered by white people for black people.[5] The pervasive but unexceptional irony of the Academy's operation was that it was controlled by white people who were committed to assisting and leading black people in a fight against white racism, poverty, and social disorganization.

The fact that the white people involved with the Mission organization and the Academy were often considered to be well meaning is irrelevant to the structural institution of racial segregation. In fact, they were not considered to be well meaning by everyone, and their impact derived from the visibility of their position, not merely from the more subtle elements of their personal motivation and intent.[6] It is not necessary to characterize the whites as "agents of evil" in order to appreciate the function they served in maintaining some of the more destructive racial stereotypes of the larger society. If students at the Academy learned arithmetic, they also learned that they learned it from a white person. If students at the Academy received a college scholarship, they also learned that it was from white people. Given this dominant role of white people in the Academy, the success it had in freeing students from their status of "high school dropouts" also can be seen to contribute to the racial oppression that the Academy's members sought to fight.[7] If you were a black dropout in the West Park area, you knew that you had to rely on the white people at Mission to do something about it, and you had to rely on them rather than on black people. This can hardly be described as a "progressive" lesson in black independence.

BARGAINING FROM THE THRESHOLD
OF SUCCESS

In the two years of operation described here (February 1967 to February 1969) the Academy changed from its initial emphasis on informal and interpersonal interaction to a more highly structured organization that could deal with more students (although less personally), that could be more clearly described to the outside world, and that gave students more reference points to the types of educational settings they had experienced previously. There were more students, a greater percentage of female students, and "better students" coming to the Academy.[8] These students worked harder at their studies than previous students had, and there was a continuous increase in the importance of college, an importance often spurred to incredible heights by a return visit of one or more of the previous year's graduates who were currently in attendance at a college in California, Utah, or some other exotic locale. In addition, the composition of the staff changed from entirely white to over half black. The staff during these two years also refined the organization of courses and the presentation of curriculum materials, providing both integration and sequencing of courses characteristic of a comprehensive curriculum. Interaction with outsiders involved in developing curricula for professional purposes (e.g., publishing houses, museums, other schools) also increased, and members of the staff were called upon more and more to appear as consultants to other educational enterprises. Such interaction motivated the staff to further refine their curriculum ideas and materials, and a number of steps were taken toward the publication of materials developed at the Academy.

The physical setting in which all this took place also underwent a number of changes. After its initial sessions in the old church, the Academy moved to a far more modern building, one complete with linoleum floors, fluorescent lighting, a large glass storefront, and brightly painted corridors and stairwells, a building that contained a great deal more usable space than had the church. More and more visitors came to this building as the Academy developed a wider and wider reputation, and some efforts were made to insure that the Academy was presented in its best light. A modern, sculptured fountain was put in the lobby; it was partly a donation of a friendly artist, but nevertheless it cost $1,500. Teachers were admonished to keep their rooms clean, and greater care was taken in displaying student art work around the building. This increasing emphasis on cleanliness and orderliness was not a spontaneous development among the staff; rather, it was the result of deliberate efforts by the Mission administration to improve the image of the Academy for purposes of raising money, gaining the respect of local residents, and increasing the effectiveness of their political posture toward conventional institutions.

Thus, the Academy was launched on a successful career. This success brought with it increased interaction with the conventional order and more demands that the operation of the school be formalized. When coupled with the timetable of the demonstration phase (which called for documentation and demonstration, rather than experimentation), these changes brought the Academy from an organizational format characterized as "one large family" to one which was more like "one small factory." As both the students and the Academy achieved what was initially considered to be "incidental" success at conventional tasks, the pressure increased to accept these as not only the major accomplishments of the Academy, but also as the guidelines for future development.

Part III
Principles

5

Making the Academy
Make Sense

In looking at organizations, the contemporary emphasis suggests that bureaucracies are "where it's at." As a result, the nonbureaucratic organozation has received little attention. In part this is due to an assumption that such smaller and less formalized organizations will either bureaucratize or perish; organizations that survive only through the ad hoc dedication and energy of particular individuals are seen to have a very short life span. The lack of attention given to these organizations is also indicative of their coordination, or lack of it, with more established and stable entities. When football schedules are planned ten years in advance, it is unlikely that a new, informal football organization will climb to national prominence during its first outing, no matter how good the team is. Similarly, accrediting bodies stipulate that a school to be must operate for a certain number of years before it can be even considered for accreditation.

The importance of these matters to organizational study is that when adopting a developmental model of organizations, which appears almost axiomatically these days, it is difficult to avoid the implicit assumption that the organization somehow "matures" or evolves to its "natural" or "final" state. What is missing from such a formulation is the recognition that the organization is just as real early in its history as it is later on. The emerging properties which may later characterize its operation are not the only critical features to examine, and to suggest that they are is to encourage both a theoretical and a methodological bias. It is, of course, easier to describe an organization when its operation has become routinized, even if the routines are less than exhaustive descriptions of the activity that occurs within it. The impact of the organization, however, stems not from how predictable and bureaucratized its functions are, but from the importance it enjoys within the social context in which it is found.

The attention given to large bureaucratic organizations also suggests the inadequacy of existing theory to address questions about goals, personal identity, and symbolic integration. When there is an official statement of these elements, the sociologist has been handed a convenient research motif. When what the "organization" says it is doing is clear, and when the rationale for its members' behavior is part of an institutional rhetoric, a simple comparison between "supposed to" and "in fact" is bound to unearth unexamined discrepancies. Official policy is always somewhat at odds with actual practice, and yet our inclination to believe officials is such that the demonstration of this fact is usually "news." Indeed, the second chapter of this book is cast in these familiar terms.

So it is but a small matter, though a continually important one, to show that things are not what they seem. We ought to move on, however, to show how things really are and why they are that way. When the subject of a study is bureaucratic, efforts to answer these questions typically involve a more detailed analysis of the "structural" characteristics of the organization. Through this familiar research there runs a vision of organizations as social facts, entities separate from and external to the humans who inhabit them. These studies show individuals fitting in, adapting to, and working within the environment of the organization. In a powerful though frequently implicit way, the organization is seen as more orderly, more coherent, and ultimately more real than the people who are engaged with it.

This is a popular approach. It centers on an image of the organization as a coherent set of behavioral patterns, external to the lives of individuals, explained by and oriented toward a simple set of official goals.[1] In contrast, I found Mission Academy to be complex, flexible, and adaptable to and expressive of the needs of individuals. I also found the people to be at least as real as the organization. Symbolic integration of organizational and personal goals was clearly in evidence, but it was not all of a piece. Rather, several models or "characters" for the school emerged, and each of these was useful to individuals in establishing behavioral priorities.[2] In the day-to-day life of the school, these characters were invoked to rationalize action, make decisions, and generate meaning. They were the school or schools in which members found themselves to be engaged. They were both creations and environments, symbolic resources that members had constructed and that were subsequently useful to those same members in locating and understanding their lives and their work.[3]

This process of creating the symbolic structures in which members then grounded their behavior was the basis for organizational integration at Mission Academy. It involved the efforts of members to make personal sense out of activity that had institutional sanction and to build into the school representations of their personal concerns. In examining this process, we will see how official goals at the Academy, many of which came from the imagination of members and from a more general movement for educational reform, became useful to individuals as larger expressions of their personal ambitions.

The complicated manner in which the conjunction of personal and official goals gave meaning to everyday life at the Academy presents a critical problem in understanding the school, both for those who worked there and for the researcher. On the one hand, there was no consistent body of tradition, routine, or even social precedent on which to base explanations of what was supposed to happen. On the other hand, there was no consistent attempt to derive, from an accepted and explicit set of goals, the ethic, means, or technology by which they might be achieved. Instead, the school was started "from scratch," and exhibited throughout its early history massive oscillations between induction and deduction about the state of its effort: at one moment, a particular classroom success would be escalated into an all-encompassing goal; at another moment, a curriculum discussion among staff members would call all classroom activity into question; and at still another moment, the students and teachers would drop everything because "one of the brothers is in jail."

BUILDING REFORM INTO THE SCHOOL: A LIMITED SUCCESS

A prime source of inspiration for those involved with Mission Academy was a social movement dedicated to educational reform. This movement has occasioned the founding of numerous experimental, alternative, or irregular schools within its broad outlines. These exhibit a great diversity, for the "crisis in education," when mapped into particular social situations, gives rise to quite different schools. In part this is a consequence of incoherent movement ideology, the often vague and ambiguous nature of many of its principles. More important, however, is advocacy of the "responsiveness" of schools to those they are seen to service and affect. The diversity of movement schools is largely a result of establishing "responsive" schools in different social settings and attempting to give substance to the intentions of quite varied, disparate, and sometimes socially or politically polarized segments of the American population.

Mission Academy was designed to operate in just such a responsive manner, but its members' conceptions of what this meant changed from time to time. Both the nature of responsiveness and the identification of those to whom the school was supposed to respond were continually discussed and modified throughout the school's development. Early statements about the Academy stressed as its goal the service the school was to perform in the surrounding community. In these accounts, it was suggested that the school was responding to the specific needs of dropouts in the West Park area:

> The Academy was born at a [Mission] evaluation conference in October, 1966. The Pastors and education experts agreed that the existing [Mission] tutoring program (800 students, 252 tutors) was not effecting real change; something more was needed. [Someone] . . . put forth the idea of a school for drop-outs. [Mission] was ready for the idea—here was a chance to get away from bandaid efforts, by attempting radical change in education dealing with the causes of the drop-out problem. There is a massive drop-out problem in the [Mission] community, with which [Mission] was well acquainted, through previous work with teens and involvement in community problems.[4]

By the end of the pilot phase, there was still an emphasis on the dropouts in West Park, but there was increased attention given to more general issues of educational reform. The community to which the school was being responsive had increased in size. The Academy was no longer simply concerned with the disadvantaged youth in the immediate geographical community, but with all students in inner-city schools. Mission administrators and pastors hoped that if the Academy were a success it would inspire other communities to develop similar schools and provide a model for reform of conventional school systems. As the school developed, this more general goal became increasingly important to those involved with the Academy—and a source of much conflict.

The emphasis on responsiveness that is characteristic of the educational reform movement—often expressed in calls for "student power" or "community control"—contains a crucial ambiguity: the determination of the group to which a school will be responsive. Those involved with the Academy were aware of how complicated such a determination could become, especially when appealing to a heterogeneous population for support and cooperation. As an early statement by Rev. Keen indicates, it was unclear whether the school would cater primarily to students interested in "getting ahead" academically or to those who wanted to stand the social order on its ear:

> The school's philosophy is flexible now, but we're approaching a decision. One of these days soon we're going to have to choose between enabling students to adapt to existing society, and turning out revolutionaries who are capable of changing it.

This dilemma was continually reexperienced throughout my association with the school. If the Academy was too radically critical of conventional educational practices (if, for example, it rejected not only grading, but also credit and credentials as symbols of academic achievement), it would lose the support of many community residents and students, most of whom wanted their experience with the school to "matter" in the more conventional social order. If, on the other hand, the school was too committed to standards of conventional academic success, it would only supplement the offerings of existing schools, performing a residual function and effectively reducing the pressure exerted by community residents to change these larger and more powerful school systems. Neither alternative was acceptable to those involved with the Academy, and constant efforts were made to keep it from deteriorating into one or the other of these ineffectual configurations.

Discussions among the staff of the Academy about the school's curriculum often focused on this dilemma between aiding individual students and changing society. When consultants from the Urban Training Center (present at the school for an in-service seminar) emphasized helping Academy students "make it" in society, Rev. Keen suggested that arrangements be made for students to accompany an executive around for a day, "to see how he *operates,*" arrangements which would include lunch for the student and perhaps dinner at the executive's home. Several staff members reacted strongly both to the general orientation of the consultants' remarks and Rev. Keen's proposal. We were critical of the implicit assumptions of individual upward mobility in these efforts and of the corresponding suggestions that the Academy provide its students with models and skills for successful competition for scarce resources. Instead, we called for an emphasis in the school on encouraging students to work collectively to change the society— changing it, in fact, to diminish the dependence of personal well-being on individual economic efforts. The meeting ended, as would other meetings of this type, on the note that these two objectives were not incompatible, and that efforts should be made to help students who wanted to "make it economically" as well as those intent on developing "revolutionary consciousness."

Behind this dilemma lay conflicting models of the Academy's constituency. It was stated that this was a community school, one which catered to the youth in the West Park area regardless of their political, social, or neighborhood persuasion. But because this resident population of dropouts was not of a single mind, they placed competing demands on the school. The academically motivated dropouts wanted everything to function smoothly and with relative impersonality; they were concerned only with getting a high school diploma and moving on to college or employment. The more politically active dropouts wanted things to be quite different, however, and they called for the cancellation of classes, special privileges, and the loan of school facilities and resources to help them achieve political reform in the community. To say that the school was a community school was to embrace the conflict that existed between and among community residents, and this appeared as a great liability to Mission administrators.

In order to protect the school from this conflict, the Academy's administrators underlined the school's commitment to extensive educational reform. Being a successful school in West Park was not enough, they argued. It was important to change Chicago's public schools, not just help a few students on the West Side. In making this claim, the Mission administrators called upon the "larger community" as their constituency. Thus, the school was seen to represent the interests of all well-intentioned high school dropouts everywhere.

Then came the determination of what "well-intentioned" meant. Did it mean those students who expressed their wholehearted commitment to overthrowing conventional schools and instituting "movement" inspired changes? Or did it mean those who were serious about their studies, who were willing to work long and hard on improving their academic skills and getting ahead in the world, to be examples for their fellow men and women? It seems clear that once the Academy was oriented toward larger reform it could no longer rely for guidance on the vicissitudes of the population of the local community. Rather, it had to act aggressively to suggest what activity was appropriate to its goals. Precluding the opportunity to take direction from all students meant that the school had to offer direction to some.

Although a number of confrontations with these issues ended with members of the staff and students affirming that all student aspirations were legitimate, not all such encounters did. In March of 1968 sixteen students were suspended from the Academy for "not being ready to participate in the Academy as serious students." This action was defended as necessary to insure that those students who wanted to learn would be able to do so. The ironies here were powerful. The Academy had prided itself for some time as a school for dropouts, a school where disadvantaged students were given a second chance, a school where you could work at your own rate and study what you wanted. In suspending these students—who were literally labelled the "not for real" students, as opposed to the "for real" students—much of the Academy's operating ideology was called into question, not only for the students, but for the staff as well.

The circumstances surrounding these proceedings were exceptional, and they drove Rev. Keen to close the school for a week due to what he perceived as a total breakdown in discipline among the students. His decision was immediately sparked by Nancy Sheen's report that someone had stolen fifty dollars from her purse, but it involved recognition of other recent thefts and an important fight that had broken out the previous Friday.

The fight directly addressed the goals of the Academy, as it made explicit the tension between students at the Academy who were working seriously for a high school diploma and acceptance into college and those who used the school primarily for its social and cultural functions. The latter group included students who had been at the Academy since its beginning, and they had developed close personal relations with Nancy. Those students intent on using the Academy as a serious preparation for college were largely new. The "old" students had constituted a formal gang at one time; as a group they engaged in harassment and intimidation of new students at the school, particularly those who showed exceptional academic abilities. The old gang was neither large enough nor diverse enough to integrate into its structure these new students who performed better in class than did the old members.

The fight itself, between Pud and Lamont, was not as vicious as the threats and contingencies surrounding it.[5] An attempt at reconciliation of the two students—and their potential constituencies, real or imagined—was unsuccessful, and there was the possibility of a gun battle in front of, inside of, or somewhere around the Academy. It was in the face of these circumstances that Rev. Keen closed the school, the only time the Academy was closed during the year other than for holidays and normal vacations. During the remainder of the year, the staff referred to this as "the crisis," and indeed it was, a crisis not only in the social order of the school but in the elaborate meaning that members found in its professed goals.

A letter was sent to the sixteen students found to be "not for real," most of whom were in the "old gang" group. The letter indicated that the entire staff of the Academy felt that they were not profiting from their association with the school, nor were the Academy and other students profiting from their presence there. In their notices of suspension, these "not for real" students were told that if they wished to be reinstated they could be, by applying for an interview and appearing with a parent or guardian for an orientation session. They were also to complete a number of academic assignments on their own, to—in Rev. Keen's words—"put them through a few hoops" before being returned to the good graces of the Academy.

At the same time, forty-seven students were found to be "for real," including Lamont, and were sent letters indicating that the school would open the following Monday and encouraging them to attend. In the letter, the staff apologized for the disruptions that had taken place during the previous week and indicated that the conflicts that had produced them had been dealt with. In anticipation of some disturbances, Rev. Keen arranged for a policeman to be in the school during the following week to insure that "not for real" students were prevented from attending.

The staff was demoralized by these proceedings, for they contradicted another very important "movement" principle—one that the staff took quite seriously as individuals: participatory democracy. In addition to being "responsive," the reform movement ideology stipulated that schools, as well as other institutions, should be operated on a cooperative basis. At the

Academy, this had been attempted with very limited success, but it was nevertheless an important ideal in the minds of the staff, the administration, and the students. The development of a healthy cooperative organization for the school was seen as the only guarantee that the school could remain responsive to those it sought to serve. The suspension of the sixteen students by the staff and administration (although some students were present when these decisions were made) seemed to clearly violate this principle.

This was a difficult week for everyone involved. At one meeting Rider stomped out, accusing the rest of the staff of turning the Academy into a "regular school." Judith refused to condone the suspensions and was particularly angry about Rev. Keen's arrangement for having policemen placed on duty in the school lobby. We all shared feelings of shame about what we had done, feelings that were not really compensated for by our recognition that we had in fact acted as some students would have wanted us to.

Members of the Academy identified with the movement; they took bits and pieces of movement rhetoric and ideology from its literature, its speakers, and its folklore. But these had to be given substance in the West Park area, and in fleshing out their alternative school there was little to go by. The two principles of "responsiveness" and "consensus" persisted, important points of correspondence between the Academy and the movement. These ideological elements established the school's membership in the "collective" enterprise, a loose fraternity of experimental, alternative, and irregular educators that has developed over the years.

The importance of this shared ideology, however primitive it (and its concomitant fraternity of educators) might have been, was that it provided a larger purpose for what might otherwise have been considered insignificant independent actions. As such, it was important not only to the integration of different shools into the reform movement, but also to the integration of parts and functions within individual schools. In some sense, it provided a rationalization for the goals of a particular school, for these represent the mapping of an ideology into a set of situationally possible actions.

This mapping process, whereby organization members select from the possible courses of action those that they feel are consistent with their ideological premises, is invariably historically grounded. As possibilities for action change—in connection with real or imagined problems arising from environment and technology—this mapping requires the continual attention of those involved. Characteristically, the effort of individuals to make sense out of and to build sense into the organization of which they are members is a process of deliberation and choice that establishes the meaning in their work.

In suspending sixteen students from a school that had previously been described as "theirs," the staff and administration of the Academy called into question not only the trust they had carefully nurtured with the students, but also the moral meaning of their work. By voiding the unwritten terms of their sustaining relationship with the larger social movement, the significance of everyday activity in the school was greatly diminished. After the school had resumed, Theodore spoke for the rest of the staff when he said, "Well, it certainly is quieter, and things move more smoothly without all those students. But ... I don't know. It's just not exciting." This lack of excitement—the energy of anticipation and dedication—was indeed missing from the school after the suspensions, for the moral order of the enterprise had been dealt a serious blow.

THE POOL OF PERSONAL GOALS

The severe costs to morale of the suspension proceedings, to the students as well as to the staff, suggest that factors other than an implicit movement ideology were important to those who worked in the Academy. Indeed this is the case, for a crucial input to Academy affairs was the set of fears, ambitions, and goals that individuals had for its operation. Those involved with the school were not doctrinaire in terms of educational philosophy or social critique, and they frequently expressed intentions for its development that were characteristic of their roles in it. The movement contributed principles of responsiveness and consensual operation, but students, teachers, and administrators elaborated these principles in terms of their personal goals and particular world views.

It should come as no surprise that the goals Academy members held for the school were never codified or made explicit. Rather, what they wanted from the school, as well as what they hoped it would be for themselves and others, was expressed in day-to-day incidents. For example, in the early spring of 1968, television reporters came to the Academy to make a brief film to be aired on the evening news. Most of their footage consisted of interviews held with students in the lobby. Seated in one of the school's formed plastic chairs, on which were focused four large floodlamps, Pud answered their questions, accompanied by the laughter and hand slapping of his fellow students:

Interviewer: Where did you go to high school before coming to [Mission]?

Pud: Sherrif, Derrick, Bellingham, and St. Charles [a regional reformatory].

Interviewer: (who was visibly amused by Pud's extensive credentials): What do you like about the Academy that makes it different from these other places?

Pud: Well, I mean, here you can work at your own rate, study what you
want . . . nobody gets on your case all the time. . . . This is *our* school
. . . we do with it what we want . . . can you dig?

Pud's remarks were echoed by Twister, Fester, Denice, and Lamont, all of
whom were interviewed in the same setting, and they contain references to
the major goals that the students held for the school. First among these was
the principle that "each student can work at his own rate." When indicating
what it was they found attractive about the school, students frequently cited
this aspect of the Academy's operation. Another common expression used by
students was that "at the Academy, you can study what you want." In
addition to these remarks, students would state, "you can do what you want;
they don't have any silly rules about no smoking, no talking, and so on";
"teachers are your friends here, not like at Sherrif where they couldn't wait
to kick you out of their class"; and "this is *our* school."

These remarks describe an ideal that was informal: where instruction was
individualized—both with respect to content and a schedule for completion;
where teachers were considered to be confederates rather than opponents;
and where there was a strong sense of "we-ness."[6] All of these characteristics
were perceived, of course, in relation to the students' previous experience
with conventional schools (in particular, the city's public high schools). Many
Academy students had been failed or rejected by these schools. In seeing
themselves as victims, they neutralized the impact of this failure. In the
alternative and unconventional schooling of the Academy, they were able to
move from this victimization to an identity that embraced general educational reform, a metaphorical movement from misfit to missionary. The
experience of being at the Academy allowed them to move from failure, to
victim, to reform advocate—both in their own minds and in their public
reputations. As advocates for educational reform, they were also good
students. Their success at the Academy showed to one and all that responsibility for their previous failure lay with the conventional schools.

Lacking from the students' goals for the school was any reference to the
amount or kind of learning that was to take place there, but students usually
emphasized "getting my diploma" when asked about what they wanted from
the Academy. The hopes they held for the Academy involved maintaining it
as an encouraging, accepting environment so that its salutory effects on their
individual academic achievement would continue. Students wanted the
Academy to provide the means for them to further their education (primarily
to receive their diplomas) on their own terms, and it was an important
institution in their lives both to the extent that it allowed them to do this and
to the extent that these terms were unacceptable to surrounding conventional
schools.

The goals that teachers held for the Academy were more complicated than those of the students. In part this was due to the remuneration provided for their services. For most of the staff, jobs at the Academy were their only source of income. Consequently, they had an interest in maintaining the financial solvency of the organization, an interest that for some took precedence over their other interests in the school.

Rider, who was better at directly expressing his emotions than was the rest of the staff, was at the same time the strongest advocate of alternative service to students and job security for himself. During the "crisis," he disrupted a staff meeting in which a proposal had been made to close down the school and direct all energies toward educational consulting. His voice breaking, his face reddened with an emotional rush of blood, Rider rose from his chair and spoke directly to the point:

> I just cannot be a part of what is going on here . . . you people are sitting around calmly discussing whether or not there's going to be a school. . . . I can't believe this. . . . there is a school and you've created it . . . and now you just want to destroy it so you can . . . how can you forget the fact that there are a lot of students in this school who *need* this school . . . and you're just going to . . . close it. A lot of good things have happened here, you can't deny that . . . you're saying that "this would be a good school—all we have to do is get rid of the students." . . . I refuse to be a part of this destruction. . . .

The staff was visibly moved by his feeling for the "special" kind of education that took place at the Academy, as well as Rider's analysis of expelling the more troublesome students. One of their objectives for the school was that it directly improve the life situations of its students, and Rider's remarks reminded us of our commitment to this goal.

During the summer of 1968 I shared with Rider a criticism that I had made of Rev. Keen.[7] Rider responded by saying:

> Well, personally I can't stand [Keen]. But, there's one thing you have to say for him: he can sure make the eagle shit. Without [Keen] out dashing around to New York, Washington, and all those other places, there wouldn't be any money to run this place. He knows how to sell this place to all those rich guys and foundations . . . he just knows how to make the eagle shit.

The continued existence of the Academy was important to the staff for personal reasons. Two members of the staff (Cockey and I) had deferments from the army for working there; Rider, Theodore, Judith, and Cookie (in addition to Cockey and I) earned their livelihood by working at the Academy; and Hal had made arrangements with a teacher training program to have his teaching experience at the Academy apply toward his MAT degree. Consequently, the staff wanted the Academy to continue to provide them with employment.

In addition to their desires to help the students and to have the Academy provide them with jobs, the staff looked to the Academy as a way of achieving larger social reforms. Involvement with the school was part of their "reformist" identity. Most of the staff said that they could "never teach in a public school" because of the harm that such schools did to students.

In order to maintain their reform identity and its rewards, it was important that the Academy be an alternative to "established" school systems. One of the most important ways in which the Academy differed from conventional schools was in its conception of the student, and the staff strongly supported the idea that students were basically adults and should be full members of the school. In fact, they supported this principle more than did the students themselves; it was more important to their identity as imaginative and "humane" teachers than it was to the students' desires to get their diplomas. The staff wanted students to be involved with running the school so that they could teach in just such a school.

The administration of the Academy, during its first eighteen months, consisted of Nancy Sheen and Rev. Keen. Their major ambition for the school was that it continue, and do so under their direction. As Nancy Sheen wrote in the *Mission Newsletter* in June 1967, "[Mission] is determined that this important demonstration of methods and approaches which work when our SYSTEM has failed not stop now when the idea has been tested and is now ready for a larger application." A similar position was revealed to me by Nancy Sheen in a personal communication in the fall of 1968; at this later date, however, she indicated that "we can't stop now until we fully prove that our methods work." Throughout the operation of the Academy, Nancy Sheen and Rev. Keen called for support of the Academy by pointing to the critical nature of the school's development; "we can't stop now" meant, in effect, "we can't stop."

The continued operation of the Academy was important to these two individuals in part because it helped hold the larger Mission organization together. Rev. Keen told me in the summer of 1968, "Boy, if it wasn't for the Academy, [Mission] might have folded on a number of occasions. This school represents the biggest visible success of [Mission] and when things get really torn apart, we can say, 'well, what about the Academy?' " Both Nancy Sheen and Rev. Keen sensibly sought to maintain the larger Mission organization; it was, in effect, their social, political, affiliative, and religious world. The "Mission Family" was not just an interesting locution; it was a real work and affinity group which protected its members, engaged in constant face-to-face interaction, shared meals and automobiles, and sought to carve out a large place for itself in the West Park area.[8]

In addition to helping Nancy Sheen and Rev. Keen maintain the involvement of the churches in the Mission organization, the Academy brought them fame and fortune. Visitors from all over the United States "look to [Mission] as a model of encumenism, and they look to the academy to see what churches can do when they get together." Their identities as reform entrepreneurs were greatly enhanced by their successful efforts to solicit funds for the Academy from large eastern foundations, their increased contact with well-known educators (e.g., Mario Fantini, Nat Hentoff), and the publicity they received in the local and national press. Nancy Sheen and Rev. Keen had been instrumental in establishing the Academy, and as its renown grew, this reflected on their contributions to its development. To the extent that they looked at the Academy as part of them (or "theirs"), they sought to maintain that part.[9]

Even though the primary goal of its administrators was to have the Academy continue, they recognized that this could not take place unless the school was recognized as a significant educational experiment, for the school was funded as a "Second Chance Model Demonstration High School." To the extent that the Academy was "just another school" it would be difficult to find funding for it, its national and local reputation as a social experiment would diminish, and it would be much less of an attraction to the Mission organization. It would also contradict the administrators' reformist identities. Thus, their objectives for the Academy for the first eighteen months included the "experimentation" and "innovation" required to guarantee the school's survival.[10]

In contrast to this, Call Strow sought to insure that the Academy developed first and foremost as an experiment designed to change the public schools. If this occasioned the end of the Academy as it was then conceived, Strow believed that this would merely be a product of natural growth. Because of his extensive contact with cultural and political organizations within the black community, and because his involvement with the Academy began well after it was on its financial feet,[11] Call Strow's goals for the Academy were more concerned with what it might become than with what it had been in the past.

Although in the few months of his administration he did not outline an explicit future for the school, Call Strow did envision the Academy becoming part of a comprehensive alternative school system for the entire city, a system that would involve five or six similar high schools, several colleges and universities, and numerous elementary schools. Preliminary discussions were begun with the departments of education at two of the largest universities in the area, and some efforts were made to secure funds for the program.

Taking these sets of personal goals together, the most commonly held and highly valued ideal for the Academy was that it continue its operation in much the same form as it had developed: as an "experimental school." This was considered by those involved with the school to be a prerequisite for achievement of their individual ambitions.[12] And, the extent to which these individuals wanted the school to continue to "experiment" was contingent on their evaluations of how such experimentation would affect efforts to achieve their personal ambitions within the school.

The term "experiment" may be inappropriate, for the dimensions that characterized the Academy as an "experimental school" became well established, and within the school itself they were considered to be conventions. A summary of these characteristics as goals of and for the Academy appears as follows:

Conventional Academic Achievement. It was hoped that the Academy would be successful in helping students "make it" academically. This involved an emphasis on programmed instruction, natural group processes, and the use of culturally relevant subject matter. Success in achieving this goal was directly related to having students take credit for their Academy experience by passing the G.E.D. examination and receiving a diploma from the state board of education.

Intervention in the Entire Social Space of the Student. Goals for the Academy included more than just the transmission of conventional subject matter to students, and it was expected that the services of the school would help to improve their total life chances (i.e., through counseling, job placement, college placement, legal assistance, and the like).

Redefinition of the Teacher-Student Relationship. Academy members felt that the technical competence of the staff should be passed on to the student. This was interpreted to include teaching techniques as well as familiarity with subject matter. In addition, it was felt that teachers should be confederates of students, not opponents.

Redefinition of the Role of "Student." A simple statement of this goal was the Academy members' support of "student power" (which was an expression of Black Power when students were black). Students were to be full members of the school and have the same civic power as teachers and administrators.

Operation of the School as a Cooperative Collective Enterprise. Associated with full membership for students, teachers, and administrators, this was an assumption of cooperative decision-making. All members of the Academy were to be involved in all decisions affecting its operation.

These characteristic goals of the school have been described as the consequence of individual translation and interpretation of responsive and consensual (in this case "cooperative") schooling. Although all these goals had their supporters, they were not always achieved in the operation of the school. To some extent, members of the Academy explained this failure as a result of lack of commitment to the goals or the inadequacy of the organization's resources. Although these explanations are not without merit—there were indeed limitations of time, money, energy, and dedication—these "failures" appear to be more the consequence of the nonenhancing or counterproductive nature of the goals themselves.

The most important contradiction contained within the set of goals that members held for the school lay between commitment to a cooperative form of organization and commitment to achieving conventional academic success. To involve students fully in the operation of the school meant that a number of normal operating principles of schools (as well as other service organizations) would be called into question. For example, it could not be assumed that teachers had appropriate expertise, that staff determinations of what was "important" subject matter were legitimate, or that the work teachers did on their teaching would be highly valued. As a result, the school's technology (its curriculum) was constantly reevaluated, questioned, examined, and modified. The consequences of this "dynamic" curriculum were debatable, but most staff and students agreed that it was dysfunctional when it changed so frequently that students did not know what was expected of them in their course work.

Alternatively, for teachers to impress upon students the need to do well in conventional school tasks undercut the more general efforts to establish parity in teacher student relationships. Given that the staff was responsible for accrediting student work, it was difficult for students and staff to experience the school as equals. In practice, their distinctive roles were augmented by differentials in background, life chances, age, and race. There existed a tension between "instructing" and "cooperating," between "teaching" and "rapping," and it often seemed that to succeed at one was to fail at the other.

ORGANIZATIONAL INTEGRATION THROUGH SERIAL ADVOCACY

The educational reform movement and its friends at the Academy had inspired the establishment of a school that sought to improve the lives of high school dropouts through its operation as an alternative to conventional schools. The functional nature of its most "alternative" aspects was clear to the Academy's members and appeared as common sense, nonideological solutions to clearly stated problems in schooling. But these objectives were never evaluated *in toto*. Their advocates never examined them as a source of potential integration or lack of integration of the Academy's goals, technology (its means), and larger purpose. The counterproductive, nonenhancing, and competitive nature of this particular set of ideals was unclear to those at the school, and as a result they were mystified about this aspect of its operation.

This mystification could have led to a number of crises in the moral order of the school. Individuals could have become frustrated with the apparent lack of success of their efforts, not realizing that they were working in two directions at once, and this did occur from time to time. Additionally, and more importantly, the integration of an individual's efforts with those of his co-workers, the school's stated purpose, and the commitment of all its members could have been called into serious question. This might suggest that the school was no more and no less than a collection of people pursuing their separate interests in personalistic contexts. The collective significance of any action would have been greatly threatened by such a failure in moral integration, but such a crisis of meaning did not occur.

The meaning of activity is derived from the context in which it occurs; a crisis in the moral order signifies not a change of context but a lack of context (although this may result from changes which seemingly threaten all frames of reference by suggesting how temporary and precarious their realities are). Fortunately, at Mission Academy individuals exhibited a remarkable capacity to change the contexts of their actions frequently, radically, and often joyfully, with the rewards of impending integration outweighing any fears of instability. The symbolic integration among various goals was accomplished not by the development of a single mission or purpose for the organization but through a characteristic set of "models" or "characters." Decisions were made on the basis of these, but none of them by itself fully integrated the goals of Academy members with the technology and operating principles of the school.

Two of these models were expressed in an article I prepared in April 1968 entitled, "Position Paper: Future of [Mission] Academy." It concluded:

> In sum, it seems that we are not only trying to change the world, but trying to change it in every way imaginable, in a short period of time, and with less than a dozen people. Maybe it's time we got ourselves together, quit trying to have everybody doing everything, and just tried to run a school for this community with one bunch of people and just tried to write curriculum and consult with another bunch. . . .

In addition to the models of "community school" and "educational research and consulting agency" implicit in the above paragraph, the character of the Academy was sometimes that of an "experimental school" or a "revolutionary training camp." These models or characters for the Academy organized some of its objectives in packages that made sense of the ambitions of its members. For example, as an experimental school the Academy was seen in terms of the redefinition of the teacher-student relationship, student power, and cooperative decision-making. But as an experimental school, the Academy was not primarily concerned with conventional academic achievement.[13] As a result, the experimental school model integrated some of the goals for the Academy into a coherent whole, but not all of them.

Similarly, the revolutionary camp model emphasized passing the expertise of the staff on to the student (where such expertise was "revolutionary consciousness"), but it did so at the expense of student power and cooperative decision-making. This model provided a close correspondence to the ideals of the staff, but the disparity between these ideals and student ambitions made it largely impractical.

The community school model emphasized intervention in the total life space of the student, and it called for active parent and civic involvement from the local community. Such involvement, however, appeared to work against Academy technology (i.e., its curriculum) and to disrupt the success-oriented learning that had been associated with it.[14]

The educational research and consulting agency model was similar to the revolutionary camp model in that it had a close correspondence to staff goals. Rather than emphasizing the transmission of staff expertise to the student, however, this agency model emphasized conventional academic achievement to the exclusion of other objectives. It was this model that inspired Rider to say that the staff thought the Academy would be a great place if they could just get rid of the students.

Although the staff and students did not explicitly articulate these various models for the Academy, the models provided significant contexts within which decisions could be made, and their capacity to "orient" action in the school was of great importance. For example, the students asked that special classes be offered which were designed only to prepare them for the G.E.D. exam, and the staff discussed its response. According to the experimental school model, the staff felt it would have to offer the courses, simply because the students had asked for them. However, Theodore and Rider called upon other staff members to think of the school as "something other than just a 'student-run school.' " Rider said, "This is a special school, and we have a commitment to what is special about it, and that is not just preparing students for the G.E.D." As a result, the staff decided to offer the course just one afternoon a week, and further stipulated that students could take it only if they were actively working in their other courses. This decision came after Rider posed the questions "What kind of school do the rest of you think this is?" The various models of the Academy provided a set of answers, and, as such, they constituted an operating identity for the school.

None of these models or characters fully integrated the objectives that member groups had for the Academy. As a consequence, the operation of the school was switched from one model to another; within a given period, all of them were utilized. This process of "serial advocacy" was manifest in an organizational concentration on one model or character at a time. As weeks and months went by, the models appeared, disappeared, and reappeared within a pattern of shifting priorities. This process drew upon the school's multiple characters to take advantage of funding opportunities, to communicate with constituencies external to the Academy, and to provide solutions to internal problems of social control.[15]

Alternative forms of integration for the Academy could have developed, but they did not. One way in which an organization can deal with a set of objectives that are not mutually enhancing is through functional segregation; this allows the organization to focus its efforts in more than one direction and institutionalizes the competition for scarce resources. It can take place horizontally (e.g., between departments of a university), or vertically (e.g., segregation of financial and teaching enterprises by the separation of administrative and teaching responsibilities). Development of such functional segregation was inhibited at the Academy by its small size (which provided for face-to-face contact between all members of the Academy every day), by the strong ethic of cooperative decision-making (which stipulated that all members were to be involved in all decisions), and by a general lack of trust among its members.

This distrust can in part be explained by the different social worlds in which the students, staff, and administration elaborated their respective egos. In addition, it can be seen as a consequence of the lack of specification of a mission for the Academy. Without a clearly defined mission, and with a strong emphasis on cooperative decision-making, it was necessary to continually assess the potential contributions of others to decisions that would infringe upon one's own "working space." In practice, this lack of trust encouraged constant surveillance of the activities of others, a process that would have been constrained by functional segregation.

Another way to integrate organizational objectives is to modify the objectives themselves. This was attempted at the Academy on a number of occasions, but the involvement of all essential personnel could only be assured through a continuing commitment to all of their objectives.

Integration can also be achieved through substitution of a common means for nonenhancing goals. For example, a service organization might achieve some degree of integration through asserting that *all* objectives would be furthered through increased contact between staff and clients; emphasis could then be placed on increasing such contact rather than on the lower order objectives. This emphasis on a common means, however, requires standardization of the setting in which the organization does its work. Irregular attendance patterns, efforts to structure experimental situations (i.e., by definition "nonstandard"), and crises precipitated by elements internal or external to the Academy all worked against such standardization. As a further inhibition of the "common means" solution to organizational integration, members of the Academy actually cherished its "uncommon" means.

The difficulties involved in integrating objectives in one of the ways described above, combined with a real capacity to segregate its efforts over time, allowed the Academy to engage in serial advocacy throughout its history. This process accounted not only for the diversity of school activities, but also for the survival of ideals that would have been rendered extinct by strict adherence to one organizational character. The survival of these goals, in turn, gave the Academy a strong capacity to adapt to new situations. There was always a version of the school that could correspond, with minor revisions, to what the situation demanded.

Serial advocacy was not without its costs, however, and the whole business created continual anxiety and frustration for the staff, administration, and students. In their efforts to develop one model as a success, they contributed to the temporary failure of another, one that in its turn would be of real significance. The fragmented character of the Academy gave it the capacity to adapt to a wide variety of situations. Like its psychological counterpart, however, fragmentation made it difficult for anyone to determine where the Academy was in terms of its own development.

6

The Academy's
Program for Reform

Time, as it appears to us every day, seems to move forward, and we usually expect "things" to move forward with it: careers, technology, the seasons, courts of law, relationships, the economy, building construction, clothing styles, and organizations, to name a few. This linear understanding of time is the axis on which we plot the points of events, and their separation and distinction provide the basis for evaluations of change.

When evaluating an organization, we want to know how well it has done what it said it was going to do. Given the passage of some time, is it accomplishing what it "means" to accomplish? We also want to know how well it is doing what it says it is doing currently. Is its self-portrayal an accurate one?

Presumptions of a direction to an organization's activities are crucial to the answers that organization members, the public, and social scientists supply for these questions. Such direction (or directions) serves to integrate the many activities of the organization into a comprehensive purpose; it provides a context in which to assess "progress" or change; it tempers "momentary" disparities between ideals and realities; and it provides an important element of coordination between the directions individuals impute to their lives and the involvement they maintain in organizations. People "going places" are not inclined to invest themselves in organizations "going nowhere."

For the people who worked at Mission Academy, it was definitely an organization that was "going places," both in the West Park area and in the larger sense of participating in a social movement for educational reform. Agreement among the staff, students, and administration about the school's movement, however, did not extend to the mechanism by which it moved. Although it was clear that the Academy was going places, it was unclear how it would get there.

A CHOICE OF STRATEGIES: "BOTTOM UP"
OR "TOP DOWN"

When explaining and describing activities in which they will be engaged, individuals frequently structure their remarks around three questions (or their functional equivalents): what to do? how to do it? and why? In some sense, an answer to the first question suggests what the "goals" of activity are. An answer to the second describes the technology involved in achieving these goals, and the third question involves statements about the purpose of the activity to the actor, its place in a larger system of meaning. If these three levels of symbolic organization are integrated within some coherent framework for action, we can call this framework a "mission."

At Mission Academy the actions of individuals were infused with purpose from the very beginnings of the school; the importance of their work was clear to everyone engaged in it. The "why?" question had been answered before the school itself was founded (or, for others, before they began working there), largely by the ideological premises of the reform movement of which the Academy was considered to be a part. In addition, there was, for some, the Christian and evangelical orientation that pervaded the larger Mission organization, an orientation that suggested that this "Mission Academy activity" enjoyed not only the positive sanction of educational reformers, but also the blessing and divine favor of "missionary" endeavors. In contrast to organizations that have clearly established goals but a lack of purpose, Mission Academy had purposeful commitment from its members long before its immediate goals were articulated.

The lack of coordination between purpose and goals for the school can be explained in part by the historical and social circumstances surrounding its development. The civil rights movement had recently galvanized collective social identities, such that you were either "for" or "against" civil rights. In much the same way, you were either "for" or "against" changing schools. In fact, a bumper sticker popular during this time simply read "SCHOOLS"; it was assumed that to raise the issue was to be aligned with the forces seeking to change them. As a result of this activist climate, the staff, students, and administration of the Academy were united "against" conventional school systems without having articulated a policy for changing them.

Efforts to elaborate the organization's policy from the depth of this pre-existant commitment brought about serious conflicts. In fact, as the preceding chapter has shown, no single model appeared comprehensively to integrate the Academy's operation in all its aspects. Instead of such holistic integration, the Academy exhibited a more piecemeal structure, one characterized by numerous models or characters rather than a single, all-encompassing mission.

In addition to the serial advocacy of these models, the operation of the school was characterized by an alternating commitment to two frequently competing constituencies. In terms of authority and position within the conventional social order, these might be called, quite simply, the "haves" and the "have-nots."[1] While these two categories had some currency at the school, there was disagreement among the Academy's members as to how they ought to be characterized and how they might best be dealt with.

The arguments for the effectiveness of each constitutency were understood by all those involved with the school. The "haves" (e.g., school principals, school board members, city administrators, university education school chairmen) were thought to be in positions of effective authority; as a result they would be able to implement Mission recommendations for reform, once convinced of their validity. The "have nots" (e.g., community residents, students at the Academy and in Chicago's extensive public and parochial school systems, political activists) were thought to be effective in resisting conventional schooling and demanding that changes be made. Large institutions need the daily cooperation of these "grass roots" people, it was argued, and by refusing to offer this cooperation, these people could exercise real power and effect significant change. The question was one of choosing a "bottom up" or a "top down" approach to educational reform.

In choosing between the two, Academy members were oriented toward differing conceptions of each constituency. By and large, there was agreement that the "haves" were rationally utilitarian. Mission administrators took the object of this utiliarianism to be "doing a good job." The staff, however, was more inclined to view these individuals as rational only in guaranteeing and increasing their personal advantage. As for the "have nots," there was even greater disagreement. The staff conceived of this group as more honest, sincere, altruistic, and genuinely concerned about human rights and human suffering—a product of their experience as oppressed people—and more capable of acting in the interests of others than were those in high positions. The Mission administrators did not wholly reject this view, but were more concerned with what they saw as the provincialism, ignorance, disorganization, and incompetence of the grass roots. Thus, while the structural power of each constituency was recognized by all those at the Academy, the staff was more inclined to cast their lot with the "have nots," while the Mission administrators saw relationships with the "haves" as more productive in the long run.

Associated with these separate loyalties were different sets of tactics—different strategies for enlisting the support of the target constituency. Given the picture that Nancy Sheen and Rev. Keen had of the "haves," it is understandable that they sought merely to "demonstrate" the validity of the Academy's program. It was assumed that politically neutral, rationally utilitarian school administrators could be swayed by documented proof of the effectiveness of alternative programs, to change public school systems for the better. It is equally understandable that the staff, given their conception of such administrators as self-interested and corrupted by power, did not follow this tack, but rather appealed to the grass roots to bring pressure to bear on the particular "haves" under which they labored.

In some sense these constituency/tactic packages represented a play for the heads of those in power versus a play for the hearts of the oppressed. The elements of romanticism in the two postures are parallel, however, for the "haves" lack hearts no more than the "have nots" lack heads. The character distortion that these conceptions suggest stemmed more from the ambiguous status of the Academy than from empirical examination of the two constituencies. In fact, it may have been derived largely from the situations in which this status was negotiated. Contact with the "haves" was usually in the form of casual, somewhat personal interviews arranged at the convenience of both parties and involving the standard politesse of such situations. Communications through letters followed an analogous formula. There was no question of pressure or threat, and it would appear that "rational," convincing discourse was the order of the day. These situations implied: "Impress me with your documentation, leave your studies with me, and I will give it my considered attention," and that is precisely what the "haves" received from Mission personnel.

With the grass roots, however, contact was likely to be made in groups and meetings, gatherings of students, parents, church members, and so on. In these situations, speaking to the "heart" through the use of strong images, apt phrases, and statements of conviction solved important problems of maintaining group attention and cohesion. Although documentation was important to such audiences, the manner in which such documentation was presented was crucial. In contrast to the "promising interview," these group meetings were matters of the moment, energizing encounters worked out in affective dynamics.

The characteristic forms of contact between the Academy and the two constituencies can be seen as a consequence of the school's position within the social order as somewhere in between the "haves" and the "have nots." Lacking the renown or political power to draw a crowd of school administrators and board members to hear their remarks, Mission personnel were obligated to see these figures individually. But, having just such a reputation within the community and among less powerful people, Academy members could speak to large audiences of the grass roots people. Behind these dynamics of social status and reputation lay the equation of institutional control: a few people with a lot of power versus a lot of people each with a little bit of power. In the balance of the effort, it was enough to convince a few "haves" in order to see some progress being made. For those working with the "have nots," numbers meant everything.

It can be seen from this analysis that the conceptions that members of the Academy held of the two major constituent ideals influenced their loyalties and further guided their tactics for enlisting support. It should also be evident, however, that such tactics and choices reinforced the original conceptions. When Mission administrators sat in closed offices talking to "big wigs," they observed civility and rationality; at the same time, the staff who were not present found additional evidence that such individuals were deceptive and self-serving. The staff gave moving speeches to responsive audiences and increased their sympathy for the oppressed, activities that simultaneously indicated to Mission administrators that such groups were easily swayed and poorly organized.[2]

Disagreement between staff and administration over the proper constituency to address and how it should be addressed, however, often overshadowed a more fundamental agreement about the arbitrary existence of the school to both efforts. Attempts to enlist the support of the two constituencies did not have to be made on the basis of an existing, ongoing alternative school. In fact, a number of instances occurred in which Academy members discussed whether or not their efforts at social change were being hampered by the day-to-day attention they gave to teaching students. At more than one meeting, arguments were presented for closing down the Academy as a school and directing all staff and administrative efforts toward meeting with the larger constituencies that were seen to be crucial factors in the school's strategies for educational reform.

The fact that this did not occur—although steps were taken to free some individuals from Academy responsibilities so that they could more effectively work with outside constituencies—may be explained in part by the great moral risks involved. As long as Mission Academy operated as a school, there were rewards to be gained from teaching, and the experiences summarized by student academic achievement were tangible, everyday testimony to the fact that something "good" was being done. Without this day-to-day validation of the Academy's members' identities as alternative educators, the success of their efforts would appear much more problematic. If they devoted all their energy to influencing a diffuse and largely unknown constituency to effect important changes in schools, the measure of their success would await the realization of those changes.

Another factor that was crucial to the Academy's survival as a school was that the area in which goals, procedures, and achievement were most clearly articulated was that of the curriculum. Although this was described throughout the Academy's history, the first attempt to codify the curriculum in one coherent document occurred in the fall of 1968 at the beginning of the demonstration phase. This was done in part as an effort to describe to the new staff (and others interested in the operation and welfare of the Academy) what the Academy was seeking to do and how it was seeking to do it. I was primarily responsible for these efforts, although other staff members contributed descriptions of the courses which they taught.

At the beginning of the document is the phrase: "Give a man a fish and he will eat today. Teach a man how to fish and he will eat forever."[3] These two lines were used in an attempt to capture the spirit of the Academy's enterprise. However, they assumed that the Academy was a school and that it was an attempt to improve upon the methods used in conventional schools.

The body of the document I wrote is a description of the Academy's curriculum. As a preface to descriptions of individual courses, I outlined five objectives of education at Mission Academy:

1. Basic skills in communication: Regardless of what vocation a person chooses, it is imperative that he be able to communicate with those around him. Our educational objective is that our students learn to listen, read, write, and to speak with facility.

2. The formation of individual and collective identity: A person must have experiences which aid him in describing himself, in appreciating "who he is."

3. An appreciation of the heritage of man and the varieties of human life. Regardless of what a person becomes, the greater his understanding is of how other people live and have lived, the greater will be the options open to him for his own action.

     This should increase his understanding of other people and enrich his cultural perspectives.

4. Skills in self-expression: The sense of mastery which a person achieves through participating in the creative arts not only encourages the development of a positive self-image, but also provides him with the skills necessary to *respond* creatively to his environment.

5. An ability to solve problems: A person should be able to think analytically and critically, and provide creative and thoughtful solutions to problems that he might face, regardless of what those problems might be.

     We would also emphasize that these five objectives are not discrete disciplines, areas of study, experiences, etc. They are all inextricably connected within the broad objective of encouraging students to become "whole people" and developing in them a sense for what is "human."

The text following this preface indicated the manner in which each of these objectives had been operationalized in terms of educational opportunities at the Academy. For example, the following passage relates the objective of "skills in self-expression" to the subject matter offerings in the school:

4. Skills in self-expression: Our subject matter is the field of creative arts. By offering our students opportunities participate in drama, art, writing, music, etc., we seek to increase their sense of mastery and provide them with the experiences and skills necessary for continued activity in these areas throughout their lives.

In some respects, this codification of the school's curriculum or technology was premature. As it was the most clearly articulated aspect of the school's operation, the curriculum assumed extraordinary importance in the subsequent development of the school. One way in which this occurred was through the use of the curriculum description as an important vehicle for relating to other organizations. Subsequent attempts to revise the curriculum or express fundamental criticism of it were then inhibited by Mission administrators who felt the organization's image and integrity to be at stake.

Thus, when I prepared a critique of the curriculum, I was told by Nancy Sheen and Rev. Keen that it was interesting but irrelevant. They said that copies of the curriculum description itself had already been sent to other organizations (among them sources of funding) and that to send those organizations the critique would be detrimental to the positive image that the school needed to maintain. As Rev. Keen said, "If a salesman told you everything that was wrong with a car, you would never buy it. We can't afford to have these negative views of the Academy as part of our advertising."

Timing and staging were very important in these matters, for Academy members were committed to reform prior to the articulation of the school's goals and operating procedures. This commitment appeared as a resource of energy and dedication to be tapped. In looking to the school for an expression of this commitment, however, the staff found very little. Disagreement about the nature and efficacy of outside constituencies made the Academy's strategies for change a problematic investment at best. The school's operation, on the other hand, offered little more than a series of almost daily crisis that called into question the selection of courses as well as whether or not there would be any courses, or credit, or even students.

The lack of direct linkage between the reasons why people came to the school and the specifics of its operation made the early articulation of the curriculum a critical event. In some sense it was seized on by students, teachers, and administrators as a welcome object for their dedication, an area of some consensus with day-to-day implications. In these dynamics, however, the curriculum did more than provide an outlet for the energy of Academy members, for it also gave increased substance to the experience of the classroom. In addition, as the most clearly articulated aspect of the school's operation it was an important instrument in the strategy for change. For all these reasons the curriculum—more than any other aspect of the school—became the symbol of what the Academy did.

The significance that the curriculum achieved within these dynamics elevated its status to that of a goal of the organization. Thus, rather than continuing to develop new curricula for educating inner-city blacks, the Academy moved to a position of maintaining the academic successes it had already achieved. Rather than continued experimentation, the dominant concern at the school became the "polishing up" of what had already been done.

In that it described what the school did, the curriculum served as a public communication to potential constituencies of the Academy. Its description did not particularly help members of the school resolve the conflict they experienced between identifying with the "haves" or the "have nots," but it certainly gave those potential constituencies something on which to base their support, or lack of it, for the school.

"RADICAL" AMBITIONS AND A "REFORM" REALITY

The conflict between members of the Academy over whether they should organize the grass roots or demonstrate the validity of educational principles to those in power did not occur in a vacuum, nor was it without reference to specific decisions about policy at the school. This conflict was grounded in a larger context through references made to existing or planned schools or schooling programs exhibiting an approach to social change that the Academy might emulate. Two of the more influential of these exemplary programs were the American Institute of Engineering and Technology (AIET) and Call Strow's conception of a super-system of alternative schools. A description of these two entities—one in operation, one only planned—should help clarify how differently individuals at the Academy conceived of their effort to achieve fundamental change in conventional schools.

The AIET, a major outlet for Manpower Defense Training funds, was located on Chicago's West Side about two miles from the Academy, so it was an easy matter to pay a visit. According to the program's director, the young men (age nineteen to twenty-nine) who enroll in the Institute have almost perfect attendance and improve their arithmetic and reading levels at a constant pace. In addition to learning basic skills in math and English up to eighth grade level, students are trained in a skill designated by the Institute and based on projected manpower needs of major industrial firms. The director spoke with pride in reporting that in six months students advanced in status from "hard core unemployed" to that of "semi-skilled laborer."

Although Rev. Keen found the director's description of the program to be very attractive, the Academy staff were disturbed by the Institute's acceptance of the conventional social order, an environment the staff had characterized as racist and exploitative. Theodore asked what he hoped would be an embarrassing question: "Why don't you offer Afro-American history here? How can young black people learn about their own heritage?" The AIET director responded by summoning a tall, thin, well-dressed black man, who entered the room and immediately lit a cigarette which hung from the director's lips. The director thanked him, introduced him to us as an associate director, and asked him to answer Theodore's question, which he did:

> Black power to me means Green power, and that's what we teach here. If you have a job, you can have money; if you have money, you can have power; and if you have power, you can be a man. For a black man, a job is Black power.[4]

Given their goal of fundamental social change, the staff of the Academy did not like hearing these remarks. They became even more discouraged when Rev. Keen asked Lamont—one of the best Academy students—what he would think of attending the Institute's school. Lamont said it would be a "good thing": as he put it, "At least if you learn a trade, you can always fall back on it. If I graduate from Mission, I don't know what I'll do."

This incident was a real blow to the staff's conception of organizing the grass roots to effect radical change. Lamont was the grass roots, and yet he was impressed by the very conventional offerings of the Institute; preferring the presumed security of a trade even to a high school diploma from the Academy.

Rev. Keen, on the other hand, was greatly inspired by the whole business and found Lamont's remarks encouraging. At a subsequent staff meeting, he proposed that arrangements be made for Academy students who would rather attend the AIET school to do so. On this occasion, Rev. Keen's enthusiasm—and his disagreement with the staff's commitment to "fundamental social change"—went even further, for he suggested that the AIET school was a model for what Mission Academy could hope to become. Both he and Nancy Sheen expressed their great admiration for the AIET program and commented on how clearly the Institute had demonstrated the effectiveness of its teaching methods.[5] As Rev. Keen put it, "They really know what they are doing. They take some student here, and they do this to him, and he comes out over here in just so much time, and they are sure of what he has learned. They've been in this business for a long time, and they know how to do it."

The staff rejected Rev. Keen's suggestions in general, but it was Judith who finally focused the sense of their critique:

I disagree with all the support you're showing for their program: I think it's really deceptive. Their organization is fundamentally different from the Academy; they are only a residual operation, attempting to deal with the consequences of a fundamentally corrupt social order rather than trying to change that social order. The students who go to their school get paid to go there, they are discouraged from attending college, and they are kept from raising their achievement levels above the eighth grade level.[6] AIET is making money, not teaching. They get paid $3,000 by the government for every student they train; that's part of the program. And, in general, . . . well, I think that their school is antithetical to the Academy, particularly in its conception of the role of the student, the role of the teacher, and the extent to which non-coercive learning can take place.

Conflict over the proper strategy for social change became more consequential during the school's demonstration phase, when the position of Strategy for Change Director was created. Nancy Sheen, who had been principal of the Academy until this point, took the position, making room for Call Strow to join the school as its principal. The separation of the day-to-day operation of the school from the larger concerns of effecting educational reform that this arrangement suggested was not very well achieved. In fact, the two positions and their incumbents were the focus of a great deal of conflict, as the following should indicate:

When he began his term as principal of the Academy, Call Strow recommended that the Academy seek to develop more significant relationships with other experimental schools, cultural institutions, and black community action groups (he had already established substantial contact with a number of these organizations previous to his employment with the Academy). During the first month of his administration, a number of black student organizations called a student strike of Chicago's public high schools. The leaders of some of these organizations were subsequently expelled or suspended from their schools, and Call Strow suggested opening the Academy to a meeting of all students in the city who were on strike.[7] Both Nancy Sheen and Rev. Keen rejected this suggestion and said that "the Academy is an experiment, not a political organization."

The implications of Call Strow's efforts were clear. If the Academy were to extend itself to other organizations through his leadership, continued relationships with these organizations might encourage the staff at the Academy to change the direction of their efforts. In particular, the balance of the school might be altered, moving from the developed, codified curriculum to something less concerned with the classroom and more concerned with political action. This would mean that the Academy's duplicating equipment would be used not to turn out math and science courses to be shown to educational administrators, but to turn out newsletters and organizational materials for the grass roots. It also meant that classrooms might become meeting rooms for black students from around the city, and it meant that Call Strow would undercut the leadership of Nancy Sheen in coordinating the school's relationships with the larger society. The Mission administrators did not want any of these things to happen, and it was in part out of fear of these developments that Call Strow was fired.

Before he left the Academy, Call Strow outlined his position even more clearly. He felt that before any significant change took place in the public schools in the city, it would be necessary to develop a comprehensive alternative school system so that students would have the option of never transferring back into the conventional schools once they had enrolled in one of the alternative schools, and so that a much larger constituency of people could be mobilized to change the public schools. As he said before he was fired, "Shit, Jon, this Academy is just a drop in the bucket. Who cares what goes on in this little place. How many students do we have? Two hundred? Three hundred? Hell, we need to get a couple thousand students and their parents involved before anything is going to change."

Firing Call Strow did not really make explicit the Academy's strategy for change. By and large, the school's means for achieving its most general goals were vague and ambiguous, and this may have been important to its survival. The immediate constituency of the Academy was so varied (with respect to socioeconomic status, political persuasion, and cultural orientation) that a more explicit and definitive statement of the school's overall mission might have spelled disaster. The Academy had to be attractive to students, teachers, parents, and foundations. If these groups were not particularly attractive to each other, they could be involved together only through self-elaboration of their roles in the school itself, and this elaboration would only be inhibited by a clear expression of how the Academy was going about changing other schools.

Without making it explicit, the firings did make more and more clear the commitment of the school to working with the "haves," to demonstrating the validity of educational practices for those in positions of conventional authority. Efforts at organizing the grass roots, those affected by their participation in particular schools, were gradually diminished; those who most strongly advocated this strategy were fired or otherwise dismissed. Call Strow, Cockey, and I (who were fired), Rider and Theodore (who resigned), and the sixteen suspended students of the year before were all more enamored of the grass roots orientation than were other members of the Academy.[8] With the advocates of organizing gone, there remained only the "demonstrators," compiling their rather casual data and writing letters to school board members.

Although some ideological discrimination may have guided the dismissal of these students and staff (as well as the two voluntary resignations), other factors seem equally important, and notable among these were bureaucratic concerns for the administration of the school. For example, when Rev. Keen expressed his admiration for the AIET program, Judith criticized his position by pointing out important ideological differences between the Institute and the Academy. In replying to her critique, however, Rev. Keen did not comment on ideology but simply restated his admiration for such a "success-ful"and "well-run" school."I wish the Academy could operate so smoothly," he said. Those who were fired or expelled and those who resigned were not just "politically" at odds with the Mission administration; they were also obstacles to the "smooth" operation of the school.

The Academy adopted as its legal title, "The Mission Academy: Educa-tional Research Project and Model Demonstration High School," and indeed this title became more and more characteristic of the school's operation. As the Mission administrators attempted to stabilize activities in the school and increase its renown among important educators, school administrators, politi-cians, and civic leaders, the Academy lost some of its contact with the grass roots constituency that had once been cultivated. Not only did the Academy look less and less to these people as a potential ally in its strategy for change, but they looked less and less to the Academy as an ally in their own struggles.

THE MISSION OF MISSION ACADEMY: THE POLITICAL LIMITS OF "PROOF"

Judging from observations made both while I was at the Academy and at other schools, this "demonstration" model of social change appears to be incomplete and naïve The numerous expressions of the need to "prove" that the Academy's techniques would work, made by Rev. Keen and Nancy Sheen,[9] appear to be part of an underelaborated model of social change—a model that assumes that the inefficiencies, inequalities, and inhumanities of the contemporary American educational enterprise are based solely on ignorance, and that knowledge alone will correct them. The Mission adminis-trators felt that if the Academy succeeded in improving the academic achieve-ment levels of high school dropouts—and proved that this had in fact been done—the public high schools would automatically adopt their recommenda-tions for change.

This "demonstration" orientation on the part of the Mission administra-tors ignores both the complicated and indirect processes by which "scien-tific" knowledge becomes incorporated into public policy, and the often complex constituencies by which the "haves" maintain their positions of social privilege and political authority. Rev. Keen and Nancy Sheen, in spite of their genuine critiques of conventional schooling, tended to see administrators as uncomplicated brokers, seeking only to negotiate policy between conflicting interest groups, but not participating in any interest group themselves.[10] What this conception ignores is that there are segments of the population whose organization as interest groups is much less complete than that of the corporate rich, professionals, labor unions, and political parties. While the "haves" may in some situations operate in the manner suggested by Keen and Sheen, they pick and choose the interest groups they are to negotiate between; and the poor, young, nonwhite, female, and elderly are seldom chosen.

In keeping with their "demonstration" orientation to social change, Rev. Keen and Nancy Sheen stressed being "aggressive towards institutions, but conciliatory towards individuals." This remark suggests not only their admiration for Richard Hauser, whose models for social change make this explicit, but also a characteristically Christian frame of reference.[11] It assumed that the "good" in people could be relied on, that "virtue" could be shared and encouraged in others, and that once the "truth" of the undertaking were known, others would see it and follow.

The inadequacy of their vision, however, lay not in an overcommitment to the "good" in people, but in a reliance on conventional administrators to see that Academy's truths as their own. The fundamentally political process of deliberate social change was dismissed. They failed to note that schools are not run nor begun nor maintained by Christian computors, but by individuals who (like the teachers, students, and administrators at the Academy) work to bring sense and meaning into the world in which they live, a world they share only in part with the students and teachers affected by their administration. It was not enough to prove that the Academy's methods worked for its own students. It would not even be enough to show that these methods would work for other students. In order to convince conventional school administrators to follow suite, it would have to be proved that Academy methods would do as much for those administrators as for the students in their schools. And, in this matter, there was plenty of room for doubt.

Part IV
People and Classes

7

Curriculum

Communication between two individuals is rarely so symmetrical that the meaning of what one says corresponds exactly to what the other hears, and communication between teachers and students is no exception. In fact, the elaborate and distilled organization of information (referred to as "subject matter" or "curriculum") that the teacher seeks to share with the student is hardly conducive to the development of this symmetry, and apprehensions about student and teacher roles may further complicate this process. It should be no surprise then, that what is learned in schools is not identical to what is taught.

This does not imply that students cannot "learn" a certain percentage of the material that an instructor is "teaching," but rather that they learn a great deal in addition. Fennessey has described some of the elements of this process as it occurs in elementary schools:

> Social habits must be learned through practice, and cultural values must be validated by perceived social support. Thus, undertaking classroom maintenance responsibilities, playing games which emphasize teamwork and sportsmanship, controlling one's attention to requirements established by someone else, working for a deferred or symbolic reward, feeling positive emotions about the flag, the policeman, the Constitution, etc.—all these are not so much knowledge as they are learned habits or attitudes. The classroom serves as the social setting in which most of this kind of learning takes place.

Students may also "learn" from the physical surroundings in which their instruction takes place. Thus, rows of desks, rectangular rooms, separate toilets and athletic facilities for men and women, the linear pattern of classrooms opening off of halls, and in general the functionally segregated physical organization of school buildings are significant aspects of the student's school experience. In some instances, these physical arrangements transmit explicit norms of behavior (e.g., individualized desks "communicate" to students that they are to be individually responsible for what occurs in their "place" in the room), and even when they do not do so explicitly, they frequently "encourage" or facilitate the development of such norms.

Conventional wisdom entertains this more general conception of education as "social learning." Movements toward educational reform have often embraced it in advocacy of educating the "whole person" or in critiques of conventional schools as "dehumanizing." Vernacular references to "social learning" abound as well, stressing the educational value of life experience (e.g., the school of hard knocks, street wise, and the like) as well as the implicit messages students get from time spent in schools (e.g., "What I really learned was how to 'psyche out' the teachers").

A more specialized understanding of "education" persists, however, and it has to do with what is deliberately taught and what students are expected to learn. These intentional elements of learning in the schools are usually called the curriculum.[1] At the Academy, this involved programmed learning, experiments with group dynamics, "experiential classes," and "cultural relevance."

PROGRAMMED INSTRUCTION: PROGRESS WITHOUT PASSION

In general, requirements for the completion of a course at Mission Academy were set by the instructor. In the beginning these were rather vague and typically stressed the kind of activity that would go on in the course rather than the performances required by a student to complete it. For example, Cockey, the English instructor, wrote the following: "English II program concerns itself with developing skills in comprehension and critical analysis of tone and style from a wide selection of authors' works" (a list of materials to be used in the course followed this brief introduction). The requirements were even less clear for completion of the Story Workshop and some of the other classes.

Students in the Academy were uncomfortable with vague statements of requirements for completion. During the first few months of the experimental phase, they worked hardest in those courses where they knew exactly what was expected of them—the elementary math and English courses, where course work was based on programmed materials. Students were encouraged by the explicit procedures for obtaining a credit in these courses, and they valued such credits highly. Attendance at basic math and English classes was usually double that of the other classes.

In addition to the high relative attendance figures, these two classes were characterized by dramatic student achievement. Test scores indicated that students working in the basic math class increased their achievement levels an average of 2.2 grade levels in the twelve weeks from October 1967 to January

TABLE 3

Arithmetic Achievement of Academy Students

Average Grade Level for Basic Math[a]	At Registration	After 12 Weeks of Academy Operation	N
Students registered in basic math	7.4	9.6	47
Students completing course work in basic math	7.5	11.7	27

[a]Average grade levels are determined by averaging individual scores on the arithmetic section of the California Test Bureau's Test of Adult Basic Education.

1968.[2] For those students who completed the math course, the improvement was even greater, an average of 4.2 grade levels in the twelve weeks (see Table 3).

Although these data show the remarkable improvement of students in terms of their grade levels of achievement (as measured by the TABE exam) they do not describe the process that brought about this improvement.[3] Students did not work through the programmed materials in the same manner, and three general patterns appeared in their efforts in the basic math class. Some students (those whose entrance exams showed the lowest scores, i.e., fourth, fifth, and sixth grade levels) simply did not have the arithmetic skills which the exam required. They had never learned, for example, how to add, subtract, multiply, or divide with fractions, decimals, large numbers, and so on. They had been in classes in public schools where these skills were taught, but they had never learned them. These students worked very slowly through the programmed books, and often required explanations in addition to those provided by the materials themselves.

A second pattern was exhibited by those students who had learned the arithmetic skills measured by the exam at one point in their educational career but had since forgotten them. These students would work very quickly through much of the programmed materials, but then they would "get stuck" on a particular kind of problem (e.g., they did not know how to divide decimals). When the problem was explained to them, however, they recognized the items at issue and quickly worked through similar problems. To these students, the basic math course was largely review; they completed the course very quickly and their grade levels of achievement showed rapid improvement.

A third pattern was exhibited by students who were very good in all but one area of arithmetic. These students were similar to those described above, in that they worked quickly through most of the instructional books, completing what was for them a basic review in most areas. These students, however, were at a complete loss with respect to one or another of the kinds of problems presented on the exam. For example, a student might score at the eleventh or twelfth grade in all areas of the exam except those that dealt with fractions, in which case he or she would do very poorly (i.e., the fourth or fifth grade level).

These three patterns seemed to correspond to different educational careers. The first group mentioned, those who knew very little, had clearly not learned arithmetic as it was taught in the schools they had attended. They were basically starting from scratch, even though they might have completed eight years of elementary education and one or two years of high school. The second group consisted of those students who had learned the arithmetic as it was taught but had forgotten it through disuse. The third group was composed largely of students who had learned the arithmetic that was taught, more or less, but who had such irregular careers (i.e., due to moving, being held back a grade, changes in curriculum, and the like) that they had in effect "missed" learning some major area of arithmetic skills. The real advantages of the programmed materials were that they allowed the teacher to work with all types of students in the same class without having their separate learning patterns conflict. As the materials were organized cumulatively, students continued to use what they had just learned when working on problems at the next level of difficulty. Consequently, it was unnecessary to place students in different classes according to their abilities, their past academic achievement, or their learning patterns.

Student performance was not recorded as systematically in the English I course as it was in the basic math course, but student learning patterns were similar to those of the math course. One distinction, however, was that fewer students came to the Academy having learned all of the language skills than came having learned all the arithmetic skills. Consequently, the number of students involved in the "starting from scratch" learning pattern was much larger for English than it was for math; as a result, students progressed more slowly in English.

The apparent success of programmed instruction in the math and English classes redirected teachers in other classes. The most direct consequence was that requirements for completion of other classes were made more clear. In Science classes, for example, I began telling students that if they successfully passed exams on each of four books used in the course, they would receive credit. Attendance rose in the science classes, and students worked more diligently after this announcement.[4] Similar arrangement for making requirements explicit met with similar successes in other classes.

At curriculum meetings, the staff expressed general satisfaction with these developments, but they also worried about a change in student attitude that accompanied the more "organized" course formats. Students began asking what was expected of them for a credit, and nothing more. As teachers who wanted to inspire students with their subject matter, who wanted the students to study with passion, we were discouraged by this turn of events. Programmed instruction obviously facilitated student learning, but for teachers it was a mixed blessing. If students only wanted credits, we mused, then what were we doing trying to run an alternative school?

The pressure exerted by dissatisfied students—as negative evaluations and nonattendance of loosely structured classes—caused all teachers to make work for their courses correspond as closely as possible to a series of units or sections such that the student could complete one unit or section, working on his own, within a class period. This message came from the students, and the staff attended to it as well as they could. By the end of the school year, the only classes that were still "open-ended" were the Story Workshop and the history class. Both of these classes, however, did move slightly in this direction. In spite of his grave reservations about doing so, Rider, the Story Workshop director, told the students that he would require at least four written "things" before they could complete the course.

It was clear that teachers at the Academy would have to learn new roles if students were going to learn new material. When student interest and achievement both pointed toward an incremental and routinized set of course requirements, the staff of the Academy took the hint. It might be more exciting to leave things up in the air and teach to the four winds, but when students drew back or simply did not appear, that excitement faded fast. Better to have students and have them working well, we argued, than to dream of others taking our passions to be their own.

GROUPS AND CLASS DISCUSSIONS

The elaborate "programming" of the curriculum of the Academy allowed students to make academic progress even though their attendance was irregular, and it gave students a clear sense of what they needed to complete the work for a class. In that both of these contributed to improving the levels of student achievement, programmed instruction was popular at the Academy. But the individualized format of this instruction was not without its liabilities, and the most serious of these was the atomization of student learning experience at the school. When discussions did not occur naturally, the staff attempted to create them through "Sharper Minds."

The "Sharper Minds Program," developed by Dan Schienfeld, is designed to build on existing peer group involvement and aggression and to transform these into teamwork and verbal ability. It does this by directing student discussions of a problematic situation within a seven step problem-solving structure. The problematic element is presented by reading a short description of a situation (e.g., "an airplane has run out of fuel"). Students are then asked to formulate as many problems as possible on the basis of this description, to chose one of these problems, and then to work on it.

The advantage of this type of discussion was that it was not cumulative; that is, it did not depend on prior preparation by the students. This was particularly attractive to the Academy staff, for the irregular attendance of students made it impossible to know ahead of time who would be in class on a given day. In addition, students differed greatly in achievement levels and rates of progress, making it difficult to design discussions around the subject matter of a course.

The Academy staff made only minimal efforts to try the "Sharper Minds" techniques in their classes, however, and these were not particularly success-ful. Three of the seven staff members each made one unsuccessful attempt to use the "Sharper Minds" process in dealing with a prepared "problematic situation." Students were very resistant to the idea and objected when it was suggested that they "put down their books for a minute to try something new." For these students, who were working individually with the pro-grammed instructional materials, this was an interruption of their work. They resented intervention of the teacher in this process, and they saw the class discussion as a "waste of time."

The only successful application of the program occurred in the Story Workshop, and this singular achievement helps identify significant elements of student reaction to the process. The Story Workshop differed from other classes in three respects: (1) students were expected to attend regularly—this meant that the same group was present for each scheduled two-hour meeting once a week; (2) the authority of the instructor was clearly outlined; and (3) it called for a great deal of verbal sharing among students within the class, communication that often involved reference to dreams, personal experi-ences, living situations, and so on. This was in stark contrast to the individual-ized, discontinuous, and impersonal instruction that students received through working with programmed materials in other classes. Students in the Story Workshop class were more trusting of other students in the class and more accustomed to the directing authority of the teacher. They were, as a result, more open to "trying something new," especially when that something new involved a process similar to what they had already been doing.

In other classes, attempts by the teacher to organize a discussion—especially if such attempts involved asking students what they thought about something—were often greeted with loud protestations that accused the teacher of trying to "psyche out" the class. Students were generally distrust-ful of teachers' inquiries about their lives and had an extensive repertoire of protective responses for such occasions. Student reactions to "discussion topics" ran the gamut from "What you gonna do? Write a book about us?"

and "Always trying to program us students" to "Fuck you, I ain't going to tell you nothin." Attempts to institute the "Sharper Minds Program" evoked the entire repertoire.

The experiences with "Sharper Minds" techniques at the Academy were not exceptional. In general, class discussions occurred infrequently, and were difficult to initiate deliberately.[5] These discussions were seen by students as interruptions of their work with programmed texts, as well as illegitimate attempts by the teacher to manipulate the class. They also represented, no doubt, a threat to those students who felt at a disadvantage in class discussions. By classifying such discussions as interruptions, students protected themselves from experiences of failure and embarrassment.

These discussions were resisted not only because of students' apprehensions about their ability to perform, but also because they entailed open engagement and confrontation with other students. Having no reason to trust such encounters, students sought to avoid them. By keeping their noses to their programmed books, students preserved their self-respect, their right to work at their own rate, and their autonomy. Discussions were "open" situations, and there were many things students wanted to keep closed.

In a more general context, students came to the Academy individually, and they usually resisted attempts by the staff to make them develop into groups. It was clear to them that it was not groups that received diplomas, but individuals. Similarly, they resisted situations in which they were expected to self-disclose to each other. Although aware of the threats these situations posed to control of their self-presentation, students were confused about the rewards of class discussions. At the Academy, credits were based on "academic work," not on "rapping."

EXPERIENTIAL CLASSES

A description of the curriculum prepared in October 1968 contains reference to courses which were to involve "experiential classes"; that is, the subject matter for these courses would be based in part on the experiences of students in the class. The courses that developed this format most extensively were social psychology, speech and debate, science, and observation and inquiry. The Story Workshop, of course, had used such a format since its inception.

Instead of following the outline I prepared for the social psychology class—one that indicated that books were to be read and papers written—the class developed into a modified t-group, and as this development took place it became more and more popular. The books assigned for the course were read by six or seven students, but the class enrollment swelled to fourteen. Instead of basing discussions on the books and the outline of discussion topics, students based them on the interaction process taking place in the classroom.

For example, I asked the students whether or not they liked Mersault in Camus' *The Stranger*. Sarah said, "He's just like Tolly" (one of the students in the class). Tolly quickly responded in an injured tone of voice, "What you mean he's just like me? What'd I do to deserve you saying that?" Sarah then went on to tell the class that Tolly did not care for his mother, that he did not seem to care about anything, and that he would spend the rest of his life "strolling around doing nothing." The rest of the class session was spent discussing Tolly, and Sarah, what they felt about each other, and what they represented to other members of the class. Thus, the prepared readings served merely as a point of departure for discussions about the relationships between students.

Subsequent class meetings followed a similar pattern. I would ask a question about one of the books and then ask the students to relate the book to one of the discussion topics. In responding to my questions, students would draw upon their own experience and make reference to their relationships with other students in the Academy. These references would involve still more students, and a general discussion would evolve. Usually, I would make some attempt to relate student remarks to the topics to be covered in the course, but these efforts were not particularly successful. For example, in one class discussion, I was trying to get the students to discuss the manner in which behavior is learned. I grew more and more impatient as they pushed the discussion aimlessly away from my general questions. Finally, greatly frustrated, I said, "Look, when a baby is born he doesn't just pop out of the womb and raise his fist in the air and say 'Black Power'," to which one of the students quickly replied, "It would be mellow if he did."

"Social psychology" to the students was by and large a chance to talk about themselves and one another in a situation in which such discussions were "safe." From their point of view, I was the guarantee of such "safety," not by representing "justice" outside of the classroom but by establishing affective boundaries within it. It was clear to them that, as a teacher, I wanted to get certain things accomplished. The thought that I could "interrupt" the group process they had initiated, and that I had some inclination to do so, allowed them to involve themselves as they otherwise would not.

The social psychology class met from February to June 1968. The next fall, Marcel, one of the newly hired instructors, taught a speech and debate class that was very popular. This class was characterized by active and often elegant discussions, but in commenting on his efforts, Marcel stated that he did not feel very qualified to teach the class; he had just decided to "give it a try."

As the course progressed, Marcel did not establish a schedule of discussion topics but rather took these from those suggested by the students. Although he felt unprepared to teach this course, he was not terrified by such "deficiency" and admitted his feelings openly to the students. They responded warmly, "assisting" him in operating the class, and Marcel developed with these students a responsive, productive relationship. Students prepared for class discussions by bringing articles, magazines, photographs, books, and the like, even though they were not instructed to do so.

Marcel had a similar experience in teaching the science course. His preparation in this area was even less substantial than for the speech course, and he admitted this to the students present at the first class meeting. He told them that he knew very little about science and so any learning in the class was going to involve all of them, not just the students. Student response to this admission was much the same as it had been for the speech class, and the science classes that Marcel taught were well liked and respected. In fact, some students remarked that they learned more in science than in any other class.[6]

The offering of a fourth course at the Academy can be seen as an attempt to maximize these experiential learning situations. This course was called "Observation and Inquiry," and it was largely developed by Cockey. The format involved setting up experimental situations in the classroom, helping students ask questions about the situation, and then suggesting answers to their questions.[7] For example, a burning candle might be put on one of the desks in the room and students instructed to ask as many questions as they could about the burning candle. They were then asked to describe the manner in which they would try to answer these questions. By analyzing the questions they asked, students became familiar with different "kinds" of inquiries (e.g., historical questions, sociological questions, ethical questions, aesthetic questions). The teacher would then evaluate their performance as a class, suggest books they might want to look at which dealt with some of the questions they asked, and point out other questions they could have asked. The purpose of the course was to develop skills in the use of the senses (observation) and to improve the students' ability to formulate questions and identify sources of information that would relate to answering them (inquiry). Student participation in the observation and inquiry course paralleled that of the psychology, speech, and science courses, and a general form of the "successful, popular, exciting, discussion-oriented class" emerges from their description.

Although students would work hard in those courses where the curriculum was clearly programmed, they did so without much excitement or "fun." When instructors interrupted work on these individualized materials, however, students resisted. In those situations where the course was organized only minimally (or, as in the case of social psychology, where there was no real effort made to stick to the ostensible topic for the class), students showed a remarkable capacity to take the initiative in "learning" something. In such situations they openly expressed their curiosity, cooperated with other students in bringing information to bear on interesting subjects, and exhibited ambition and energy in organizing their learning experiences.

There were additional characteristics of these "successful" situations (i.e., in terms of excitement, high student interest, and collective participation) at the Academy, but they appear to be consequences of the structural elements mentioned above. It was important, for example, that "relevant" topics be the subject of such discussions. But relevancy was not a simple matter. In any given class, it had to be worked out within the moment, and the process, much to the dismay of earnest teachers, was not cumulative. A topic discussed with enthusiasm and intelligence on one day would be met the next day by student groans and feigned "fatigue collapses" onto a desk or table (dramatic, but invariably cushioned by skillfully placed arms).

Thus, "relevance" in these successful, experiential classes was derived from the experience of being in the class, that day, and during that hour.[8] The room for "relevance" was provided by loosely structured class situations, and the social process of experiential classes relied on the attention given to individual experience of students and teachers.

Another characteristic of these experiential classes was the maintenance of important affective boundaries. While curriculum materials themselves were largely responsible for this in the programmed courses, the teacher was crucial to establishing such conditions in the experiential classes. The engrossing discussions that took place in these classes did not, and probably could not, take place spontaneously among students in the Academy (e.g., during their lunch period, before and after school). Discussions of personal experiences in spontaneous groups would be too open-ended for students to feel safe, particularly within the climate of general mistrust that students shared for each other. Within the classroom, however, the teacher could serve as a symbol of the boundaries of discourse, removing interaction from the contingencies, dangers, and consequentiality of "real life." In order to be successful in this effort, however, teachers had to refrain from asking students overly personal questions. To ask such a question posed a profound threat: not only in that honest responses might reveal incriminating details, but also in that it compromised the teacher as a symbol of the "safe" boundaries of the situation.

The importance of the teacher to the bounded definition of the situation extended to the title or subject matter of the course, for if the discussion-oriented courses had been identified merely as such, they would not have been successful. On numerous occasions, the staff of the Academy had offered courses designed to stimulate class discussions; often the titles of these courses were explicit references to their purpose, such as "hot-talk" and "operation roundtable." Students did not attend these classes with any regularity or enthusiasm, and they were shortly discontinued.

The dynamics of these class discussions at Mission Academy can be stated as follows: It was necessary for a course to have a purpose other than that of discussion in order for a discussion to take place. Courses in psychology, speech, science, and observation and inquiry, for example, were organized around certain areas of subject matter. In these classes a teacher stated that the students would learn something about the subject, and students then felt free to attend and participate. If left to their own devices at this point, they frequently found "real" issues of great interest. When issues were imposed by the teacher or the subject matter of the course, however, they balked. Paradoxically, in order for students to participate enthusiastically in a discussion of a relevant topic, the suggested topic for discussion had to be irrelevant.

The manner in which teachers precipitated this useful dilemma can be seen from the previous description of successful "experiential classes." In the psychology class, an intention was stated, but it was not followed through. That is, the topic of discussion for one session of the course would be "roles," but the discussion would not be restricted to that topic and, in fact, would wander around until a more relevant topic was located. In the speech and the science courses, the instructor stated his goals for the course to the students and then indicated his own ignorance of the subject matter. In this case an intention was articulated for student work in the course, but then the teacher described his own inability to stick to that intention. In the observation and inquiry course, the "experimental situation" was designed by the teacher, but the responses to it were left largely up to the students. Thus, in each of these classes, a very tentative attempt to direct the discussion around a particular topic of no relevance provided the assurance of affective boundaries that the students required before fully engaging in a relevant discussion.

This suggests a certain correspondence between class "discussions" and the dynamics of game playing, a correspondence seen most clearly in the structure of the participant's involvement. In the "experiential" classes, the outcome of interaction was not only problematic, but also related to the contributions of the individuals involved. These characteristics of the situation stemmed from the relationship of the experiential classes to other offerings. Had students been graded for "classroom discussion," it is unlikely that the experiential classes would have had the vitality they appeared to have, for the most timid, casual, or genuine question would have had consequences for credit extending far beyond the "boundaries" of the class.

The creation of these "game" conditions was not the result of deliberate planning by those who taught at Mission Academy but stemmed from the conflicting demands placed on teachers by students and colleagues. The rewards a teacher received from students were that they liked the class he or she taught and actively participated in it. In order to receive these rewards, teachers were inclined to do what students wanted in the actual classroom. The rewards received from other teachers, however, were that they thought he or she was doing a "good job," and even in an "experimental secondary school" this job had something to do with teaching a particular subject. Thus, the teachers in these courses chose subject matter to meet the expectations of other teachers, and they failed to restrict classroom discussion to that subject matter in order to meet expectations of students. As a result of role conflict, teachers in "experiential classes" adopted a strategy that inadvertently engaged students in class discussions—and engaged them more effectively than had deliberate efforts to do so.

This explanation of the success of "experiential classes" is based on the role strain experienced by some teachers in the Academy, but it does not explain the way in which this strain worked selectively to make only some classes successes. Some courses did not develop into "experiential classes" because they were already so well developed as individualized programmed instruction. The English, math, and Afro-American history classes, for example, all had developed very elaborate programmed materials. Even though the teachers of these classes experienced the same role strain as did those of the experiential classes, they had such an investment in the prepared curriculum materials that they could not easily abandon their subject. In addition, the intensity of role strain was minimized in these courses by student expectations that their programmed format would remain unchanged and that this "hard work" was important to academic progress. Although impossible to demonstrate empirically, it may have been that without these programmed "hard-work" classes, students would not have been as comfortable in other classes where it might seem that "nothing was accomplished."

CULTURAL RELEVANCE

In taking part of its inspiration from popular critiques of public school education, Mission embraced the concept of "culturally relevant" curriculum. Staff members at the Academy were very critical of attempts to teach inner-city high school students with texts emphasizing suburban situations. Not only were inner-city students black and suburban students white, but the socioeconomic differential between the two places of residence was considered to represent different "values."

Early in the development of the Academy (September 1967) a representative of an educational materials publishing organization had suggested that the staff should develop its own curriculum materials in areas where there were no "relevant" materials available. Partly as a result of this professional encouragement, the staff began to gather curriculum materials that they thought were relevant to inner-city black students, and the first area in which this was fully realized was Afro-American history. Theodore, the instructor, was an associate of the Du Sable Museum of Afro-American History in Chicago, and he had access to a great many documents and artifacts that were integrated into the course he taught. The students responded warmly to this effort to teach them about their Afro-American heritage, and Theodore, even though he was white, became something of a cultural hero in the school.

Spurred on by the success of this class, and by collective student achievement as represented in a student production of "Scenes from the Life of Malcolm X," the Academy staff sought to make all classes "culturally relevant." An attempt was made to find culturally relevant curriculum materials for teaching science, English, history, arithmetic, and art. Although such efforts may have been well-intentioned, they were not based on a careful analysis of the "culture" to which relevance was to be related. Efforts to base the student's academic tasks on a stereotypical view of his or her ghetto living space were not only unsuccessful, but also were considered to be inadequate from one very important point of view: that of the student.

Cockey, the English teacher, made an effort to select for his students as many reading assignments as possible from "black literature." Students initially responded quite enthusiastically to the selections he assigned. As many works of great literature (whether black or white) are found to be too vulgar or "advanced" for use in conventional schools, students were excited and often surprised to read in books the words they previously had only heard spoken or seen written on the walls of buildings. Students were also fascinated to find as scenes of great literature the everyday occurrences of their personal lives. One student who was reading Claude Brown's *Manchild in the Promised Land* said in a very excited voice, "Hey have you read this? Have you *read* this? This is *me* man, this is really *me*. This is my life put down right here!"

After the initial excitement that students showed for black literature (at the Academy this included works by Richard Wright, Claude Brown, Leroi Jones, Langston Hughes, Gwendolyn Brooks, Malcolm X, and James Baldwin, among others), student interest in these works would wane. This is not to say that they quit reading, but simply that they began asking broader questions about what they were reading. They were no longer interested in reading just to identify with characters and situations in literature. This change appeared in their changing appreciation of black literature and in their desire to read "something else." Rather than praise Claude Brown in the manner described above, students were more likely to express their admiration for a subtle turn of events portrayed by Leroi Jones or an insightful line written by Langston Hughes. They also asked about other writers of whom they had heard, such as Shakespeare, Plato, William Faulkner, Ernest Hemingway, Eldridge Cleaver, and J. D. Salinger; they read the works of these writers as avidly as they had the exclusively "black literature" that they had at first found so stimulating.

This development of student appreciation and interest in the English class was paralleled by performance in the Story Workshop class. The first book used in this class was Richard Wright's *Black Boy*. The great interest students took in reading this book continued as they read selections from Homer, Kafka, Camus, and Orwell. Although the significance of the culturally relevant reading matter at the Academy should not be underemphasized, it served primarily as a point of entry for the student to the experience of reading. Once comfortable with the written language, students did not limit themselves to the popular black literature but actually extended themselves to read more serious and difficult works by black authors and books written by men and women who had little in common with stereotypical descriptions of inner-city "culture"—writers who wrote about Europe, Russia, England, and California, some of whom lived decades or centuries earlier.

A similar account can be made of the efforts to make the science course culturally relevant. Hal and I, the science teachers, went to speak to several curriculum specialists in the School of Education of the University of Chicago. We asked these specialists how students at the Academy might be better prepared in the sciences, and how we could develop curriculum materials that would achieve this purpose. The responses of the university educators were always the same: "Make the curriculum culturally relevant."

In spite of these recommendations, we decided to make the curriculum correspond to some of our own pedagogical and intellectual interests rather than to so-called "inner-city interests." As an introduction to the science courses, we developed a unit on "observation." This required students to look at photographs and ask as many questions as they could about each picture. No effort was made to choose photographs that depicted stereotypical ghetto scenes (i.e., pool halls, switchblades, run-down tenements, graffiti on the buildings, black people, broken sidewalks, or policemen performing a stop-and-frisk). Rather, photographs were selected that were enigmatic, colorful, illustrative of some scientific principle, humorous, rich in detail, or fantastic. The response was very enthusiastic, and students actually fought over who would get to study a particular photograph next. Further, the selection of photographs by the students for special attention did not exhibit an "inner-city" cultural bias. The most popular ones were not the most culturally relevant but rather the most striking and the most likely to be included in collections of professionally judged quality photographs.

The mathematics classes offer a further qualification on the purported necessity of using culturally relevant material to teach inner-city students.

Some "culturally relevant" curriculum materials stressed asking the student to generalize from his or her experience in handling money to the more abstract matters of the real number system. My attempts to use these materials at the Academy were not unsuccessful, but the students preferred working on problems without monetary coefficients. In fact, they were most excited by the programmed materials in modern algebra, referring to this course as "philosophical mathematics." Even students who had not finished the basic math course (which dealt with arithmetic fundamentals) worked on their own with the modern mathematics books.

These descriptions of student response to curriculum developments at Mission Academy indicate that the cultural relevance of instructional materials is not crucial to their success. Students at the Academy had well developed intellects and were capable of dealing intelligently with almost any subject if they wanted to. The value of culturally relevant material lay primarily in that it allowed the student to develop a new definition of an academic area that he or she had previously found to be boring, insipid, or defeating. This is clearly shown in student response to the mathematics course described above. If the students were told that it was "algebra" they were studying, they would reply, "Oh, I can't do that. I flunked that three times"; or "Algebra! I can't do that! I haven't even passed essential [basic math]." However, when they would call the course "philosophical mathematics," or when I called it "formal mathematical rules," they would apply themselves with great energy and they learned a great deal.

Student response to curriculum, according to the experiences described above, does not seem to rest on finding the key to cultural relevance but rather in providing options for the students to define their tasks and subject matter in new ways. Student intelligence could be enthusiastically applied to all subjects, with a few exceptions, and the exceptions themselves point to a partial explanation of the value of culturally relevant instructional materials. "Algebra" symbolized to many students their own failures in public schools; "mathematical rules" or "philosophical mathematics" did not. Reading highly distilled, censored versions of the "classics" symbolized to many students their past failures in high school English classes; reading exciting, colorful novels written in honest vulgar language did not. Reading thick, highly verbal science texts symbolized to many students their past failures in high school science courses; looking at photographs and asking questions did not. Although students might say, "I never could do that and never will," the staff at the Academy learned to take this as an indication of the quality of the teaching materials and not as a statement about the student's capabilities. The answer was not to deny the students' statements, but to find new, less threatening vehicles for teaching.

DERIVED CURRICULUM: BLACKS
AND STUDENTS

Although it sought to deal with the total life space of the student, the greatest "success" that Mission Academy achieved, in the eyes of its members, came in the classroom. The use of programmed, individualized instructional materials was particularly effective in teaching Academy students basic skills in mathematics and English. Unfortunately, the well-organized and incremental nature of these curriculum materials encouraged students to concern themselves only with the completion of requirements. This came as a disappointment to the Academy staff who sought to "inspire" their students. After having made the process whereby a student would receive a credit in a course quite explicit, the faculty bemoaned the fact that a student would not deviate from the well-defined path to engage in an enthusiastic discussion of the subject.

Attempts were made to "revitalize" the discussion-oriented learning that had taken place prior to the expanded use of programmed materials, but these were not particularly successful. Such discussions did take place, however, in classes in which the instructor was effective in acting as a symbol of affective boundedness and showing respect for student opinions but was ineffective in holding student discussion to a particular topic. This teaching pattern can be seen as a structural dimension of desire for esteem from the class and from colleagues. To receive this esteem from colleagues the teacher had to select a topic for discussion; to receive it from students, he had to give it up.

In addition to the use of programmed materials and experimental classroom formats, the Academy sought to increase levels of student motivation through the use of "culturally relevant" curriculum materials. The most significant contribution of these materials was to the process whereby students and teachers sought to transform student self-images of cumulative failure. Culturally relevant materials (as well as some "culturally irrelevant materials") served to give students new definitions for tasks at which they had previously experienced failure. Once the impediment of the students' self-image of failure was removed, they did not limit themselves to learning material that was culturally relevant. In fact, they exhibited an intelligence that enabled them to think and speak critically about any material with which they might be presented—including Shakespeare, Plato, molecular biology, boolean algebra, and the philosophy of science—if they desired to do so.

The implications of these findings are of significance to more general issues in contemporary education. For example, one of the common criticisms of black studies programs, minority studies majors, and what might generally be termed "special interest education," is that such programs lower the academic demands placed on students; it is argued that this results in a general lowering of academic standards for the sponsoring institutions. At the crux of this criticism is the assumption that student work and interest will be limited to the superficial "special interest" that has generated the course or program. I suggest that this assumption stems from an unsophisticated understanding of black culture (or "special interest culture"), the culture to which things are to be made "relevant."

At Mission Academy, students did not limit themselves in culturally relevant courses to what was superficially characterized as "culturally relevant" material; Homer and biochemistry were not dismissed by the same black students who were excited by an introduction to "black culture." In fact, these students seemed to incorporate these apparently "foreign" elements into their active and vital black appreciation of culture. This suggests that much of what is presently considered "culturally irrelevant" material is indeed part of black culture, but a part made inaccessible by institutional insensitivity to more immediate black interests and ambitions.

The experiment at Mission Academy supports the contention that a large part of "black culture" is no more and no less than American culture, Western culture, as experienced by blacks. Just as whites adopt or emphasize cultural elements that at a particular moment appear relevant to them (e.g., George Washington and the Potomac; the U.S. Constitution), so do blacks (e.g., slavery and Nat Turner; the Declaration of Independence). And, just as these preferred elements are in a state of constant debate among whites, so too are they among blacks. It is important that individuals are not deprived of the opportunity to participate in such debates, and blacks must continue to have opportunities to define, in their own terms, black culture.

Black culture is not a diminutive form of white culture; it is not somehow less "basic," "real," or "fundamental" than what whites have presumed to call "culture itself" or "American culture"; and it must be recognized that the white experience of American society is itself a "special interest" experience. The culture to which things are to be made relevant is not so simple that it can be accurately portrayed by a bit of Afro-American history here, a black studies program there, and a proportional selection of brown faces in an elementary school reading book, important though these may be in particular situations. To suggest that it is indeed so simple is to participate in a yet more elaborate form of racism than that which has made necessary these remedial efforts in the last few years.

But "black culture" is only an example. The general issues are those of schooling—the source, structure, and functions of the curriculum. In this respect, the culture of the school and the dynamics of student-teacher interaction seem to have been critical to the relatively high level of student achievement at this alternative school. The particulars of the Academy's

man or woman in terms of aptitude for college or employment; it records all the "character" variables requested by organizations seeking new members: ability to relate to others, conscientiousness, evidence of leadership and responsibility, willingness to follow orders, and so on. More than any other contemporary institution, schools process the young, plucking out not only the bright and accommodating as college material, but also the emotionally disturbed, recalcitrant, obstreperous, overly critical, and disruptive as social rejects. To be a dropout is not merely to be sealed away from a particular school, but to have demonstrated failure as a mini-citizen and to suffer for it.

In assessing the conditions of his failure, the student is confronted not only with the correlative withdrawal of privilege, but also with the spectre of "responsibility" for his status, for there is no lack of admonishments for students who leave school. These appear both in educational journals (as articles designed to assist teachers and counselors in "curbing the dropout problem") and in subways, on telephone poles, and in magazines: "Boy: drop out from school and that is what they'll call you for the rest of your life," we are told.[1] There appears to be some lack of coordination, however, between those who exhort students to stay in schools and those who counsel school districts and the public in matters of school facilities. Can we imagine what the schools would look like if indeed those who do drop out did not? The school in question, the urban school that is successful in keeping all its students, with its classrooms initially designed for 20 or 30 students (currently holding 35 to 45), would be jammed to the walls with 70 or more students to a room.

Limited facilities suggest that some students will have to be excluded; the curve, that profoundly ironic appelation of the normal distribution, provides the mechanism for their dismissal. In attempting to solve problems of social control in the school, teachers and administrators characteristically process students in such a way that "potential dropouts" are clearly identified. The curve—which operates in terms of character, personality, and nonacademic behavior as well as test scores—becomes the rationalization for eliminating troublemakers, malcontents, the slow to learn, and undesirables of any shape or form. In addition, school can be hard enough on students to prompt them to leave of their own "free will"; this drastically reduces the number that administrators have to explicitly kick out.

Although Americans have a strong sense of the rightness of equality of opportunity in education, it appears that schools are more characterized by "mass processing" than they are by "mass education." To process a child requires only very limited interaction; often students are "identified" and categorized within the first year or so. To educate a child should take much longer.

To view schools as the helping hands that bring the poor and disadvantaged up from the despair and poverty of their nonschool lives is naïve; examples of this process occurring are important, of course, but hardly characteristic of the statistical norm. Some social critiques have suggested an obverse view, that schools seek only to rationalize the status of the elite and insure that the poor remain so. Although this may in fact be a function of schools, it seems equally naïve to suggest that this is their deliberate intent. It appears more realistic to envision schools as sifting and sorting devices, slightly rational in their construction, but characterized by all the prejudices, predispositions, and inhumanities of the larger society.

There are examples, of course, of individuals who did "take advantage" of the rationality of the school to demonstrate their exceptional ability and who subsequently received rewards greatly in excess of those he or she might have received without schooling. For every one of these Sunday supplement success stories, there is a corresponding failure story of the child of the wealthy and educated who did poorly and dropped out. All of these, however, are exceptions to the bulk of student careers, in which the coefficients of social class are maintained, and perhaps strengthened through rationalization, in the day-to-day affairs of students and teachers.[2]

It is in this conception of the school as a problematic institution, with its series of trials and tests, that students appear as hustlers and victims. On the one hand, they can—by exceptional energy, accommodation, and ingenuity— impress the "gatekeepers" as gifted, intelligent, and "likely to succeed." Given the fundamentally competitive nature of the trials and tests they encounter, however, such success necessarily implicates their fellow students. A "promising" student in this process is only "more promising" than his or her fellows. Likewise, a "poor student" or a "failure" is identified by being less capable than others. As a result, for every student who hustles to the top of the institutional pile, another student is coaxed, led, or shoved to the bottom. For every successful hustler there is a victim.

In a larger sense, all students are victimized by the terms of their relationships, terms that have stipulated long before they arrived that there would indeed be winners and losers. But this competition is not limited to schools, and ex-students find it equally characteristic of more "adult" aspects of American economic life. It is no surprise that conventional schools reflect this competitive and victimizing ethos of the larger society. What is of interest, however, is that such forms are so pervasive that alternative and experimental schools themselves are contaminated, in spite of their intentions to the contrary. Not only were local West Side high schools a competitive terrain for students, but so was Mission Academy, a school created as an alternative. The manner in which this conventional process was built into the Academy is illuminated by a description of the backgrounds of the students and the experiential and institutional dimensions of their careers.

YOUNG, BLACK, AND DROPOUTS

At Mission Academy, students were recruited through posters placed in pool halls, store windows, churches, and on telephone poles; through word of mouth contact; through radio announcements; and through loose and informal associations among public high school counselors, mental health workers, probation officers, and local policemen. This form of recruitment functioned to select a student body that was largely from the surrounding area,[3] that was predominantly male and black,[4] and that had an average age a little over eighteen years.[5] The majority of these students had completed less than one full year of high school credit.[6] Eighty-one percent of the students had attended only one high school previous to the Academy, and they had been out of school an average of 17.7 months before coming to Mission.[7]

Each student had his own reasons for coming, but one of them was usually to get a high school diploma. Some said they wanted to come, others said they were made to attend the school by parents, relatives, or probation officers.[8] Still others were referred to the school by mental health workers, high school counselors, and community organizers.[9] Some students, particularly those who had been involved with the Academy since its founding, used the school as a social and cultural center, which they frequented to "hang out" with their age-mates. Enrollment in the school also guaranteed a selective service student deferment for males under the age of 20 who were otherwise eligible for the draft. All these things "mattered" to students and potential students. Although it is doubtful whether any of the students would have attended if their work at the Academy could not lead to a diploma, the diploma itself is inadequate to explain the variety of motivations and expectations of enrolling students.

The students' backgrounds do not provide a complete explanation of their behavior in the school, but they do suggest parameters by which student experience at the Academy can be evaluated. It was very important, for example, that these students were in middle and late adolescence. Not only were they the youth of the community, but they were the young in their individual families, and a wide range of parental ambitions rode with them. In characteristic fashion, their parents hoped for and somehow expected greater success from their children than they themselves had achieved.[10] In their pre-adult status, the students could still imagine changes in their future that would derive from their "potential" to be competent, able, adult citizens. They could imagine that the Academy was the place that this potential, heretofore unrealized, would finally be tapped.

While for many this was a fresh start, it was not a first start. Students brought with them to the Academy a number of starts and failures. In addition to the stigma attached to their status as dropouts, most students had suffered a long series of previous frustrations and defeats in individual classes throughout their academic life. In addition, students coming to the Academy frequently expressed despair and bitterness over what they held to be their general incompetence as adults and specific inabilities to read, write, or do arithmetic. These 18 year old students scored consistently below the eighth grade level on the diagnostic entrance exams, with the exception of the male students' scores on the reading portion of the exam which were slightly above that level.[11] It was clear that if these students were possessed of great potential, they had not benefited from past institutional experiences in which it had been clearly demonstrated.

A third factor critical to their engagement with the school was their "blackness" and their awareness of it. In one sense, being black in America helped students make sense of the institutional failures they had experienced. These young men and women knew that blacks were discriminated against in this society. As Mose, one of the Academy poets, would say, "Everybody know/If you're white, it's all right./If you're black, stay back." Racist dynamics of the larger society explained to students why they were dropouts—though it did not always do so accurately—for it emphasized the collective nature of their status. This had an important energizing and motivating effect on students, for they saw that their personal failures were something more than personal. In perceiving the systematic nature of their failures, they were able to recognize their individual potentials for success in altered circumstances. To the extent that the Academy provided such circumstances, they were free to think that it was here, in a school free of the defeating black stereotypes of conventional schools, that they could achieve according to the full measure of their personal capabilities.

The Academy developed some reputation in the surrounding community for being a nourishing environment for black students, and one indication of this is that the academic preparedness of students entering the Academy improved throughout its operation. In the year from November 1967 to November 1968, scores on the diagnostic entrance tests increased by about one and one-half grade levels, and this appears in part as a response to the Academy's success-oriented image that developed over this period of time. Several of the students enrolling in 1968 were in their last year of high school and scored rather well on the diagnostic exams. These students dropped out of their public high school to avoid the oppression they experienced there and came to the Academy in hopes of obtaining one of the college scholarships that previous graduates had received. At their public school, these students reported, very few students were encouraged to attend college, counselors refused to give others necessary information and assistance in filling out college forms, and classes were boring and "irrelevant." At the Academy, all students who wanted to go to college were encouraged and assisted, and classes were more interesting. With a reasonable chance of passing the G.E.D. exam and getting a diploma, these students found the Academy to be a better environment than the public school. These students were, nevertheless, dropouts, and they thought of themselves as such. Their decision to leave the public high school was not a simple one. "Dropping out" was not the obvious thing to do, nor was it recommended by their fellow students at the Academy. Although these "good" students said they left of their own free choice, most other Academy students continued to express curiosity about the "real" reasons for their exit from public schools.

These factors of youth, conventional school failure, and blackness provided a set of terms by which an individual student defined and explained his or her behavior. A simplistic formula for how these variables related to each other did not emerge within the student culture of the school. All three were fundamental to the student's sense of self, and none of them were to be dismissed through mental gymnastics. As much as they may have liked to, students could not avoid seeing themselves in these terms. They could not forget that they were black, that they were young, and that they were dropouts. What they could do, and what they did do, was to manipulate the meanings of each of these elements to generate affirmative definitions of their struggle, their place, and their future.

FOUR STUDENTS

Encouraging students to attend college was not the only important difference between the Academy and the surrounding conventional schools. In most conventional schools, students are promoted from one grade to the next in the company of others of relatively the same age. This age-grading is the basic element of "lockstep" progress, a process by which all individuals of a particular age group are located at the same level of academic achievement. In conventional schools students are expected to "keep up" with the rest of their age-mates. Student advancement in these schools is the advancement of classes (e.g., the class of 1957, the eighth grade class of 1970), and students who do not conform to the advancement pattern of their class are treated as residual cases.

A "class" orientation to student advancement was clearly absent from Mission Academy. Students progressed through course sequences not by growing older but by completing the work required for the courses. They were not age-graded, and students at a given level of academic achievement were characterized by a range of chronological ages. As there was no age-graded "class" pattern at the Academy, there was no residual class of students who could be identified by their lack of conformity to such a pattern. Student advancement at the Academy was by and large the advancement of individual students, not of particular age-groups.

A description of student careers at the school must take into account this individualized process of academic advancement. There was no single "normal" student career, but rather a number of kinds of careers, each of which differed from the others in major respects. To prepare a natural history of student involvement in the Academy, it is thus necessary to identify the social categories corresponding to common experiences in the school.

To provide a more elaborate picture of the social fabric from which these categories can be derived, the abbreviated careers of four students will be presented. These were selected as being representative of students at the Academy in a number of dimensions: their educational preparation before coming to the Academy; their role in the student culture of the school; their academic performance; the inclusive periods of their attendance; their intellectual curiosity; and their careers subsequent to departure from the school. Informed by the particular lives of these four students (Pud, Sarah, Mose, and Lamont) we will try to construct the meaning and demeaning of "being a student" at the Academy.

PUD

Pud was tall and lanky and moved with a slow, very deliberate rolling gait. He presented an image of toughness and "no nonsense" without any element of harshness, cruelty, or viciousness. Although he was not afraid to laugh, he was never silly, and was in many ways one of the more serious students in the school. I first met him in September 1967 when he walked into one of the staff orientation meetings wearing matching pants and shirt in a bright blue knit. Pud walked around the edges of the room, turned his head to say "What's happening, Theodore?" and then pulled up a chair next to Nancy, turned it around so that it faced backwards, and straddled it. Nancy said, "What's happening Pud?" and he answered, "Nothing, same as always."

Pud's initials were P.R., and this gave Rev. Keen the opportunity to refer to him as "Pulaski Road," a place where Pud was often to be found hanging out in one of the pool halls. He enrolled in the Academy during the first portion of the pilot phase and thus was one of its first students. Many of the original members of the Academy were recruited from the street corners around the old church, and Pud was one of the leaders of these students in their activities on the street, a leadership that carried over into the Academy itself. When the students produced "Scenes from the Life of Malcolm X," Pud was one of the main organizers. When a number of students wanted musical instruments, Pud was their spokesman; when Nancy agreed to provide them, he received, for his efforts, a saxophone.

Previous to his involvement with the Academy, Pud had been in and out of a number of public schools and correctional institutions. He had spent no more than three years in any one school and had amassed fewer than one full year of high school credits. His reading and math levels were below the sixth grade. He lived within a few blocks of the Academy, had a reputation among the local youth for his proficiency in fighting (he had won a golden gloves competition), and a reputation among local policemen as a "troublemaker." During the pilot phase he made very little academic improvement, but his efforts as a student leader were well respected by Nancy and the returning staff.

During the summer months between the pilot phase and the experimental phase, Pud worked at Happy Hills Farm with three other Academy students. While on a brief vacation from the farm, he returned to Chicago where a local wine-head attacked him with a tire-iron, and Pud allegedly stabbed him. The man later died, and Pud was charged with third-degree murder. In August of 1967 he stood trial and was acquitted of the charge.[12] Nancy and Rev. Keen invested a great deal of time and energy in arranging for his defense at the trial, and Nancy often recounted how this experience had brought Pud and her much "closer together."

When the Academy reopened in the fall of 1967, Pud was there, and he was still very much a leader. At the initial orientation trip to Happy Hills Farm, $40 was stolen from one of the camp directors. A student meeting was called to deal with the theft, and Pud automatically chaired it. When students returned from the orientation sessions, a meeting was called in the Academy building, and Pud also automatically chaired that meeting. A local newspaper printed at this time a photograph of a number of Academy students pointing out the deteriorated quality of curbs and gutters in the West Park community, and Pud was prominent among them.

During the month of October, Pud worked diligently in all his classes. At one student meeting he gave a brief speech attesting to his own desire to work seriously toward his diploma and suggesting that if there were any students present who were not going to take this seriously "they could leave fast." As his initial achievement levels were quite low, the improvement he made during this period of time was not quite enough to complete any of the basic courses. Other students (such as Lamont), who were more prepared before coming to the Academy, were able to complete the basic courses by expending the same amount of energy. Partly as a result of frustration with the seemingly "endless" nature of his tasks (frustration which was accentuated by the performance of students like Lamont), Pud applied himself to his courses less and less. His attendance at the Academy, which had been very regular through October, became less regular and less frequent through the month of November, and his academic work suffered accordingly. When in December the staff drew up a "danger list" of students who were not working hard enough on their studies, Pud was on the list.

After the Christmas recess, Pud's attendance at the Academy was highly irregular and infrequent. He would appear for lunch or after school once or twice a week. Toward the end of January, he made what in retrospect appears as a "final assault" on his academic work, attending classes every day and applying himself seriously to the programmed texts in basic math and English. At the end of this week he took the final exam for the math class and failed it for the third time. When I told him how he had done, he took no encouragement from the fact that his scores on the three tests showed a steady improvement over the months, going from slightly below the sixth grade level to the ninth grade level. Students were required to pass this exam at the tenth grade level to receive credit for the course, and Pud knew it. "Don't give me any of this bull shit," he said, "Go on, tell me I flunked it, I flunked it didn't I? That's all there is to it. I flunked it. Well, fuck you," and with that he stalked out of the room. This signaled the end of his academic involvement with the Academy.

During the months of February and March 1968, Pud worked at various jobs in the surrounding area. Once or twice a week he would drop by the Academy on his lunch hour or while running an errand for his employer, and once he drove by in a Good Humor ice cream truck while he was employed selling ice cream. During these social calls, he was often stoned or drunk and spent all of his time "talking up" girls in the school and laughing with his former schoolmates. In April, during one of these visits, he precipitated a fight with Lamont, and when the "for real" and "not for real" students were identified during the crisis in April, he was found to be "not for real."

As far as the Academy was concerned, this ended Pud's career, and so it was with a peculiar ambivalence that Mission administrators and teachers listened to accounts by Nancy Sheen of how Pud had steered rioters away from the Mission building after Dr. King's assassination. Although he would drop by every other month or so, he was considered to be a "former" student and was barred from participating in Academy functions. When the school opened the following fall for the demonstration phase, he did not attempt to reenroll. Students at the Academy who still saw him socially reported that he worked from time to time in factories in Chicago and that he was "making good money." The last time I saw him, in the fall of 1968, he was roaring down Madison in a 1961 Chevrolet convertible with the top down, steering with one hand, and waving casually with the other to a group of friends standing on the corner.

SARAH

The first time I saw Sarah she was leaning up against a piano on which Fester was playing one of his original jazz compositions. She was wearing a brightly colored red, pink, and orange dress, and as she stared off across the room at nothing in particular, she madly chewed a piece of gum. I remarked to Cockey that none of the male students, who usually applied themselves with great energy to "talking up" the female students, would bother her. She was known as a "tough broad."

Sarah was another of the "original" members of the Academy. During the pilot phase, it was reported (by Nancy and Theodore) that she was a very difficult person with whom to deal. They said that she would not pay attention in class, that she almost invariably came to school stoned, and that if a teacher would directly ask her to cooperate she would "throw a fit." A similar evaluation of her was made by instructors in an Upward Bound program of which she was a member. From their reports, her disposition had much improved during the few months of the pilot phase, and they thanked the Academy for the "good influence" it was exerting on her.

I am unfamiliar with the particulars of Sarah's selection into the Upward Bound program. However, unless hers was an exceptional case, she was selected on the basis of recommendations of high school teachers and counselors as a student with a lot of "potential." After participating in the program for one summer (in 1966), Sarah found her former public school education "boring," and she dropped out of school in the following December. She continued her involvement with the Upward Bound program through the following summer, and reenrolled in the Academy in September 1967.

During the first few months of the school year (1967-1968), Sarah neither attended classes nor worked in them with any consistency. However, in the month of December, she began working on basic math and English. She progressed well in these classes and completed them by the end of January. At the beginning of the experimental phase (September 1967) tests indicated that her reading and math levels were at about the seventh grade level. Thus, she improved her achievement scores on the math test three grade levels in the first four months of the school year.

In addition to showing academic improvement and a greater attention to academic work, Sarah changed her social role at the Academy as the year progressed. Early in 1968 she changed her straightened hairstyle to that of a "natural," and she expressed herself with facility in the rhetoric and forms of Black Power. Her initially hostile expressions toward teachers were softened, and she became a very cooperative person. In February and March she would often help teachers by tutoring some of the less advanced students in a class on a one-to-one basis. And in January she was elected as one of four members of the student governing board. Students in the school considered her to be a "nice, friendly person," and they generally looked forward to seeing her in class.

Toward the end of March, Slinky, a male student who was one of the least academically oriented in the entire student body, began paying a lot of attention to Sarah. Previous to this, no male student appeared confident enough to make a play for her, and those who offered the most tentative gestures in that direction were rebuffed with a strong, "Get away from me before I smash your face!" Sarah did not reject Slinky, and the two of them could sometimes be seen holding hands as they walked through the building. During this period of time, Sarah also held a birthday party for herself (at my apartment) to which a number of the Academy students were invited. She appeared at the party with Jerome, a boy she had been "going with" for several months and who worked in a local retail store. Slinky was not present, and no one asked where he was.

During the process of identifying the "for real" and "not for real" students, Sarah played a passive but responsible role. As a member of the student board of directors, she was present during the meetings, and she did not openly resist the efforts of the staff to eject some students from the school. During the weeks after this meeting, however, Sarah's attendance at the Academy became less regular and she often slept at a desk or table when she did come to class. Except in her drama class, she did little work in the remaining weeks, but she had completed enough courses to be awarded a Level Two Diploma at graduation.

Sarah did not come to the graduation ceremony held in May 1968, at which she was awarded not only a Level Two Diploma, but also an award for being the most outstanding student in the drama class. I took her diploma and the $20 check for the drama award and went to see her the next day. She was baby-sitting her younger brother and sister while her mother was out, and when she opened the door and saw me she was quite surprised but quickly invited me in. This was a dark room, sparsely furnished with two chairs, a low small table and a console record player. Sarah went over and turned down the volume, Aretha Franklin dropped off in the distance, and we talked, a bit of light coming in through the yellowed window shades and partially drawn curtains. When I asked her why she didn't come to the graduation ceremony, she said, "Hell, I didn't think I was gonna get no diploma, and it looks like I got two of 'em. And one of 'em is for twenty dollars!"

Sarah was one of the twelve students who were to go to California on a field trip shortly after graduation. I asked her if she still intended to go. "I just don't know," she said. "I'll hafta ask my mother when she gets back." This was the day before the group was to leave, but the next morning, when a total of eleven students loaded into two small station wagons and a microbus, she was among them. During the field trip, Sarah took the role that she had previously taken during the first part of the year and was very friendly, cooperative, and highly amusing. She was in high spirits during most of the trip and provided the group with a great deal of interpersonal stimulation.

Once a week or so during the summer, Sarah would drop by the night school and say hello to the Academy graduates who were teaching there. She complained about her mother and about living at home and reported that she was no longer going to the Upward Bound activities. On one of her evening visits in August of 1968, she appeared at the Academy with her hair straightened for the first time since January of that year. I asked her about it, and she replied, "I got married. Nothing better to do; get away from my crazy house. It's better than doing nothin all summer." Her husband, Jerome, would not let her wear her hair in a natural, she continued, and so she had changed it for him. She expressed no desire to continue her educational career at this time, even though she had previously made application to a college she had visited while on the field trip to California. When I asked her what she was going to be doing during the next year or so, she replied, "Nothin, I guess, just bein' a wife. Don't sound too exciting does it? Well, I guess it ain't."

The last time I saw her was in November 1968. She crossed the street to say hello, and I asked her how she was. She replied, "Same as always. Nothin ever changes around here. You know, we shoulda stayed in California. That was fun."

MOSE

Mose was a real money-maker for the Academy. Whenever Nancy Sheen or Rev. Keen wanted to show what good things the Academy was doing, they pointed to Mose. I first met him at an orientation session at the beginning of the experimental phase. The session had been called as an "open house," an event where new students and their parents could meet the Academy staff. Mose walked in through the side door of the church building and came up the steps following a fortyish white couple; the older black man following Mose was his father. The white couple asked a number of questions about the school (e.g., "Is it accredited?" "How do you teach English?" "Do you give grades?"), and the three staff members who were present at this time did our best to answer them. After fifteen minutes or so of these questions and answers, the couple turned to Mose and asked if there were anything he wanted to ask about the Academy. He just shrugged his shoulders to say, "No, it seems all right." His father then asked, in a very deliberate but involuted way, what a person could do after graduating from the Academy. And we, the staff, told him that a graduate of the Academy could do pretty much what he or she wanted to do.

Mose came to Mission Academy in order to set up an electronics shop for repairing radios and television sets. At our initial meeting, the white couple who had accompanied him told us that he had put together a radio kit. In an effort to sell the school to him, we told Mose that he could do whatever he wanted to do: if he wanted to work with electronics, then he could. This seemed to excite him a great deal, and he left the session only to return in an hour with Darnell, a friend of his who also wanted "to study electronics."

In all his months of attending the Academy, Mose never had a single class session in electronics, nor did he ever have a radio repair shop. The staff of the Academy were simply unprepared to establish such a shop by themselves, and they were unable to provide the additional facilities and personnel required to operate one from their limited resources. Mose's test scores indicated a reading level of about the third grade and a math level of about the sixth grade. Previous to attending the Academy, he had attended a number of public schools and had spent some time at a regional correctional institute. His public school transcript indicated that he was "educable but mentally handicapped."

Mose had registered for "art" because he needed something to complete his class schedule. At first he expressed a fear of working on a large, empty, clean sheet of paper but soon had filled a number of such sheets with brightly colored creations that were entirely his own. The drawings, executed in pastel charcoal, were hung around the Academy and gave him an instant identity. He became very excited with "art" and often worked on drawings and paintings at home that he brought to school the following day. During the first few months of the school year, he worked only in art and in Story Workshop class; although his attendance was regular, by Christmas of 1967 he had made very little progress toward a diploma.

After the Academy moved to the "new building," Mose became the unofficial director of the art room (under my supervision). In this capacity, he initiated what was subsequently referred to as the "art room orgy," a "decorating" party that involved Sarah, Twister, Lamont, a couple of passers-by and me, and which left the walls of the art room completely covered with a variety of designs, solid color areas, and graffiti.

In January 1968, Mose still spent all of his class time in the art room or in the Story Workshop room. He developed a close relationship with Rider, the workshop director, and he wrote a number of very witty, colorful, and imaginative poems and short stories. Rider encouraged his writing efforts, and Mose wrote more and more. Toward the end of the month, Rider suggested to Mose that he should work on some courses other than art and Story Workshop; Mose agreed to give it a try and began working in the basic math and English classes at that time. Within the next few months, he improved a great deal in math and received his credit for completing the course in April; he had raised his achievement level in math a little more than four grade levels in the period of four months. His improvement in English was more precipitous, and it was most visibly exhibited by his ever-expanding appetite for reading. Throughout the rest of the school year, he became more and more involved in the academic program and received a Level Two Diploma at graduation.

Although Mose had developed academically during the school year, he did not fully come into his own socially until he went on the field trip to California. At the beginning of the trip, he was used by the other ten students as the butt for their jokes and was ridiculed at the slightest invitation. His idiosyncratic speech patterns were mimicked, and most of the students baited him constantly. For example, other students would ask him a ridiculous question, to which Mose would reply, "It all depends." The students would then say, "Hey Mose, it all depends," and break into peals of laughter. But by the time the students returned to Chicago (the field trip took ten days), Mose had become a person of real stature in the group. He remained an outsider to some of the more superficial interpersonal exchanges, but students respected his eccentricity as the mark of genius and imagination. Rather than parrotting his peculiarly enigmatic speech, students who went on the field trip came to use it as their own.

During the summer of 1968, Mose paid occasional visits to the school and spoke briefly with the Academy graduates involved in the summer program. He worked in some of the summer school classes to prepare himself for the G.E.D. exam. He intended to enroll in a college in California in the fall, and he attended some of the precollege counseling sessions that were held at this time. When he could not raise the money for his plane fare to California, however, he rejected the idea of attending school there.

Nancy Sheen had contacted a Midwestern scholarship service and described Mose's creative talents and financial need. They responded by offering him a partial scholarship to the Art Institute of Chicago, and he began classes there in January 1969. Mose found the classes stultifying and boring, and his attendance at the school was sporadic. After several months, he left and took a job teaching art to small children in a Catholic elementary school. At first he worked for no pay, but after a month or two, he was compensated for his efforts with a small salary.

In the summer of 1969, Mose worked in the summer program administered by Mission, and he applied again for scholarships to attend college. He was awarded a full scholarship for the fall by a regional scholarship foundation, and in September he enrolled at Columbia College, a small creative arts college in Chicago. His work there was satisfactory, and he continued his studies with an expanded schedule through the spring semester. Through the college, he has become involved with a young muralist, and they formed a group to paint a number of large murals around the city.

In March 1970 Mose moved away from his family's home in the West Park area and took an apartment by himself on the north side of Chicago. He has continued painting and writing to the present date, and his apartment walls are covered with his own works. Early in the summer of 1970 he sold some of his drawings, and his writing has appeared in a literary journal published by the college he attends. One of his more recent contacts with Mission Academy was to solicit the support of Mission administrators for the group of muralists of which he is a member. As a result of these efforts, Mose and his associates executed a large mural on the side of the Mission building.

LAMONT

As part of an assignment in composition, Lamont wrote a description of his first day at Mission Academy:

My first day at Mission

For me it was an experience I'll never forget.

The first person I met was [Theodore], maybe that were my first impression that the school was a section-A nut house. I mean, [Theodore] triped all over hisself trying to be friendly, my sister and me used to call him the mad prof. Can you picture a white cat standing in the door way of a church in an all black neighborhood, standing there with open arms telling you come in, come in. Right then and their I wanted to turn around and say forget it, but their was [Roberta] my sister telling me to come on—well, not telling me, twisting my arm is more like it. Well, we interduced each other our name and [Theodore] said to call him by his first name, so he took me on back to [Nancy's] office, who supprised me because she was so young.

I filled out the application and told [Cookie] to brief me on the school. So [Cookie] gives me a whole line of bull of how I can make it if I want to but it was up to me and on and on. The only word I got out of it was this one word—you see, he was trying to talk real hip I guess because I looked like a gangster or something, but like I was saying he kept saying "well, wire me up" if I have any problems. But it turns out that he got wired up, literally.

Anyway, on the way out I met [Suzanne] and her and my sister got to rapping and I was standing in a daze looking around the place, when someone came up and rang a bell and then it seemed like well all hell broke loose, people started coming out of rooms up stairs, and from the basement, and started playing the piano, flutes, and going through this rite of hand shaking and wearing afro robes hanging on the railings up stairs hollering and cussing and smoking in the church. I thought to myself, this is a school? So right then and their I made up my mind not to come.

The day he described was early in October 1967, shortly after the students had returned from the trip to Happy Hills Farm, and in spite of his initial reaction, he came back. I first met Lamont two days later when he appeared in my basic math class; I hurriedly gave him abbreviated directions for working with the programmed materials and went on to work with some other student. At the end of the class period, the bell was rung, and all the students left except for Lamont. I asked him what class he had next, and he told me that he had no idea. I then noticed that he did not have a programmed book, and I asked him why not. Lamont answered that he did not know where they were, and he did not want to interrupt me by asking. He had sat through the entire class without saying a word, without having a book, and without feeling that this was an unnatural situation. He later recounted that his greatest shock in that class was that I had come to him after class and actually had spoken to him.

Previous to enrolling in the Academy, Lamont had attended a number of public elementary schools and Derrick High School. He had been kicked out of Derrick in the fall of 1966 for smoking. Shortly thereafter he had been arrested for car theft and had pulled a gun on the arresting policeman. Tried on a number of charges, he had been found guilty and sentenced to several months in a correctional institution. He was released from custody in August 1967. When he took the entrance exams in October 1967, his scores indicated achievement levels of the seventh grade in mathematics and reading. He had accumulated a little more than one full year of high school credits.

Lamont worked very hard, and by the middle of November he had finished all the work for the math course. He took the final exam and scored above the eleventh grade level, an improvement of four grade levels in about six weeks. In addition to his efforts in the math class, he was one of two students who worked consistently in the science course. I was impressed with his capacity to learn academic material, and I asked him if he had ever thought about going to college. He replied "College? Are you serious? Hell no, I never thought about it. I just want to get my diploma and go learn a trade, maybe be a turret-lathe operator."

By December, Lamont had established himself as one of the best students in the school. The staff suggested that he take the Scholastic Aptitude Tests in case he decided that he would like to attend college the following year. He filled out an application and spent a few hours with me preparing for the exam, but he did not show up to take it. I asked him why he had missed it, and he replied, "Well, you see, my old man didn't want me to. He said he had work for me to do that day, and that if I didn't help him, he'd put me out of the house and never let me back in."

Although he showed no interest in "student politics" and usually did not attend student meetings, Lamont became more outgoing as the weeks passed. He was considered by the staff to be one of the most trustworthy students, and he worked as an assistant to Suzanne in operating the Academy cafeteria. He was the only student in the school who was trusted to handle sales in the cafeteria, but his insistence that students pay for what they bought often provoked hostile exchanges with those who attempted to take food without paying. One such exchange led to the serious fight between Pud and Lamont in April 1968. Although he was suspended for one week after the fight, Lamont was identified as a "for real" student.

At the graduation ceremony in May, Lamont was one of two student speakers. In addition, he received all three levels of Mission diplomas, a certificate indicating that he had passed the G.E.D. exam, and an award for being the "most outstanding student for the year." Lamont went on the field trip to California, and when he returned he worked as a teacher in the Mission Summer School. During the trip to California, Lamont and five other students had been interviewed for admission to a university in Utah for the coming academic year, and these students participated in the precollege counseling sessions during the summer. In June, however, Lamont told me that he had decided that he could not go to college, because he was not "good enough." He said that this was not only his own opinion, but also that of his family and friends. Two of the other students who planned to attend college in the fall assured him that if they could make it, he certainly could, and Lamont admitted to their wisdom.

Throughout the summer, Lamont continued his involvement with the precollege counseling sessions and showed competence in his teaching position. In August, he reported to me that he would not be able to attend college because he had been arrested for purchasing a stolen battery. However, he was sentenced only to a period of probation, and his probation officer approved his forthcoming enrollment in the university. His intentions of enrolling were almost frustrated a week before he was to leave when, at a farewell party held at his sister Gloria's house, a drunk guest attempted to involve him in a gun battle. But Gloria had had the foresight to hide his gun, and that prevented him from participating in the incident.

Lamont enrolled in the university in October 1968, along with five other former Academy students. He was an immediate social success and was elected president of his dormitory and freshman class representative to the university student government. His academic work was sporadic but satisfactory, and he finished the first quarter with a B average.[13] In an interview held during the Christmas recess, he expressed his dissatisfaction with the university. He cited in particular, the "boring and irrelevant" nature of his academic work (although he enjoyed an introductory philosophy course), the intimidating manners of white students, and the lack of a significant number of black students and a sense of black culture.[14]

During the winter quarter, Lamont was identified as a "disciplinary problem" by one of the deans of the university. This judgment was based on threats he had made to white students who had harassed him and because he had taken an unauthorized trip to California. Lamont reported to me that the white students overreacted to everything he said and that he felt physically threatened in the dormitory because of "reactionary white racists" who had burned a cross on one black student's door. The university had not made any attempt to discipline the person who burned the cross, he said, and it looked as though they did not care about protecting black students as much as they did about protecting white ones.

During the spring quarter, Lamont and the other Mission students made an effort to organize the fifty or so black students at the university into an active interest group. Lamont was chosen spokesman for the group, and he also began assisting the admissions office in an effort to increase the enrollment of minority students. Although lacking a few credits from the number required for "normal" academic progress, by the end of the academic year his work was satisfactory, and he returned to Chicago to work during the summer for a black social action agency on the West Side.

In the fall of 1969, Lamont returned to the university to begin his sophomore year. As the months passed, his academic work deteriorated from what it had been before, and he became further and further dissatisfied with the timidity and obsequiousness—what he called the "whiteness"—of other black students at the university. During the winter quarter, he married Elaine, one of the other five Mission students on that campus, a girl with whom he had enjoyed an "off and on" relationship for well over a year. In April, thoroughly frustrated by his academic deficiencies and an apparently disappointing marriage, Lamont left the university by himself to return to Chicago, where he again joined the black agency he had worked for during the previous summer. I asked him why he had left, and he told me, "It was just too much, too much for me to take. Just too many white people there, and you can't trust one of them."

MAKING SPACE TO MAKE IT ALONE

By and large, students came to the Academy in order to receive a diploma. They went away after receiving a diploma; they would not have come if they thought it impossible to get one; and when it seemed completely out of reach the students became deeply frustrated. In addition, activities that appeared to direct them away from the diploma were frequently resisted and often attacked (e.g., class discussions in the Sharper Minds Program). This did not mean that students applied themselves exclusively to completing their academic work, but it was important to them to think that they did and to view other activities as "interruptions," "breaks," or "digressions." The most important aspect of the students' self images at the Academy was the development of competencies leading to a diploma, skills and abilities manifested in academic progress.

A number of factors worked against maintaining this academic self-image as a positive one. Most of the students at the Academy had been told for a significant period of their lives that they were academically incompetent. This message was brought to them by a succession of public school teachers who placed them in the lower half of their classes or in categories of no retreat such as "educable but mentally handicapped." Their parents usually took these evaluations at face value, and many were convinced that their children were in fact mentally "defective." The development of this status of defeat often culminated in dismissal from public schools, an event that ascribed to these young people the notorious label "dropout." If students were to review their past schooling, they would find many more situations characterizing them as academic failures than situations showing them to be successes.

In addition to the cumulative factor of the students' previous educational experience, competition with others for recognition made feelings of academic competence ephemeral. Competition for academic rewards was not peculiar to the Academy, but the emphasis on individualized instruction heightened its salience for the students in some unsuspected ways. Even though no grades were given, students used the slightest evaluative remarks of instructors as a basis for invidious or enhancing comparisons with other students in the school. Pud was frustrated to the point of dropping out of the Academy not merely by flunking the math test, but by the fact that many other students had passed it. Lamont was made more confident of his potential to do well in college not only by having passed the G.E.D. exam, but also by recognizing the superiority of his achievements over those of others who were also going to college.

Interactions between students were not mediated by a well-developed student culture, one that could provide a stable normative order for competition and status mobility. Instead, students at the school were moral pioneers, laying claim here and there to whatever holdings they could. Life on such a social frontier was anything but orderly, gentle, or cooperative, and anxiety about their academic "standing" was only part of the identity struggle in which students engaged.

Sexual identities, for example, were fraught with powerful fears. As a result, sexual ambiguity met with vicious and violent attacks. Walter, a meek young student who was smaller than others, worked part time in a flower shop. Other males, responding to his somewhat effeminate manner, constantly attacked him both verbally and physically, though the staff did their best to prevent or stop such actions. Female students frequently joined the males in calling Walter a "sissy" and in ridiculing him in whatever ways they could. Occasionally, some energetic male would attack him in a total rage, screaming at him, hitting him, and demanding that he fight back or be killed.[15]

Walter carried no lasting physical scars from these encounters, but he often left the building crying after receiving such abuse; I am sure he suffered deep emotional wounds. The staff never fully acknowledged the terror he must have felt, but passed it off in the terms by which Nancy Sheen described it: "Walter has *real* problems, deep, deep, psychological problems, and the best that we can hope for is to get him placed in a job where he'll be accepted."

Walter's torment at the hands of his fellow students was part of the moral pioneering described above, the creation of social categories out of the frontier of personal encounters. Over a period of time, this produced a variety of social characters or types that students in the school could use in "understanding" their own behavior and that of others. The manner in which these categories and labels operate in more conventional schools is well-known; words such as "red-hot," "goody-two-shoes," "Jock," "freak," "teacher's pet," "M-R," "remedial," all serve to identify individuals as social types and to specify predictable characters.

At the Academy, however, these categories were relatively under-elaborated. There was a lack not only of perjorative labels (e.g., troublemaker, slow learner, dumb), but also of affirmative ones (e.g., college prep, good student, valedictorian). Encounters among students in conventional schools can be based on identification of individuals as representative of existing and predictable social types, a process that leaves room for a range of acceptable behavior. At the Academy, however, such encounters involved creation of the social types themselves. In the absence of established labeling systems, students at the school understandably brought great emotional intensity to individual encounters, events that brought crucial moral values into the open. These were individuals insuring not only that the rules of social intercourse were obeyed, but also haggling, arguing and sometimes fighting over what the rules themselves were going to be.

The lack of useful social categories at the school can be explained in part by the resistance the staff showed to their development. After all, in theory this was a school where students were treated as individuals, not types. And, in practice, the staff was loathe to violate this principle, doing so only under extreme circumstances (such as those surrounding the "crisis" leading to identification of "for real" and "not for real" students). One of the staff's critiques of conventional schools was that their social organization relied heavily on the typing and labeling of students and ignored individual imaginations and potential. And, to some extent, the efforts of the staff and students to keep the Academy from developing in this direction were successful. The integrity of individual students was respected, and invidious comparisons between social types were generally taboo.

Suspended judgments about "kinds" and "types" of students, however, did not extinguish competitive social processes, and without these intermediate symbols, comparisons were focused on the individuals themselves. In a school where social types were not a priori good or bad, students had a hard time knowing where they stood.

The idea was that students would "stand" together, but that kind of collective spirit was hard to achieve at the Academy. In its absence, students were likely to feel good about themselves and their academic skills to the extent that they felt they were better than someone else. Such gains over a previous self-image of failure were hard to maintain, however, for this "out-doing" others strategy was in no way institutionalized. There was no "normal" Academy career to measure one's progress against; there were no grades given for class work; and there were no "college prep" courses or other symbols of high academic standing. In addition, there was the power of Academy rhetoric, an affirmation of the idea that everyone was equal. Taken together, these features gave no support for the idea that there were "really good students" or "really bad students" at the school, and even those who seemed to do better than others were very cautious in thinking of themselves as academically competent.

A student at the Academy was thus caught in the middle of a vicious cycle, a product of which was diffuse feelings of distrust for other students. To begin with, certain "safety" mechanisms were lacking at the school: no evaluative labels were allowed; academic competition was not condoned; and there was not enough collective or communal spirit among students to generate emotional "free space." There was, however, a deep need for students to demonstrate the fact that they were doing good academic work, a need that they brought to the school but one that the staff would have invented for them had they not. And, staff ideals to the contrary, individual students also needed to find a "place" for themselves in the social organization of the school and a place among their peers.

At the Academy, academic competence was a matter of individual effort and responsibility; credits and diplomas were handed out to individuals, not to groups. What this meant was that students were expected to stand alone, without comparatively testing their newly felt competence, an expectation that was simply unrealistic. Without a pecking order, it was indeed hard to peck, and the staff saw this as an important accomplishment of the Academy. What this view underestimated, however, was the need students felt to do just that. After years of being put down, it was not enough to be told that everyone was equal. As a result, the school was unsuccessful in keeping students from pecking, but it did keep them confused—not only about where to begin, but also about where the next peck might be coming from.

To some extent, students felt good about their abilities as they worked

through courses and saw their credits mount up. They also took encouragement from the experience of learning things they had not imagined they
could learn. But these highly personal, inner rewards needed outside
referents. The institutional structure of the school did not formally provide
them, and students worked at them informally (as best they could) in the
form of unacknowledged competition with each other. In their own minds,
they could find places where their newly developed skills improved their
social standing; in their school, they appeared to go along with the idea that
"everyone is equal."

The irony of the Academy's design was thus the students' central reality:
The school was founded to give them a second chance to get their diploma
and improve their lot, and that is why they came. Within the school, however,
experiences of "getting ahead" of other students were morally unacceptable,
and none of the Academy's organizational features rewarded such contests.[16]
When students fell into unacknowledged competition with each other, they
worked in a climate of distrust. The circle was made complete when such
distrust inhibited the development of the communality they might have
experienced in self-governance, affinity, or community action projects. The
lack of these collective activities kept the cycle from winding down or
breaking down over time, and the dynamics of student distrust were a
persistent feature of the school. Instead of standing together as a group—the
hope of those founding the school—students stood alone and well apart from
each other.

There were exceptions to the suspicious, individualized and competitive
fabric of student culture at Mission Academy. On field trips, such as those to
California, Washington, D.C., Kalamazoo, Michigan, and Happy Hills Farm,
the students opened up emotionally and developed close friendships. No
doubt the "marathon encounter" characteristics of these trips (e.g., driving
from Chicago to California and back in ten days) were important to this
process; the trips forced openness and trust out of the sheer intensity of
twenty-four hours a day interaction. But institutional factors were equally
important, for the value of these trips was wholly collective; no "credit" was
assigned on an individual basis. In contrast to the academic program of the
school, students on the field trips completed the experience together. There
were no differential "rates of progress" or "levels of achievement," and
traveling across country was not taking them toward a diploma.

Students would often say that they had learned more on the field trip than
they had in all their classes, but I found not a single reference to having learned
more from a field trip than had another student. That form of comparative
remark appears to have been reserved for the work done in the classroom.
Thus, when the collective spirit could flourish, it did perform as expected,
giving each student a place without generating a rigid status hierarchy.

Students clearly differentiated themselves on these trips, to be sure, but when the linearity of credits and diploma work were absent, they did so horizontally and not vertically.

Another exception to distrustful interactions was to be found in the relations between students and teachers within the context of academic work. Teachers appeared as "confederates" to students, a role nurtured with some care. The programming of course materials allowed teachers to actually help students learn, to work with them to meet competency requirements for completion of the course. This was in contrast to conventional situations in which the teacher acts as the sole judge of a student's performance and where the criteria for his judgment remain obscure. At the Academy, when course requirements were clearly specified, the teacher worked together to achieve them. When they were not (e.g., the experiential classes), the teacher was still able to cut through the distrust among students by insuring that interaction was affectively bounded.

Student and teacher backgrounds may have had little in common, but the serious business of the Academy—and the lives of those who were involved with it—created opportunities for students and teachers to cooperate and support each other. While students had distrust for the staff as a whole, as well they might, their trust of teachers as individual rarely wavered.

The student experience of the Academy was thus more a "second chance" at academic success than it was a "liberation" from conventional academic achievement. This second chance was offered under conditions that differed greatly from those of conventional schools, but this did not change the basic nature of the task and the goal toward which it was directed. Although students were free of many of the odious restrictions that had been placed on them in previous schooling (e.g., prohibitions against the use of certain words, wearing certain clothes, wearing certain hair styles, or student initiated assembly), they were not freed from a competitive process of academic advancement, nor were they freed from its consequences for interpersonal relations. For those who could take advantage of this second chance to affirm a sense of academic competence, the maintenance of this affirmation was problematic at best. Outside the walls of the Academy, under the weight of unpromising responses from family, friends, and conventional institutions, students were likely to revert to "the tried and true," a sense of themselves as academic failures. Student experience at the Academy was much more likely to show a student how he or she "might behave" as a good student than it was to completely transform a career of institutional failure into one of legitimate success.

And self-image was not all that mattered. Hustling credits and diplomas from the Academy helped a student out, but it did not free him from more general struggles. Hustling kept a young black person from falling under and ending up sick, dead, in jail, or in prison, but it was not a highway to success. Rather than "getting ahead," when viewed in the context of the American social order, hustling at Mission Academy helped a disadvantaged student stay even with the more middle-class members of his cohort. Although there were important day-to-day successes, the differential management of economic, social, and political resources in the larger society kept everyone a victim. For a young black to succeed at Mission Academy meant survival and not much more.

9

Teachers

The image of the young teacher-to-be, sallying forth with enthusiasm and idealism, is a familiar one to American readers. The sequel, in which the teacher suffers profound disillusionment in a first teaching assignment, is no less well known. In that these images capture something about maturation, they parallel similar accounts of the experiences of neophyte farmers, soldiers, criminals, salespeople, and so on. In addition, they call attention to the inadequacy of formal training as preparation for working in the "real world," a fact to which most graduates of formal training will readily attest. There is one aspect of these images, however, that distinguishes the teacher's career from the more general patterns of maturation and professional development, and that is the problematic and dramatic nature of the raw material with which he or she works. For the teacher, these are groups of live, active or sullen, verbal or speechless, human beings, all of them working and scheming to survive as undamaged as possible.

The peculiarities of the naïve teacher's disillusionment are that he or she has identified with the generous and genuine curiosity of potential students, with a personal excitement for learning projected onto their own, and with a belief in a shared idealism. Thus the spectacular crunch. Although other teachers may give warning, and, in retrospect, assist in understanding the terrifying events of disappointment, it is ultimately the individual teacher's failure with students that stands at the heart of the matter.

In an attempt to understand why things are not working out as planned, the disillusioned teacher may settle on the idea that his or her students are "dumber" than had been imagined. He or she may also find, however, that the school is a mysteriously inhibiting environment in which to teach. The analysis rarely goes beyond this point, and that itself is of great importance, for it illustrates the most poignant inadequacy of conventional schools. Not only are most schools hard on students, but they are also poor places in which to learn how to teach. The social organization of educational institutions rarely provides a teacher with the opportunity to experiment and make sense of errors in judgment. He or she is left confused by both failures and successes and remains inarticulate about the peculiar rewards received from the work, the students, and fellow teachers.

In contrast to more conventional schools, Mission Academy was an ideal place to learn to teach. Those who worked there used the climate of experimentation, reflective meetings, their colleagues, and responsive students to develop into effective and gratified teachers. The importance of these elements was not that they removed the possibility of teacher disillusionment, but that they allowed teachers to learn from such experiences. With their efforts to become better teachers supported by the ideology and social organization of the school, Academy staff members found the inspiration for their activism bound into the teaching environment. In finding their work meaningful, they uncovered a great resource, one which enabled them to confront the realities of the students, the community, and the Mission organization with imagination and wit.

JOINING THE ACADEMY, MISSION, AND THE COMMUNITY

During the pilot and experimental phase, the Academy took on staff members in a highly informal and largely personal manner. A teacher's first interaction with the school was usually with Nancy Sheen—some were referred to her by friends and acquaintances and arranged to meet her at the school, others she encountered on one of her many speaking engagements. Interviews were held between the prospective staff member and Nancy at the Academy, and these included any others from the Mission organization who happened to be around at the time. The interviews were usually informal and indirect, and staff were frequently told at that time whether or not they could expect to have a job when the school opened in the fall.

The impression that this process made on the individual staff member was that he or she was being hired solely on the basis of Nancy's personal evaluation. Such an impression—accurate at least in part—encouraged the staff to think that a teaching position at the Academy was a matter of personal privilege and that continued employment was contingent on maintaining a good relationship with Nancy Sheen. Under these circumstances, her effective authority as principal of the Academy was augmented. Not only was Nancy Sheen seen to occupy a powerful *position* in the school, but she was also seen as an important and powerful *person* in the school, the Mission organization, and the larger community.

The informal and personal hiring practices of the experimental and pilot phases were replaced by a more formal administrative mechanism during the demonstration phase. Although the terms of employment for returning teachers were set by Nancy Sheen and Rev. Keen, new staff were hired by the Personnel Committee. (This committee was created out of the membership of the Academy Advisory Board, and it was recognized by the larger Mission organization as a "step forward.") Meetings with prospective candidates were established much as before, by word of mouth, but advertisements were also placed in local papers. Interested candidates still had their first experience with the school through Nancy Sheen or Rev. Keen, but only one person was excluded from consideration at that stage of the process.[1] Ten applicants, all of them black, were interviewed for positions at the Academy, and five of them were hired.

The increased formality of the process and the involvement of additional people—the Personnel Committee had eight members, most of whom attended regularly—functioned to decrease the apparent role of personal privilege in hiring. Newly hired staff members felt that they had been hired by an organization, not by an individual, and they were likely to see their role at the Academy in more "professional" terms than did the returning staff.

During the demonstration phase, these differences between the way in which the "new staff" was hired and the way in which the "old staff" had been hired resulted in a division between the two groups of teachers, one that was reflected in their conceptions of their jobs. The returning staff was accustomed to "living the job" at the Academy twenty-four hours a day. The new staff, in contrast, "quit working" when they left the building, and were not very receptive to extending their working hours to meet "exceptional circumstances."

For example, in interviewing and hiring, the Personnel Committee neglected to tell the staff members that the Academy also operated four nights a week as a night school. After having been hired, the new staff were appraised of this and asked to select which night of the week they could teach, but they refused to do so, insisting that this was not part of the "job" for which they had been hired. Although the old or returning staff were also hired without mention of the night school, they agreed to work there. The Mission administrators assumed that the old staff was well aware that there was a night school at the Academy and that it was unnecessary to make their involvement with it explicit when renewing their appointments. This argument had some persuasive effect, but the main reason for their willingness to work at night stemmed from the conception they had of their jobs as functionally diffuse. By and large they felt that they had been hired to be "people" in the school, not "teachers." Indeed, they would be people who taught, but the teaching they would do was by no means limited to normal class hours.

This division between the old staff and new staff during the demonstration phase was visible in other areas as well. Not only had the teachers joined the school in taking a job, but they had also joined the "Mission Family," as they were told from time to time. The building in which the school operated was owned not by the school itself but by the larger Mission organization. During the experimental phase, the work of the old staff in renovating, repairing, and maintaining the building had been considerable. The new staff, however, resisted taking on these building maintenance activities. As Marcel put it, "Hell, I was hired to teach, not to be some goddamn janitor." The Mission Family concept—which also involved casual and open reference to Nancy Sheen as "Mother Mission"—did not impress the new staff. In contrast to the old staff, who saw the school as a place where they would work out what their job meant through trial and error, the new staff knew what they had been hired for, and as far as they were concerned they did it in the classroom during regular school hours.

There was a larger context in which these staff differences took on increased meaning, and that was the relationship between the staff and the surrounding community of the West Park area. The returning white staff was lacking one significant alternative that existed for the new black staff: an appeal to their right to be in the community. As a consequence, in establishing their legitimacy in the area, the white staff relied a great deal on Nancy Sheen and Rev. Keen, who had lived in the area longer than the staff and who had extensive community relationships through the Mission organization. While the new staff could join the community through the street, a public place where they could mix and mingle with the residents as fellow blacks, the old staff could only join through existing community organizations and the people responsible for their maintenance. While the new staff could call upon the blacks in the West Park area as allies, the old staff was left anxious with the precarious legitimacy negotiated by Nancy Sheen and Rev. Keen out of their Mission efforts.

Superimposition of the terms of their "welcome" in the community and the situation of personal privilege in which they felt they were hired heightened the affective ties between the two Mission administrators and the returning staff. Nancy Sheen and Rev. Keen were not only their administrators, but also the pipeline through which they pumped their reputation to the larger Mission organization and the community itself. The emotional ties that developed out of this functionally important relationship would simply support greater demands for time and energy than would the more clearly contractual relationship that existed between Mission administrators and the new staff.

A similar situation would appear to have existed within the school itself (in terms of the relationships between teachers and students), but here the teachers' specific competence cut across racial lines. Although for its first two years of operation the Academy staff was predominantly white—and the students were almost entirely black—a sense of "welcome" and "joining" occurred that frequently transcended this racial split. Students were committed to getting a high school diploma, and to the extent that they saw Academy teachers as helpful to them, they were willing to think of them as useful, competent, respectable, friendly, and even trustworthy. Because they were in some sense confederates in a common and important task, the students and teachers in the school managed to act, in many instances, irrespective of the racial schism that they represented institutionally.

The rewards of this "expert belonging" were not lost on the staff, and one of the ways in which they attempted to deal with the precarious and second-hand welcome that Nancy Sheen and Rev. Keen had created for them was through development and presentation of their teaching skills. Staff members felt it incumbent upon them to develop innovative and successful teaching techniques, not only to receive approval from their colleagues, but also in the hopes that status as an exceptional teacher would somehow transcend an a priori status as a white and a stranger in the West Park area. In this respect, they attempted to recreate, on an individual basis, the process by which Mission had established its own legitimacy in the area. The orientation sessions (described earlier, p.63) had made their point, and the Academy teachers largely accepted the terms by which they had been introduced into the community's racial dynamics: service for protection. In this world—where a good teacher would be more welcome than an average or a poor teacher— decisions by the staff to invest extraordinary amounts of time, energy, and imagination in their teaching appeared as common sense.

Being a "good teacher" or a competent professional was necessary but not sufficient for establishing the sense of welcome that the Academy staff desired. In fact, there existed in West Park a form of "double bind" that valued staff members for their skill on the one hand, and on the other expected them to be not only skilled but also dedicated and loyal to community residents. To the extent that residents were suspicious of "professionals from outside the community," it was necessary to demonstrate sincerity, sympathy, and enthusiasm for the particulars of West Park black life. To the extent that residents were suspicious of politically motivated outsiders coming in to "get them organized," however, it was necessary to demonstrate dedication to one's profession and exhibit great competence and cool in professional tasks. To some extent, to succeed in one direction undercut success in the other, and the teachers at the Academy anxiously walked the tightrope between the unwelcome statuses of the political "trouble-maker" and the exploitative and unresponsive "slick professional."

The tension between these two unacceptable extremes was not solely the product of the politics of the community. It should be remembered that staff members were hired by the Mission organization not just for their teaching skills but also for their dedication to educational reform. The tightrope operated inside the school as well as outside. In the context of the American social order, it represents an anxiety and ambivalence clearly alive in much of the social conflict of the 1960s. Crucial moral issues were cast in terms of the conjunction, or lack of it, of instrumental skills and political allegiance. In the Academy, as well as elsewhere, questions were being raised about taking personal responsibility for organizational, professional, and societal goals.

The Academy itself assisted staff in dealing with these issues by making the political intent of their actions clear to the larger community. Given that it was established out of a critique of conventional education, the very presence of a teacher at the Academy was a demonstration of sympathy for the "cause" in the West Park area. The staff experienced the luxury of concentrating on their profession in an organization that provided them with a political identity acceptable to the surrounding community. Teachers in the public schools were not so fortunate, and they had to demonstrate not only that they were good teachers, but also that they were in some sense "against" the institution for which they worked.

At the Academy, it appeared, at least to the older staff, that the more they put into joining the school, the Mission, and the community, the more lasting and stable their welcome would become. The situation was made to order for teachers who wanted to be dedicated to their students and their craft.

TEACHING AS TRAINING FOR TEACHING

By and large, the Academy staff learned to teach at the Academy itself. If teaching experience previous to the Academy had been summed for the eleven staff members working during the experimental phases, the total would have been less than five full years. Only one of the five new staff hired for the demonstration phase had any previous teaching experience, and it was not in the areas she was to teach at the school. Of the sixteen Academy teachers involved with the school during the experimental and demonstration phases, only two had participated in teacher training programs.

This lack of teaching experience and formal preparation for teaching was not simply a consequence of the "stage of life" represented by Academy staff members. Although seven of the eleven experimental phase staff members were twenty-three years old or younger, the remaining four were thirty-one, thirty-nine, fifty-one, and "around sixty." This was not a group of dedicated teachers who were just getting around to doing what they had always wanted to do, but a collection of individuals who had worked on a variety of jobs and exhibited complex career patterns. Theodore had been a grocery store clerk and a museum researcher; he had done newspaper work and had held a number of odd jobs that enabled him to organize labor unions and community organizations, an activity that he had been engaged in for some twenty-five or thirty years before coming to the Academy. Rider had worked for a printing establishment before becoming the proprietor of a candy store, an enterprise that he sold after teaching at the Academy for a year and a half. Martha, the eldest member on the staff, was a retired public school librarian. The new staff joining the Academy at the beginning of the demonstration phase came from jobs where they had worked as a bus driver, an accountant, a receptionist, a probation officer, and a graduate student at Northwestern University.

The educational backgrounds of the staff members were also varied, and, with the exceptions of Hal and Judith, they did not indicate conventional preparation for teaching careers. Theodore had received a B.A. in journalism for the University of Wisconsin. Judith, Hal, and I had also received B.A.s from accredited colleges and universities; Hal's degree was in biology, and Judith and I were awarded degrees in the social sciences. Cockey had completed the requirements for a B.A. from a Catholic seminary, but his dismissal from the institution just prior to graduation kept him from receiving the degree. Both Suzanne and Martha had completed a number of years of college and had received provisional certification as teachers in their areas of specialization. Cookie had not completed high school, nor had Rider, and Candy and Betsy were working toward their B.A.s at Kalamazoo College. Although Judith, Hal, and I were working toward advanced degrees at the time we were employed by the Academy, none of us at that time saw these degrees as leading to a career in teaching. The new staff for the demonstration phase had all been to college, but only two had graduated with the B.A. degree.

Rather than stressing educational preparation, conventional teaching credentials and training, or previous teaching experience in selecting staff for the Academy, Nancy Sheen and Rev. Keen stated that they wanted people who could "actually teach." According to their statements, they looked for individuals who were energetic and intelligent, who had "extensive inner resources," and who were dedicated to teaching.[2]

The combination of the personality and character variables listed above was viewed within a context of experience in certain kinds of activities. Nancy once told me that she looked for particular kinds of people for particular jobs. Thus, Cookie was hired because he was black and had previous experience working with young black people in producing musical revues and the like, but he was hired to fill a particular need at the school. With his "qualifications," he would not have been hired to teach math or English or any of the academic courses: he was barely twenty-one years old and had not studied academic material at the college level. When the "collective productions" he was supposed to organize proved to be unpopular among the students, he was given a leave of absence from the Academy.

Cookie's case was somewhat of an exception. The usual formula was that someone was hired who said that he had studied a subject in college and could teach it. Competence was sometimes checked by reference to college transcripts and letters of reference, but this practice varied. The real nature of the teacher's job, the description of what he or she was supposed to do in the classroom, was left largely undefined. It was assumed that the Academy staff would work individually and collectively to discover what it was that they were going to do and how best to do it.

A critical factor in the amount of energy that teachers at the Academy committed to this process of learning how to teach was that attendance at the school was noncompulsory. Students would attend a class only if they thought it was entertaining or productive. Their direct response, through attending or not attending, made student evaluations an important reference point for teachers, much more so than if students had been coerced into showing up for class. In a sense, the "responsive" structure of student attendance created an important learning environment for the teacher. Rather than waiting until the end of the term, if not several years, to find out what students thought of the class, the teacher at the Academy would find out immediately. Such prompt feedback was very useful to the staff not only in evaluating the success of various techniques, but also in making visible the rewards of teaching. A teacher knew that if students did attend, it was because he or she was doing something well, not just because it was "class time."

Had they taught under such circumstances without opportunities to discuss with other teachers the day-to-day encounters that they survived with students, the Academy staff might have been less enthusiastic and resourceful in their efforts. To place one's reputation in the balance on a daily basis—as opposed to the yearly basis in schools where administrators are by and large the sole judges of a teacher's competence—took courage, and this courage was nurtured by the staff's collective spirit, identity, and social enterprise. Knowing that other teachers suffered the same pains and enjoyed the same rewards was a comfort to the individual teacher, and this knowledge was communicated clearly and frequently at staff meetings. By getting together as a group two or three times a week to discuss what was happening in the school, the teachers at the Academy supported each other's ambitions and visions. Such meetings also gave a continuity to instructional effort that might otherwise have been lacking. And, in the long run, these meetings raised the level of sophistication of the staff as educators by helping them identify the personal, structural, and serendipitous elements of the teaching process.

The orientation toward establishing a community reputation for expertise and for dedication, the learning mechanism of noncompulsory student attendance, and the frequent staff meetings were all instrumental in the development of competent, communicative, and gratified teachers at the Academy. Beyond a basic familiarity with proposed subject matter[3]—and in some cases irrespective of it—these structural elements appear to be critical to understanding the successful teaching done at the school.

There is another matter that merits attention, however, for the only "sought after" attributes that a potential staff member could present to the interviewing Mission personnel were those that had to do with interpersonal skills, statements of dedication, and "dynamism." This was made clear to staff members not only at the time of their hiring (e.g., a candidate was invariably asked questions such as: What do you *really* like doing? What turns you on? What would you like to teach here if you could teach anything you wanted to?), but throughout their involvement with the school, Rev. Keen and Nancy Sheen often complimented the staff by saying that they had never seen "such a dedicated and dynamic group of people who could really work together well."

It may be that the Mission administrators were able to find exceptionally dynamic and interpersonally skilled individuals whom they then hired as staff for the school. But even if this were not the case, the staff incorporated these qualities into their individual self-images. Teachers at the Academy thought of themselves as energetic, interpersonally skilled, and dedicated to teaching as an enterprise and to educational reform. Their continued involvement with the school provided them with a continuing demonstration that this was indeed a valid self-image. The sense of satisfaction that they took in this validation was important to their growth as individuals and as a staff, as well as to their contributions to the development of the total school. We were more than willing to work hard and creatively at our teaching, for we were recognized by our supervisors and each other as hard workers and creative teachers.

MEANINGFUL WORK:
AN ORGANIZATIONAL RESOURCE

The experience of joining the school and community and learning to teach at the Academy were important ingredients of staff culture, a pattern of behavior and perception that gave meaning to involvement with the school. This culture served to integrate, in a rewarding manner, a teacher's decisions to join the school and remain with the experience of being there five days a week. In the first case, the staff was involved with the Academy as a thing in itself; staff participation (based on salary, commitment to educational reform, and the role the Academy played in that reform) appeared as dedication to the organization. In the second case, however, the staff was involved with individuals in the school, and participation was based on the rewards of this interaction. The context of the first case—that of dedication—was the larger if not total life space of the staff member; the context of the second—interactions with others—was mostly confined to the school building itself.

To some extent, staff members were selected on the basis of the dedication they could be expected to exhibit and experience at the Academy. Mission administrators also stressed the contribution that teachers would be making to fundamental social change, making it easy for prospective staff members to select themselves in or out of "educational reform." The Academy was advertised as a place where social criticism could be galvanized into social action, where teachers could teach without formal constraints on their efforts that were characteristic of public schools, and where "exciting changes could take place" in the lives of students.

All this worked to recruit individuals who were already sympathetic to the broader movement for educational reform in which the Academy participated. This sympathy was one of the two most significant features of staff participation, and it was largely responsible for their willingness to make extensive contributions of time and energy to the students and the school. Although staff members did not compare their teaching situations with those of teachers in other experimental schools, comparisons with public schools were made continually. Often these referred to stereotypical dimensions of public school conventionality (e.g., dress codes, no smoking rules, prohibitions against vulgar language), but they usually focused on the opportunities for a concerned individual to teach students effectively. Staff members would often remark, "I just couldn't ever teach in a public school. How could you stand just going through the motions of teaching? At Mission you can really do something for the students; they can learn something here." In a very important respect, staff members worked at the Academy in order to help students and to reform American schools.

The staff of the Academy can be characterized, like the students, as misfits—individuals maladjusted to the conventional social order and the institutions that maintained its existence.[4] As a result, the conventional rewards that the Academy provided were not in themselves adequate to insure continued staff involvement with the school.[5] When these conventional rewards were coupled with an ideological commitment to social change, however, their attractiveness increased. The staff members found the Academy to be a place where they could "have their cake and eat it, too." Not only could they work toward general educational reform, but they could do so within an organization that provided them with financial security.

The staff's participation in the school was functionally similar to that of the students in one respect: Neither the opportunity for conventional rewards nor the opportunity to "experiment with education" were enough in themselves to insure full participation. In another respect, however, the two groups differed greatly. For the student, the assumption that his or her involvement with the Academy would lead to a high school diploma was often reward enough. Students accepted the Academy as preparation for something better—a better job, more education, or more money. For the staff, however, working at the Academy was not seen to lead anywhere in particular, and they required immediate remuneration.

The fact that the staff received more immediate rewards for their work at the Academy points to the supply and demand characteristics of schooling. As a result of compulsory education and the importance of educational credentials to upward mobility, students come cheaply. In fact, in some cases, students pay for both the experience of being in a school and the credentials they receive. Alternatively, the experience of teaching in a school does not carry with it a process of systematic credentialization. The very limited supply of individuals who see teaching as a personally rewarding enterprise in and of itself requires that teachers be paid to do what students are paying to do: work in schools.

The Academy was able to involve about 400 dropouts in its first two years without offering one student salary. In order to retain seventeen staff members during this same period of time, the Academy had to provide salaries for fourteen of them. Being a "misfit" teacher at the Academy was far more profitable than being a "misfit" student. Teachers could more easily transform their status from "misfit" to "missionary" than could students, and missionaries got paid.

It should come as no surprise, then, to find that staff members were more likely to "experiment with education" than were students. After all, the staff were paid to do just that, and students would receive conventional rewards only if the experiment were successful (and, even then, in less tangible forms). In one sense the staff could not lose, and yet it was unclear whether or not students were going to win. As a result, staff involvement with the school was characterized by a deep dedication and a firm commitment to innovative programs; this differed greatly from the involvement of the students.

A second major feature of staff culture was the meaning of their interaction within the school building. Whenever a staff member had an observation to make about the Academy, it seemed important that other staff members share it. When one teacher thought things were "going well" it was important that other teachers thought so also. Disagreement among the staff was generally thought to be a bad thing, and Nancy Sheen often characterized dissensus as a "threat to the survival of the school."

There were a number of factors that encouraged this taste for unanimity, and one of the most important was the staff position as a minority within the school. There were ten to twelve staff members and three to six times that many students in the school building at any one time. In addition, the four to six white staff members were the only whites frequenting the building, exclusive of guests and Mission pastors. The staff members perceived their minority position as a vulnerable one, not only because they were fewer than the students, but also because they were "whiter." Establishing unanimity among themselves was seen as a powerful and necessary protective mechanism. If a teacher did not have the support of fellow staff members, he or she effectively had no support, for there was no other place to go to get it.

The minority position of the staff members was exacerbated by the ambiguity of their jobs. Teachers' tasks at Mission Academy were functionally diffuse; this created large areas of staff responsibility that were not clearly within their jurisdiction. The existence of these "contested areas"— they were contested with students and administrators—meant that efforts to perform their duties often required appeals to fellow teachers for support. For example, when Cockey wanted the door of his classroom closed because of noise in the adjoining hall, Twister objected, telling him that it was not "Cockey's classroom" but that of the students. Cockey said he could not teach with the door open and went to close it. Twister leaped up from his desk and slugged Cockey in the jaw, knocking him to the ground. Cockey could not appeal to students in the class, for they were afraid of retributions from Twister, and the conflict was left hanging and unresolved through the rest of the day. The next day, however, the entire staff called a teaching strike to show their support for Cockey. This was effective in forcing students to recognize the rights of staff members to organize activities within the classrooms.

The ambiguity of staff roles in the Academy fed into a more general confusion about mechanisms of social control. Because it sought to operate as a student-oriented school, the Academy advocated a democratic model for decision-making. Institutionalizing this model was supposed to involve democratic processes as well. Failure to engage students fully in the process of institutionalization, however, did not lead to abandoning the model, but only confused the manner in which decisions were "supposed" to be made. The lack of formal, clearly defined norms for decision-making and enforcement created an atmosphere in which the only power available was that of "groupness." When conflict emerged, civil intimidation was the order of the day, and the staff accurately recognized its power to be based on the appearance of group cohesion. In conflicts between teachers and students, the staff could invariably rely on having less dissension to deal with than did the students. Student struggles to achieve consensus around their side of an issue were usually no match for the united front presented by the staff.

The high value placed on unanimity in the staff culture may have been inspired by issues of social control, but achievement of this "like-mindedness" was facilitated by structured interaction. The staff met often as a group, and it frequently met in opposition to other groups. At least three meetings were held each week, and in exceptional situations this number was increased. The meetings focused on the development of curriculum, individual teaching, problem students in the school, efforts to develop experimental programs, and the relationship between the Academy and conventional institutions. By constantly comparing its own operation with that of more "conventional staffs," the Academy teachers affirmed their group identity; an awareness of the "threats" to experimental education increased the salience of that identity to their normal behavior in the school.

Staff culture at Mission Academy can be seen as a structure in which staff identity could be elaborated, both with respect to a general commitment to the Academy and with respect to day-to-day interactions within the school. This identity assisted individual staff members in making critical decisions, supported them in the face of community hostility, and favorably related their status to that of teachers in conventional schools. Within these terms it made teaching in the school "meaningful work" for those who did so, and it rewarded teachers for caring deeply about what they were doing.

This deep "caring" about teaching at the Academy did not occur in a vacuum, nor should it be dismissed in assessing the factors important to the school's success and survival. Students and teachers at the school confronted a large carryover of "conventional school" mentality among themselves and others, as well as a profound confusion about how they might best relate to each other. The political climate in which they came together was both highly charged and ambiguous, and the ideal of cooperative administration was an unlikely direction to take among the strangers and, in some cases, avowed enemies who involved themselves with the school. Given these circumstances, the Academy's persistent success is hard to explain without reference to the deep commitment that individuals made to its operation.

In the same manner that the social organization of the school helped teachers learn how to teach, the staff culture—and the sense of "meaningful work" at its core—encouraged them to care about students, courses, other teachers, and the future of the school. This was a formidable resource, to say the least.

A "SECOND CHANCE" FOR TEACHERS

The careers of individual staff members changed as a result of their participation in the Academy. Rider, by demonstrating exceptional skill in directing the Story Workshop, secured a teaching position at Columbia College in Chicago and subsequently sold his candy store. Largely as a result of my work in curriculum development, I also found a position at Columbia College. Cockey taught at two "experimental" Catholic schools on the West Side before making his way to New York and an acting career, and Theodore continued his work with the Museum of Afro-American History. Instructors joining the Academy at the beginning of the demonstration phase remained at the school for some time longer, and a few are still there. Their failure to resist significantly the firing of Call Strow led to a temporary but deep split with the staff who left or were fired at that time. Call Strow worked through a fellowship to study American Literature at an eastern university; he is currently consulting his way from school to school as well as writing a novel and some plays.

At the end of the experimental phase, Cookie, Judith, Hal, and Suzanne left the Academy. Cookie has since worked at a number of jobs, including counselor in a program to train dropouts for careers in the telephone company. Judith moved to Boston and found work as an educational consultant; she has become increasingly active in the women's liberation movement and other radical political enterprises. She is currently completing requirements for a Ph.D. in sociology. Hal worked as "Human Relations Coordinator" for Springfield, Ohio, and as director of a poverty program in a suburb of Chicago; he is currently enrolled in a graduate program in sociology at Berkeley. Suzanne has been largely occupied with raising her two children, one of whom was born in the summer of 1968.

The activities of staff members subsequent to their departure from the Academy indicate that their professional careers were enhanced by their experiences at the school. In addition to the full-time occupational involvements described above, all of the former teachers at the Academy have extended or expanded their reputations as "educational experts."

The Academy was not accredited, and it provided no formal credentials for individuals who taught there, but participation in the Academy has appeared as an attractive element in the professional résumés of staff members. In this respect, the Academy served the upwardly mobile aspirations of the staff as well as those of the students. Mission Academy was identified, after all, as a "second chance" school. It seems that the staff used this second chance at least as well as did the students.[6] We may have come to the Academy as misfit teachers in search of alternative education, but we left as missionaries of reform, and we were not afraid to say so.

Part V
Spirit

10

Getting and
Keeping Order

We call upon a variety of strategies in our efforts to create and maintain social order. Two of the more dominant are those of "controlling human behavior" and "understanding collective human process." Order in conventional schools has typically been seen as a problem of control; understanding and collective process are seen as resources to be used by those in control—but not as ends in themselves.

It is here that many problems arise. To the extent that social order in schools is grounded in institutional and authoritative control, teachers will be expected to control students and administrators to control teachers. As Willard Waller has put it, "the school is continually threatened because it is autocratic, and it has to be autocratic because it is threatened."

If social order in schools were based more on an understanding of collective process and less on institutional authority and control, the jobs of teachers and administrators would be that much easier. James Herndon worked out this alternative kind of order with his students in a conventional school, and he was fired for it. In an interview with his principal—a hearing granted after he was told that his work was unsatisfactory—Herndon was criticized for having no control over his students.

This hearing took place in the spring, and it occurred after the school had erupted in a series of riots. The control-based order in most classrooms broke down, but Herndon's students did not join in these riots, and his classes continued much as usual. As he told the principal, "no one in my class had rioted; no one locked me out, or threw my hat out the window. None of this happened in my classes. So who had better control?"

The principal's response to this argument is illuminating, and it exemplifies the deep commitment to social order based on control held by those in charge of conventional schools. As Herndon writes, "He wasn't impressed. He knew there had been riots; he knew I'd had none. It didn't matter—in fact, it proved his point. . . . A riot meant that some order had been imposed, some control established, since it was against that control that the children were rebelling. It followed that as I was allowing them to do as they pleased it was unnecessary for them to riot. . . . [Even if] the class had worked out their own system of doing things, I should realize that wasn't what he thought desirable. The opposite, in fact."[1]

In general, the "control" and "process" conceptions of order are associated with contrasting ideas about human nature, human potential, the legitimacy of feelings and conflict, "hard" and "soft" structures, hierarchical and democratic organizations, work and play, and so on. At heart, there is at least some notion in the case for control that the ideal course of events is not the one natural to those involved, but a program designed by others of exceptional wisdom. And with an orientation toward collective process we are left with the notion that groups of people left to their own resources and imaginations are usually at their best.

Associated with advocacy of each of these two types of order in schools is a distinctive conception of "student nature." For those committed to control, students appear to be a very mixed lot, ranging from the good to the depraved. For society as we know it to survive, they argue, the good have to be sorted out from the bad. The good may then excel within existing social structures and provide strength and leadership for the nation, while the bad may be rehabilitated or removed from arenas of normal social intercourse. On the other hand, those calling for understanding and collective process see in students a youthful dignity and nobility. The suggestion here is that all youth, under favorable conditions, can blossom into creative, socially aware, and constructive citizens. One position emphasizes discipline, the other guidance. One blames students for the crisis in education; the other blames the schools.

There is a common sense appropriateness of these correlations between conceptions of the social order and conceptions of students, but this is slightly deceptive. We have at least two possible strategies for finding order in the world, and, as it happens, for finding it in schools: authoritative control and process-focused understanding. And we are faced with at least two conceptions of the mass of students: basically mixed and in need of sorting, and basically good and in need only of encouragement. We might ask why school administrators (and many teachers in conventional schools) typically emphasize control of the mixed lot, while alternative teachers and educational activists define the situation in terms of understanding and encouraging all students. Correspondence between their positions in the schooling business and their attachment to these concepts is suggestive of the kind of analysis that we need to make. What are the intervening factors that emphasize—on the one hand—not only control, but also the "good" and the "bad" and—on the other hand—not only understanding, but also categorical nobility?

What appear to members of one camp as destructive and chaotic social situations appear to the other as vital, life-enhancing learning. What appears to one as the careful selection of qualified students appears to the other as the discriminatory destruction of individual experience and imagination. And finally, to one group a teaching job is a difficult and precarious struggle against the natural inclinations of youth, while for the other it is a joyous and rewarding commitment to the natural course of events.

At Mission Academy, there was a strong affirmation of the dignity and the enormous, unrealized potential of today's youth. Everyone who worked there thought that students deserved our sympathy, understanding, and encouragement in their encounters with conventional schools and "life itself." It is of particular interest, given this agreement, that while students and teachers at the school were largely content with an order based on collective process, Mission administrators were not. They were ill at ease with a social order that was understandable and predictable but out of their hands. As a consequence, they were continually involved in efforts to better control the behavior of other members of the Academy.

It is additionally interesting that within the Academy itself, students, teachers, and administrators all experienced deep ambivalence over actions that indicated that some students were less deserving than others. At the Academy, everyone was supposed to be equal. When decisions were made suggesting that they were not, the moral order of the school came apart. In working to reintegrate that order, individuals at the school developed an interim process, one in which the most important values were those of "fairness" and "trust."

Everyone at the Academy was committed to the basic dignity of students and to understanding their collective process. We worked, however, in a school that at times, operated in contradiction to that commitment. As a result, we had to find exceptional ways to explain the failures of the school to live up to its ideals, ways that made some sense, but not so much that they could threaten the basic commitment to collective process. The moral order had to be repaired, but it would not do to have the repair job look better than the original. After all, this was an alternative school; the ideal of collective process was absolutely essential to insuring the continued participation of its members.

In the Academy's new building, one room in the basement had been reserved for an art room. The room was about twenty feet square, and it contained a number of exposed overhead pipes running along the ceiling. The walls were unfinished concrete block, and the floor was concrete. All of these characteristics were important to its selection as the "art room." The Mission administrators assumed that space would be at a premium in the new building, and they did not want a dominating activity (such as painting with its attendant smells, smears, and constructions) to take place in a multipurpose room. This room was not particularly useful as a multipurpose area, and on that basis it was selected as the art room.

Few students expressed interest in taking art courses, and only Mose showed enthusiasm for working there. As a rule, students rarely came to the room. If they noticed that someone was already in it, they might stop for a moment to chat, but they did little painting or drawing. In early December 1967, however, five students and I participated in what was later referred to as the "art room orgy." After an hour and a half of concentrated activity, the walls, floor, and ceiling were painted in brightly colored designs, about half of which consisted of large signatures of the students involved, some of them taking up the length of one of the four walls. In addition, other "signatures" were left in red, yellow, blue, and green enamel: footprints, handprints, self-portraits, and pet slogans (e.g., "God's not dead, he's just a high school drop-out"). All this had begun with Mose painting a design on one of the walls as we talked. One by one, the other students followed suit until the five of us were totally involved in the painting—and not a little "zipped" from the fumes in that close space.

At some point we finished, totally exhausted and satiated with spreading color and meaning around the room. In standing back and looking at it all, we were quite impressed; the room was transformed. We decided to surprise Nancy and Rev. Keen with our handiwork, and Mose went to get them from a meeting in which they were involved. The rest of us waited in anticipation as their steps came down the basement stairs and their heads poked into the room. They appeared to be totally bewildered, but Nancy's first remarks were: "Gee, this is great, really great!" Rev. Keen looked around for several minutes, pulling lightly on his goatee, and then said that he hoped the paint on the floor was not wet or it would be tracked all through the building. He and Nancy both stated that it was "good that there was a place in the building where this could take place." Afterwards, however, Rev. Keen expressed to me his concern that once the students had acted so freely and disrespectfully of property in one context, they might feel encouraged to do so in other contexts; he hoped that this "painting-things-up business" was not going to spread.

The reactions of Nancy Sheen and Rev. Keen to the spectacle of the brightly painted room and its equally brightly painted students reflected important concerns about social order in the Academy. Although they approved of the "spontaneous" and "vital" aspects of the event, they did so with great misgivings. In the first place, they worried about "contagion" and wondered whether the art room orgy would inspire other students to commit similar acts of beautifying vandalism. They felt that the Academy could withstand such expressive and spontaneous behavior only on a very small scale. In addition, the "excessive vitality" manifested in the careless manner in which the walls, floor, and ceiling of the room were painted gave them pause. Such vitality represented a threat to the low-key politesse that they encouraged as a mechanism of social control. Finally, they were concerned about the dissolution of physical domains which these vital and contagious elements might bring about. The lack of respect for "property" that they saw in the art room orgy constituted a threat to their own control of the building, a structure they relied on to define the limits and scheduling of acceptable behavior.

In an earlier section, I described the manner in which the building mediated efforts of Academy members to establish their own versions of order in the school. Students, teachers, and administrators each sought to define building spaces in such a way that behavior within them conformed to their own ideal. The indirect "defining the situation" process which this entailed was also manifest in efforts to draft explicit rules for conduct and to organize classroom activity.

RULE-CREATING AND RHETORIC:
THE DENIAL OF INDIVIDUAL DEVIANCE

At Mission Academy, rules for student conduct were created in four situations. In three of these situations they were generated by the students, and in the fourth they were initiated by the faculty. All of the situations can be characterized as crises in the social order of the school, and the creation of rules can be seen to have provided solutions to the crises.

The first set of rules came out of a meeting in which students were asked to elect a representative group of leaders and to establish standards for behavior. The meeting was called by the staff during the first week of school, and, at Nancy's suggestion, it was chaired by Cookie. When he asked for the election to begin, a number of students protested, asking that it be postponed to a later date so they could have more time to get to know each other. The staff members argued against this, even though it made sense to them. They wanted the elections held right then and there, so that not another day would go by without official student leaders.

Elected student representatives were very important to the staff, who hoped such official leaders could be made responsible for student conduct as well as the expression of student interest at the Academy. By resisting the election, students were not only disagreeing with teachers, but also actually threatening the staff's conception of how social order would develop in the school. As far as the teachers and administrators were concerned, this order would be based on cooperation and the sharing of power and responsibility.

After over an hour of discussion about the elections, Nancy Sheen moved the agenda to the second task, that of making up the rules by which students wanted the Academy to operate. Students redirected their efforts and came up with the following five rules:

1. No visitors allowed in building unless a guest of students or teachers.

2. RESPECT for sisters; no swearing.[2]

3. Any brother who fights another brother will suffer the consequences.

4. No weapons allowed in the building; they must be deposited at the front desk.

5. No "reefers" or alcoholic beverages allowed in the building.[3]

After presenting this list of rules, the students were granted the postponement they had requested; the elections were called for two weeks from that day, and the meeting was dismissed.

A second set of rules emerged from a confrontation between teachers and students on December 18, 1967. The staff had called a meeting at which they recommended the suspension for one month of a number of students who had completed an "insufficient" amount of work. The students were outraged and interpreted this recommendation as a failure in cooperation by the staff. Accusations were traded back and forth, and the students finally asked the staff to leave the room, insisting that we let them take care of this matter themselves. The staff complied, and by the next morning, the students presented us with a new set of rules.

1. All conclusions drawn up by vote of the majority.

2. Discussion on *no* boycott unless necessary—unanimous.

3. All rules made stand when signed by student body.

4. No smoking pot or drinking in the building or cussing.

5. No students kicked out unless signed by student body.

6. A meeting every month on students (end of month) on probations and students decide on outcome of them *only*.

7. No disturbing others in class.

The staff asked how these rules were to be enforced, and the students assured them that "we'll take care of that." The staff pressed the students to elaborate the process by which rules would be enforced and the consequences for an individual who broke the rules, but the students would say no more than "it will be taken care of." Finally, the staff accepted the set of rules as a gesture of good faith, and cooperation between the two groups was restored.

The third set of rules came out of the incident in which Cockey was slugged in the mouth by Twister, one of the more aggressive students. The staff responded to this with outrage and a strike. Teachers showed up for work the following morning and sat in their classrooms, but they refused to teach. Students were outraged in turn and demanded to be taught. When the teachers refused, the students ran from one room to the next announcing an all-student meeting to be held immediately in the history room.

This student meeting resulted in another set of rules, similar to the list cited above, and a call for new elections of student representatives. In addition, the students stated that their rules for the Academy applied to teachers as well as students, and they imposed a twenty-five cent fine on anyone who engaged in swearing or cursing. The staff accepted this as another expression of student cooperation and returned to their teaching duties.

The fourth set of rules was the product of events surrounding the real "crisis" of the year, the closing of the Academy for one week and the expulsion of sixteen students. Students who were considered to be "not for real" were not allowed to return to the Academy when it reopened. Letters were sent to all "for real" students asking them to return the following Monday and apologizing for the disruptions which had occurred. Another letter was sent to all "not for real" students (by registered mail) indicating to them that the staff felt that neither they nor the Academy would profit from their continued presence in the school and suggesting that they might apply to a number of vocational training programs in Chicago.

In these actions, the staff established the following rules:

1. Students had to show measurable progress if they were to remain in the Academy; they could not literally "work at their own rate" whatever that rate might be.

2. Students who disturbed or disrupted the normal operation of a class would be suspended from the school.

These rules were unique in that they were enforced. Individual students were classified (ex post facto) as deviants for violating these rules and were subsequently expelled and suspended.

In all four cases, creation of rules for behavior occurred as a strategy for reestablishing order. In each rule-creating situation, a crisis in the social order was perceived and rules were suggested as a solution. In three of the four situations they were accepted without being enforced.

At Mission Academy, rules existed without offices or mechanisms for their enforcement, and individuals who violated them were not negatively sanctioned. Their continued importance to establishing social order stemmed not from their power to guide behavior, but from a more complicated bargaining process, one which reestablished cooperation between the students and staff in the normal operation of the Academy. In this process, the rules meant two things to the staff: that the students had thought about the issues involved in cooperatively administering the school, and, in that the rules were accepted in good faith, the students would be ashamed of themselves if they did not act according to them.

These two products of "rule creating" were very important. In the first place, the staff included among its objectives a clear sense of "consciousness raising." Teachers felt that students had been demoralized and dehumanized by conventional school systems and that the Academy could counteract these effects by encouraging students to think of themselves as potent and effective citizens. One of the staff goals for raising the issue of student participation was that students "deal with these issues." As a result, teachers were pleased when the students called meetings to make up lists of rules for their own behavior. These activities indicated that the students were seriously dealing with the problem of social control.

"Rule creating" without enforcement was also important to the staff because of the way it side-stepped the treatment of individual students as deviants. The staff felt that the imposition of arbitrary and petty rules for behavior had forced many Academy students out of conventional schools. In their efforts to convince these students that the schools had failed them, and not vice versa, Academy teachers were loathe to take actions that would indicate to a student that he or she was indeed a failure—a deviant not only in the conventional school system, but also at Mission Academy. The Academy was created to deal not only with individual dropouts, but also with the "dropout problem"; it was to provide a model for reform of conventional schools. If it had its own dropout problem, it was argued, the Academy's credibility as a model for reform would be greatly diminished.

As a result of these two factors, the staff accepted the student created rules as acts of good faith and thereby established their cooperation with the students in the operation of the school. This functioned to remove considerations of individual deviance and to emphasize the collective responsibility of all students for each student's behavior. This bargaining process was not entirely one of good faith, however, for the staff was well aware of the difficulty students would have in enforcing their rules. Part of the strength of this dynamic stemmed from the staff's anticipation that students would be compromised by advocacy of the rules and their subsequent inability to enforce them. Within this context, the act of creating the rules compromised the students as a group, underlining their inability to govern themselves in spite of their high ambitions.

In some sense, the staff was setting the students up for experiences of collective shame and failure. As much as we hoped they would, we never really believed that the students were going to take charge of the authority they worked within. And in some unintended way, the understandable failure of their efforts was almost punishment enough for transgressions that did occur. Rather than provisions for sanctioning individuals, they offered us the promise of collective shame, and we took them up on it.

The rules emerging from one of the four rule-creating situations were enforced. In this case, however, the rules were created and administered by the staff, sometimes with the assistance of local police. Teachers felt that if we merely stated our rules without enforcing them, we would be seriously compromised. The staff took care of itself. We acted to prevent the kind of "punishment" we knew was in store for the students in similar situations.

The creation of rules took place within the larger context of the school's operational rhetoric. Students stayed with the school in part because they felt that it was "theirs." In addition to the use of slogans (e.g., "It's our school" "You can work at your own rate" "You can study what you want" and "No one flunks out of [Mission]"), the students defined their presence in the school in positive terms with the locution "I'm an artist, baby." They used these inspirational slogans and rhetoric to define the situation in attractive terms, and there was general agreement among students, teachers, and Mission administrators that the resulting positive student self-image was a crucial factor in the school's success.

When teachers accepted "rule creating" as a commitment by students to share the work of running the school, they did not do so primarily to compromise student ambitions—even though that may have been inevitable. It was not so much that teachers let students get away with shaming themselves, but that they acted to preserve the Academy's image as "student centered." When students let go of that image, teachers would do their best to bring it back.

ORDER IN THE CLASSROOM: THE EVOCATION OF CONSENSUS

One of the most striking changes that occurred with the move to the new building was that teachers became the proprietors of classrooms and teachers' desks. When Pud first entered the science and math room in the new building, he stopped, drew back, and mimed astonishment and incredulity. "This sure does look like a real classroom now," he said. "Now you can be a *real* teacher, you got a *real* desk. That sure is something." Along with the other teachers, I was glad to have (at last) a desk in which to keep my materials, but the notion that this was a step back toward the conventional classroom was not lost on me.

The ideology of the Academy stressed that it was a "student-oriented school." Additional endorsements of Black Power and "student power" by both the administrators and staff made attempts by white teachers to impose order in their classrooms appear contradictory if not hypocritical. Teachers themselves felt ambivalent about controlling their classes, and this ambivalence was no doubt communicated to the students, making the task difficult. Teachers and students also feared the retribution from a student singled out and admonished for disruptive behavior, a fear nutured, no doubt, by the knowledge that students could take the "student centered" rhetoric of the school and use it as a solid base for their own indignation.[4] As a result, teachers seldom attempted to control the behavior of students in their classes by directly asserting their authority. Rather, they sought to define the classroom environment in such a way that disruptive behavior would appear to be selfish, inconsiderate, or even counterrevolutionary.

At Mission Academy there were factors in addition to those outlined above that functioned to reduce the teachers' ability to act in authoritarian ways. One of these was the exceptional heterogeneity of students with respect to age, educational background, aptitude, and motivation. This heterogeneity encouraged the teacher who wanted to be effective to deal with each student as an individual, and this made any position of generalized authority difficult to maintain. If every student were an exceptional case, authoritative rules would be difficult to enforce.

In most schools, a differentiated grading system provides the teacher with a certain amount of leverage. At Mission Academy, however, grades could not be used as sanctions, for they were not used to evaluate student work. Students either completed the work for a course or they did not complete it. The only sanction a teacher could impose on a student was the fact of his cooperation or noncooperation in teaching the student material required to complete the course. To withhold cooperation in teaching went clearly against the normative structure of the school, and teachers usually felt their greatest responsibility to be that of teaching those who wanted to learn.

Instead of trying to maintain order through the exercise of their traditional authority, teachers sought to define classroom behavior such that disruptive activities were consensually "reproachable." Teachers would remind a disruptive student that he or she was making it difficult for "other students to get their high school diplomas"; they would tell the class that some disruptive students were making it impossible for them to teach the rest of the class; and they would say that disruptive students were selfish, looking only to themselves and ignoring the interests of other students, black people, and so on. Although statements such as these would not bring a disturbance immediately to an end, they usually were very effective within five to ten minutes. Other members of the class frequently would voice their disaffection for a disruptive student, and the "guilty" student would then leave; sometimes the accused student would defend against the teacher's criticism by being a "good student" for the rest of the day.

In addition to their efforts to define the classroom situation—such that class members themselves would negatively sanction untoward or disruptive behavior—teachers emphasized, in their individual communications with students, orderly and consistent academic progress. The use of programmed instructional materials gave this emphasis an institutional context, one that had real impact. For example, a teacher would inform an unserious student that his or her present rate of progress would require working for a period of at least four years to finish the course in question. Confronting students in this way, with the reality of their own schedule for achievement, often had the intended effect, and the student would find renewed energy and commitment for the work. In their efforts to create orderly classrooms, teachers used the highly organized and incremental structure of the instructional materials to program student behavior. Once a student accepted the goal of getting a diploma, the teacher could outline the steps required to achieve it.

Teachers at Mission Academy were successful in managing orderly classes without appearing to be authoritarian. Within the context of ambivalence about their roles, fears of personal retribution, and the structural characteristics of Academy classes, they established and maintained order by defining the classroom as a place for "serious learning." What teachers saw as disruptive they identified as a threat to serious learning, and the students themselves usually brought the disruptors back into line. By keeping ambitions for the high school diploma in the foreground of classroom interactions, teachers encouraged the student behavior they wanted without "dressing down" individual students and without appearing to be "strict." By treating the students they taught as adults—and making this point explicit—they did encourage the performance of adult roles in the classroom. Clearly, they were not in control of their classes, and yet a careful observer would soon note the complex ways in which they were definitely in charge.

THE SYMBOLIC SEIGE: EXTERNAL THREATS AND ACADEMY POLITICS

The establishment of a normative structure for behavior at the Academy had consequences for the development of the school as well as the larger Mission organization. By condoning behavior prohibited in most conventional schools, the Academy developed a reputation for being "way out." Visitors usually commented on or inquired about the lack of Academy prohibitions against smoking, the casual manner in which students sat around in classes, irregular attendance patterns, the diverse styles of clothing worn by both teachers and students, the free flow of uncensored conversation (at times full of obscenities), and students addressing teachers by their first names. The conflict over allocation of building space—often made visible with signs and posters declaring rooms to belong to one group or another (e.g., "This is the student lounge, only for students and their guests")—was often interpreted by outsiders as indicative of a lack of social control. The free-form arrangement of tables and chairs in classrooms was seen in much the same light.

As the rules for behavior in the school were obviously codified by the students, and due to the casual and undeferential manner in which students addressed teachers, the school was identified as a place where there was "no order." Outside reaction to these more public aspects of the school was less intense, no doubt, than such reaction would have been to a number of events known only to members of the school (e.g., the smoking of marihuana in the men's room, Twister slugging Cockey in the mouth).

Parents, students, and community residents were deeply suspicious of the distinctive social order which emerged at the school. They used details of this order and the process that generated it as grounds for expressing serious reservations about the Academy's educational enterprise. Usually these involved criticism of the Academy staff for being too lax or "liberal" with the students. When Twister slugged Cockey and received no formal punishment, for example, Cassiona (one of the Academy's more vocal students) told a group of students and teachers that he should have been expelled: "And, nothing happened to him, did it? He's still here just like nothing happened. That ain't right? He should have been kicked right on out of here for slugging a teacher. That's what would have happened at any other school!"

On another occasion, a mother of one of the students demanded that the teachers explain why they let students read whatever they wanted to at the Academy. She thought that it was the staff's responsibility to censor the materials that students read, and she was particularly concerned that the students might get "wrong ideas" put into their heads.[5] These attempts to change the normative order of the school were generally resisted by the staff, Nancy Sheen, and, later, Call Strow.

Outside criticism, however, did make the Academy staff wonder how much outsiders should know. There was a general feeling that if those outside the school knew about everything that went on inside, they would do their best to shut it down.

Perhaps the most damaging suspicions about the Academy, as far as students were concerned, came from the parents. Many, in fact, did not believe their children were attending a school; they thought this was just another in a series of fantastic explanations given by their children when asked where they spent their time. Nukey told me, for example, that his mother simply would not believe he was attending school; she thought he was always at the pool hall.

Students took to heart their parents unfamiliarity with the school, and, as the academic year came to a close, they made plans to show them what the Academy was all about. To do this, they held a "real" graduation, complete with robes, a banquet, and guest speakers.

The event was a complete success, and the parents were duly impressed. Several of them told me that, before coming to the ceremony, they could not believe such a school existed, one where students could work at their own rate and where their own children had done so well. The effect their earlier disbelief had had on the students is hard to determine. It seems unlikely, however, that it worked to the student's academic advantage.

The Academy's reputation as a "way out" place also had consequences for its relationship with conventional institutions of social control. Fire code inspectors often walked through the building looking for violations which would authorize them to close the school or at least exert some influence over its operation. Policemen frequently stopped and questioned students who were on their way to the Academy, ending the interrogation by telling the students not to come around this area of the city again or by placing them in jail on whatever charges they thought were appropriate.[6] Students who transferred to the Academy from the surrounding public schools reported that their former public school teachers and counselors had warned them about getting involved with a "bunch of crazy revolutionaries like those at Mission Academy."

This low-level harassment which the Academy received as a result of its reputation as a "way out" school, however, did not come from the official policies of neighboring institutions. The administrators of the local police precinct, neighboring high schools and elementary schools, and social work agencies all expressed their official support of the Academy. In addition, they offered their cooperation to those who worked there. The bad reputation of the school was more a popular one, an image of the school most salient to passers-by and low-level employees of social welfare agencies in the immediate area.

The staff, students, and administrators of the Academy gave a great deal of significance to the harassment they received from those outside the school, however, and exceptional behavior was often justified on the basis of the "precariousness" of the school's survival. This was particularly true of a number of arbitrary actions taken by Mission administrators. It was within a "crisis mentality" that a group of them took the extralegal steps necessary to fire Call Strow, Cockey, and me early in 1969. It was out of similar thinking, however, that Call was hired in the first place.

The outside threats were real, but their importance emerged through the manner in which they were perceived and portrayed. By maintaining a sense of imminent danger, members of the school were able to make crucial decisions without taking full responsibility for them. By building up threats from outside the school—at least in the minds of its members—administrators provided themselves with golden opportunities to rule. The Academy's survival was indeed precarious from time to time, but this did not stem primarily from its relationship with neighboring institutions of social control. Here the school certainly had enemies, but it also had friends. Belief in this precariousness, however, was essential to the manner in which the school was governed. With its strong emphasis on cooperative management, a state of continual crisis was the only workable ground for legitimizing continued control by Mission Administrators.

In a sense this process involved a closed cycle: the more independence and initiative the staff and students exercised in the school, the more the school would appear to violate the norms of the surrounding community. The more these norms appeared to be violated, the easier it was for the Mission administrators to characterize the Academy as "vulnerable." As the Academy's survival appeared more and more precarious, the administrators assumed greater powers and the independence and initiative that could be exercised by students and teachers was reduced. The cycle did not even rely on actual intervention from conventional institutions, for the students and staff clearly recognized the conventional norms that were being violated. Rev. Keen was listened to when he once told the staff, "When push comes to shove, I've got the checkbook. And when I can't raise any money for this place because of a bunch of goof-offs working here, there won't be any checks for you."

In promoting their own conceptions of reliable behavior in the school, students, teachers, and administrators manipulated the resources that they had at their disposal. The normative order emerging from this process was not a simple product, however, for different groups had different resources. The Mission administrators had more control over the building than did either teachers or students, and they used this to fight for their version of the well-ordered school. Teachers at the Academy used their verbal facility and interpersonal skills to construct rewards and sanctions within classrooms and to define in their own terms the events that occurred within the school. Students found that they could manipulate the sympathies of the staff and administration, exercising the built-in imperatives of the reform movement out of which the school was founded.

Working both against each other and together, these groups created a reasonable but contested order in the school. The symbols and resources that individuals manipulated did not necessarily imply different forms of order, but those who used them wanted different things from the Academy. In a school conceived out of an ideology emphasizing consensual and responsive operation, these symbolic resources were especially important, for they allowed order to be achieved without the appearance of authoritarian imposition.

All this came together in a sort of game, one in which the students would call upon the righteousness of their position, the administration would respond in terms of the reality of the building, and the staff would interpret in terms of "what was really at issue and what should be done." When one of the three groups appeared to be losing an important point, it would augment its particular resources by calling upon the appropriate factors external to the school itself. While actively involved in this game-like process of promoting particular conceptions of order, it was difficult to examine or confront the nature and allocation of the symbolic resources themselves. The day to day exchanges of righteousness, interpretation, and control of the physical plant created a rich and exciting environment in which to hold forth.

Dealing with Unreality

This book began with an account of the contradictions between the structure of authority at Mission Academy and the school's ideology of cooperative and shared administration. Now that a more complete description of the school is before the reader, it seems appropriate to return to these concerns, for a number of questions remain unresolved. The social order of the Academy has been outlined and illustrated, and we can begin to describe the manner in which it articulated individual experiences. The focus of this chapter, then, is the role played by trust, interpersonal process, and politics in the social reality of the Academy.

TRUST AND MISTRUST: LIVING THE ACADEMY'S UNREALITY

There was a strong element of unreality to Mission Academy. The numerous references made to the school being "weird" in terms of its alternative format point to part of it, but these do not capture the essential sense of unreality that people experienced while they worked there. Rather, remarks about the school being "way out" were really based on self-conscious comparisons of the Academy with conventional schools. Beyond these comparative statements there was a more important sense of unreality, one which was noticed not by standing back and looking at the Academy's peculiar development in the universe of conventional schools, but which emerged from ambiguities and contradictions in the school's day-to-day operation.

Rider captured the essence of this unreality in a marvelous image that he was happy to share with Cockey and me. As he put it:

> You know what [Mission] Academy is really about? Well, I'll tell you what it's about. Someday, there is going to be a huge riot, and the building is going to be totally demolished. All you'll be able to see will be the charred foundations marking the place where the walls used to

stand. And, Monday morning, we will all be here at nine o'clock, just as always, sitting around in the space that used to be the conference room, having our Monday morning faculty meeting. And [Nancy] will say, "Because of the events of the last few days, I think that we will have to modify some of our course offerings." And the meeting will go on, and on; and no one, *no one* will say a word about the fact that the building is totally, utterly destroyed. *That* is what [Mission] Academy is all about.

What Rider captured in his image was the fundamental contradiction between "normal," everyday, agreeable, rationally structured collaboration between members of the Academy and the "exceptional"—sometimes violent—irrational, and noncooperative crises which erupted on a regular basis. It was as if there were two sets of norms, each appearing absurd within the context of the other. One set applied to the so-called "normal" interaction at the school. This involved the acceptance of what another person said as an honest statement, general trust of other people, an understanding that everyone was well-intentioned, and a recognition of common purpose. The other set applied to the "crises" at the Academy. Under these conditions, there was general mistrust, what a person said was always thought to be deceptive, individuals were thought to be self-seeking and ill-intentioned, and there was some vague notion of a fundamental conflict of interests. It is not too great a simplification to say that these two normative modes corresponded to the presence or absence of trust in the school. Not only were crises characterized by a lack of trust, but a lack of trust was characterized as a crisis.

These alternating normative structures provided a context in which Academy members engaged in something akin to "deep play" as described by Clifford Geertz. Situations of "trust" and "mistrust" reflected and exemplified the important fears and anxieties of those involved. Members of the Academy were afraid of something happening which would harm them emotionally, physically, or socially. These fears were difficult to acknowledge, however, for they implied a failure in the kind of human relations that the school sought to construct. When the official structure of the school neither reflected these fears nor encouraged their expression, the social order appeared to all those involved with it as a precarious one, a volatile structure which was liable to tip over into chaos for the slightest reason.

Individuals had a great stake in this order, for it protected their social and physical beings. As a consequence, its precariousness engendered super-vigilance; even if one could not prevent the collapse, one might be able to spot when it was coming and strike a protective pose.

In their super-vigilance, however, members of the Academy toyed and gambled with the very loss of trust they feared so much, and it was important to them that they did. Trust was very serious business. The "game" of the matter was not really to win—no one was keeping score, nor could they have—but to stay alive to the elements of deepest meaning in all that was done. It may have seemed foolhardy to play with trust, but Academy members could not resist experiencing the fundamentally precarious condition of their mutual accommodations. It was the truth of their lives. If it were not made clear officially, this truth would be told through the crises and social emergencies that regularly punctuated the school's "normal" operation.

The fears people had about "something happening" to them in the school were in part the normal fears that individuals develop when they have insufficient information about factors they know to be important to their lives and livlihood. At the Academy, "other members" constituted one such important factor. In the balance of it all, teachers, students, and administrators knew very little about each other, and yet were deeply interdependent. Although there were open and caring interpersonal engagements, the school had a profound lack of a collective political process. The staff had frequent and successful meetings of its own, but was not effective in meeting together with students and administration. Students showed a clear capacity to engage in constructive political processes among themselves, but this did not carry over to their dealings with the staff. Mission administrators participated in a similar pattern.

As students, teachers, and administrators, members of the Academy went their separate ways. Their willingness and capacity to do so, however, stemmed in large part from the belief that what was really important was not their organizational roles but their appreciation for each other as "people."

This was well and good, and many individuals were gifted in their ability to appreciate each other in this way. It remained a wholly individual matter, however, for the official organization of the school gave no collective substance to these "people first" relationships. There were, for example, no provisions under normalcy for bringing everyone together on a regular basis to discuss the operation of the school. One of the three groups might call a meeting to which representatives from the other two were welcome, but there were no "scheduled" meetings of the whole. So-called "all school" meetings were rare, and they provided no opportunity for truly collective decision-making. Usually such meetings were called by the staff to pass on to the students some important information (e.g., the schedule of a field trip, announcements of college entrance examinations), and they never included Mission Council administrators.

As part of attempts at the Academy to deemphasize traditional differences among students, teachers, and administrators, no formal provisions were made for these groups to relate to each other. This was combined with a lack of organizational settings in which all members of the school could get together and discuss its operation. With collective settings for neither "groups" nor "people," real collective process was effectively absent. Without this process, it is understandable that individuals worried about just what it was that the students, administrators, or teachers were going to do next.

The lack of understanding among functional groups was common, but it was most clearly underscored within the framework of a "crisis." Although there was interpersonal interaction in the school under "normal" trust and politesse, a "crisis" involved breaking off this interaction. As everyone was a member of a group, this meant that cross-group understandings were disrupted.

Crises thus took the following form: When a lack of trust was precipitated (or accumulated, as the case may be), groups did not come together to hash things out; rather, they retreated from each other to work out independent solutions. Frequently there were brief confrontations of all members of the school, but these usually lasted only a few minutes and succeeded only in raising the levels of mistrust among the groups to the point where it made sense to split apart. After separating, different groups might produce a series of ultimata, but no productive encounters ever emerged from such lists. The demands were neither explicitly accepted nor rejected by other groups, but rather were left to "die on the vine." A week later, under more "normal" conditions, they would be almost forgotten.

It is important to note that situations of crisis were considered to be exceptions to the so-called normal operation of the school, even though there was about as much of one as there was of the other. Had crises appeared less frequently, and had trust been less important, the dual characteristic of the school's normative structure would not have emerged as clearly as it did. Given that about half of the days were seen to occur within the context of one or another crisis, however, the rules for behaving in crises had some substance.

The unreality of the Academy for those who worked there involved the inadequacy of organizational and personal ideologies to explain the school's operation. It was not just that there were breakdowns in trust, but also that these were unexplained by the assumptions of normal activity. Likewise, trust itself seemed absurd within the norms of crises. Under conditions of normalcy, crises could not be imagined, and in the heat of a crisis, normalcy seemed impossible. When crises occurred and experience existed that was contrary to the dominant moral order, they were denied, distorted, or rationalized as exceptional to the normal functioning of the school. When this exceptional behavior occurred at least as often as normal behavior, conditions for the unreality of experience at the school were clearly formed.

The dual systems of moral order at the Academy were not the only factors contributing to unreality. In addition, there was an interpersonal climate that discouraged conflict and expressions of hostility, that called instead for enthusiasm and politesse. Rev. Keen and Nancy Sheen were particularly influential in setting this tone, establishing priorities for topics to be discussed and then cutting off discussions before they became too heated. Their intervention in the natural dynamics of the groups' processes was another inhibiting factor on the development of trust among individuals at the Academy. Interrupted feelings of hostility and anger were given increased potency. When individuals were kept from acting through their negative feelings, there remained the sense that not everything was being made clear.

Here again appeared the controling rationale of the Mission administrators: anger begets anger, hostility begets hostility, and conflict begets conflict. What the Academy did not need, they argued, was conflict among those involved with it. As Nancy Sheen said on a number of occasions, "There are enough problems out there in the world without us getting into arguments here."

The reasons for the lack of a well-developed political or interpersonal process at the school reflect in turn the fears of those in control. In effect, there was a "safe" agenda that had been set up largely by Rev. Keen and Nancy Sheen, the individuals with the greatest control over the operation of the school. It consisted of topics that could be discussed, places where discussions could be held, and acceptable levels of emotional intensity. This elaborate schedule was designed to control elements they thought might spark fundamental disruptions of the school's operation, an operation for which they held themselves responsible. As a result, however, trust was maintained only as long as members of the Academy thought in terms of the safe agenda. By linking "normalcy" to their own agenda, they built into their administration a significant vulnerability. When an event upset the limited concerns of the safe agenda, trust evaporated, and members of the school retreated into their own groups to wait for the crisis to pass.

At issue in these crises were all the things that untrusting people can imagine doing to others or having done to themselves. Given their critical reading of the social order, although from different points of view, both staff and students had rich imaginations in these terms.

When the acceptable agenda went unchallenged, all previous crises were unacknowledged. A past crisis never appeared on a "normal" agenda, the fear being that this was asking for trouble. In this, students and staff provided essential cooperation. Combined efforts were quite successful. It remained for individuals alone to determine whether a crisis had been a major one or a minor one. In playing with trust, however, members of the school could not resist testing the order; this was not designed primarily to gauge the strength of disorder, but to make disorder visible, if only for a moment. By nudging our fears into life, we made partners of our lives and the school.

THE BUSINESS AND THE SPIRIT OF
MISSION ACADEMY

"Cooperation" was the keynote of Mission Academy—on paper. When the school was still housed in the old church, Nancy Sheen made a large sign, which hung at the front of the assembly hall with the word "Harambe" on it. She explained to the staff and students that this should be the Academy motto: the Swahili word for "work together." With their continual emphasis on the "Mission Family" and the diffuse responsibilities of teachers and students, Mission administrators attempted to substantiate the ideal of a cooperatively administered school. This ideal was also shared by students and teachers, each of whom found it to be one of the attractive elements of the Academy.[1] The most common reference members made to the distinctiveness of the Academy—with respect to conventional schools—was to the cooperative manner in which it was governed: "Everyone has a say."

In fact, power and authority were not held in some common trust between students, faculty, and the administration.[2] This is not to say that no cooperation existed between these groups in the operation of the school, but merely to point out that the form this cooperation took was hardly consistent with the ideals expressed by its members. The ideals referred to the self-conscious and willful sharing of administrative duties among individuals who found themselves to be involved in a common cause. This form of cooperation involves a strong element of trust, and it was expected to emerge from recognition, among members, of their common condition and mutual interest. At the Academy, however, trust was far too important and problematic a variable on which to base continued cooperation.

Instead of this cooperation, there existed a cycle of suspicion, one which related the lack of collective political process and the lack of depth in interpersonal processes to a lack of trust in the normal affairs of individuals. The mistrust made the political and interpersonal processes difficult, and this encouraged feelings of mistrust. Had there not been strong inducements to at least "act" in a trusting way, it is hard to imagine the school functioning at all. Given a condition in which everyone was afraid of something "bad" happening, it is rather remarkable that individuals worked out a way of appearing to be trusting about half of the time.

There were exceptions, however, to the mistrusting cycle which characterized relations at the school, and these provide an important clue to the kind of social order established there. The most stable experiences of trust at the Academy were those between a teacher and a student in a totally academic context. Students learned to trust Academy teachers, to feel confident that they would neither intimidate them nor criticize them for what they did not yet know. This was encouraged by the programmed instructional materials, for these allowed the teacher to be a confederate of the student in trying to assimilate the subject matter. Of additional importance were teachers' personal efforts to show students that "as students" their imagination and experience would be respected.

Trust between individual teachers and students was based on exchange; the teacher was paid, and the student was taught. Where the transactions between individuals involved clearly defined rewards such as these, trust could be more easily established. In such situations, each party knew what to expect from the other, and it was clear what was at issue. Students and teachers alike felt that student mastery over subject matter was a worthwhile goal, and both were rewarded when this was seen to develop.

This exchange basis of social relations was tried out very early in the Academy's development, not only in academic matters but in terms of student commitment to the school itself. The original Academy students were effectively bribed to attend classes by the promise of a week of camping in the country and the possibility of getting a high school diploma. Additional student incentives and rewards were offered as the school developed. In the summer of 1967, Nancy Sheen rented a number of musical instruments for students who expressed an interest in learning how to play, and money was loaned to students to finance their trip to EXPO 67. The students agreed to pay part of the rental fee for the instruments, but many did not follow through. In addition, one of the most common exchanges taking place between Academy students and staff involved the collection of bond money for a student being held in jail. As often as once or twice a week, students would go from one classroom to the next and report: "One of the brothers is in jail and we need your help to get him out." By contributing to these frequent and short-lived causes, teachers exchanged their money for recognition as "mellow people," sympathetic to the oppressed condition of the black students.[3]

The effect of these "exchanges" was that they allowed the school to function even though general trust among its members was deeply problematic. In effect, there were "trustworthy" situations (such as the classroom), and important exchanges (such as bail money), which generally survived the frequent and dramatic untrusting crises.

Exchange processes between the staff and the Mission administration were complicated by the fact that the staff believed in what they were doing. As a result, they felt awkward in asking for conventional rewards (e.g., money) for their labor. The Mission administrators took advantage of this by always phrasing a request for additional time or energy in terms of the "critical situation" which the Academy was currently facing, and the word "overtime" did not exist at the school. Administrators could rely on the staff's commitment to educational reform to insure their continued involvement with the school, and teachers themselves were loathe to call this into question, as it made them appear selfish and inconsiderate of others who were in greater need than they. In short, altruism was the order of the day.

Being a member of the Academy was neither painless nor effortless. A lot of work was required, and involvement with the school required huge quantities of psychic and physical energy. Trust in the school was a problem, interpersonal relationships were rather truncated, and no one was making a fortune off the school's operation. Given these conditions, the day-to-day rewards of altruism and small-scale symbolic exchanges were very important, even though personal involvement in them might be much less than complete. While the spirit of the Academy swung back and forth in frequent crises, its business exhibited a nervous but visible stability.

What the school offered was not a close-knit, agreeable, trusting group of individuals who had deeply rewarding personal relationships. The Academy had the potential for such a sense of community to develop, but there were a number of important factors working against it. Rather, the school offered resources of immense importance to individuals in their lives outside the Academy. For the poor who were placed in jail—guilty or innocent—and who did not have the wealth to get out, it offered bail. For those who had been denied opportunities normally provided by schools, albeit in limited amounts, it offered: musical instruments, clubs, a chance to learn to read and write, high school diplomas, and the possibility of going on to college. For those who had no place to work out their conceptions of alternative schooling, the Academy offered a place to teach and do so. And for those who had a sense of the accumulated wrongs done to a people because of their skin color, the school provided opportunities for being useful to blacks and working through the school to improve their lot. It was out of factors such as these that individuals constructed meaningful careers at the school, and that meaning gave both persistence and inspiration to their efforts.

The question remains as to why the rather stable "exchanges" system was unacceptable to members as the primary explanation for the operation of the school. Although Rev. Keen frequently advocated this rationale, Nancy Sheen, the staff, and the students resisted it strongly.[4] This resistance stemmed in part from associations of "exchange" with the exploitative relationships by which Academy members characterized the world outside the school. Exchange meant giving and taking, and those at the Academy feared that these kinds of connections invited abuse. Rather than staying with exchanges and trying to make them equitable, they tried to transcend such mundane transactions by ignoring their contribution to the school. If we were reduced to making deals with students, then how could our educational ideals of passionate and self-initiated learning ever survive?

Another factor to be considered, however, is that an "exchange theory" of the school reduced the practical importance of collective trust and undercut its symbolic centrality. For exchange to operate—equitable or not—students, teachers, and administrators would have to respect mutual obligations, rights, and contracts. They would not, however, have to like each other, nor would they need to trust each other. In fact, operating the Academy on such a basis would make it much less dependent on the very kind of collective trust that was so hard to come by. Rev. Keen was no doubt aware of this but saw explicit exchange as the way to run the school in a more orderly fashion.

The teachers at the Academy, however, did not even debate the logic of Keen's argument. Instead their resistance to exchange was couched in the romantic terms that had brought them to the school in the first place. Exchange would "cheapen" the Academy's educational offering, would commercialize love of teaching and learning, and would destroy any chance of transcending, at the school, the most exploitative and alienating processes of the American social order. This critique, of course, was no more romantic than Keen's vision of the orderly school, the meaning of which still remained in doubt, but it integrated more completely the reform sensibilities teachers had brought to the Academy. Without a foundation and affirmation of "collective trust," the school was on its own. With it, the Academy was part of changing America.

A central dimension of members' experiences of the school was thus a commitment to collective trust. This belief allowed them to connect their own efforts to those in other alternative schools; it preserved their pedagogical ideals; it kept the Academy's social process open in strange ways; it encouraged students to feel trustworthy and cared about; and, most importantly, it granted everyone dignity. The understanding that trust was behind it all implied that the school was not so much a business enterprise as a spiritual crusade, a missionary effort of truly mythic proportions, and one in which we could all play a part.

It is in this context that the "deep play" of those at the school achieved its real impact. The spirit of educational reform—indeed, the spirit of social possibility itself—had to be kept alive in order for individuals to participate in it. The business of the school threatened this spirit by implying that we were deep in the middle of the social order rather than perched on its edge. And yet, it was the social order itself we were to change. In gambling with collective trust, we risked not only our persons and status in the school, but also the meaning of what we were doing. Without risking that meaning, however, it died.

The game was complex and involuted, but the risks were real and immediate. We could fail to stay "alternative." We could be so "alternative" that we had no impact on those outside the school. We could disintegrate and watch individuals fall away from what was once a school. Risking these failures gave meaning and excitement to our efforts at success, a fact we worked with within as well as out of the school. By playing with collective trust, by taking our chances with the spirit of reform, we stayed scared, committed, and full of excitement. Had we opted for the safe school (the orderly exchange of goods and services), the life of the project would have passed away.

The school's frequent crises were thus not only failures to achieve the collective trust to which we were pledged, but affirmative expressions of the symbolic system in which we worked. While the business of the school brought us from one day to the next, the crises brought us to peaks of our collective potential for meaning. Credits, salaries and diplomas—all cast in terms of alternatives to conventional schooling—got us through the week, but the ephemeral presence of collective trust took us to the frontier of our worlds. As missionaries and misfits, bound together beyond reason, we knew we dealt with things that mattered. The spirit of reform was alive.

Part VI
Interpretations

An Alternative School

A friend of mine, a graduate student in political science at the time, once questioned me about the future of the Academy's students, "What's going to happen to these kids after they leave [Mission]," he said, "and they find themselves in the real world of dog eat dog? Aren't they just going to be more frustrated by the fact that they enjoyed themselves and had a good learning experience at the Academy? Do you really think they will be able to take it?"

This is a frequently asked question and it expresses the common fear that reform efforts will sacrifice personal careers in an effort to bring about institutional change. In the case of the Academy, I think the fear is misdirected. The students did not seem to be weakened as persons by their alternative schooling, and it would be as persons that they confronted the realities of life outside or beyond the school.

The question of what happened to Academy students in the balance of their lives, however, is totally in order. Katania was questioned by a Western University student about the relationship between her "experimental high school" and the "conventional" demands of the university. "If you come here," she was asked, "do you think that you can completely adapt to this conventional institution?" Katania responded, "I hope not," and further remarked that the institution would have to do some of the adapting itself.

That particular confrontation between Academy graduates and a more conventional school was highly complex. It engendered profound changes for both the students and the university in what was ultimately an unsuccessful effort at mutual accommodation. There are other features of the school's impact on students that are more clear-cut.

In its first two years, thirty of the Academy's students earned a state certified high school diploma through their efforts in the school and in passing the G.E.D. exam. Over twenty students began college in the fall of 1968. Over a hundred students raised their reading and arithmetic levels an appreciable amount (over one grade level), and some of these students improved three or four grade levels in a matter of as many months. These accomplishments are clear. In these terms the Academy demonstrated that it could provide meaningful educational opportunities for students who had failed or had been failed by conventional schools.

The problems of the future are perhaps suggested by the experiences of those who went to college, about half of whom dropped out at least temporarily during their first two years. Although academic deficiencies were often cited by students or by administrators as the immediate cause for student withdrawal, it seems clear that this was only the most explicit manifestation of the students' general alienation from the collegiate environment. These students had demonstrated at the Academy that they were capable of college level work and that they would work seriously and consistently on their courses. And, in small college classes which were discussion-oriented, particularly those taught by instructors sensitive to racial hostility and honest about it, the Academy graduates did very well. But competitive grading, institutional living arrangements, lockstep academic processes, explicit hostility and condescension from white students, and authoritarian and inaccessible teachers provided real obstacles for the students attempting to do high quality academic work. In those courses or colleges where the environmental impediments to the students' performance were taken seriously and efforts made to alleviate them, the students continued to perform at a level equal to or above that of their work at the Academy. In other courses or colleges, where administrators and teachers assumed that student academic performance was simply a reflection of previous preparation and "innate capabilities," the Academy graduates did not fare so well.

In this there would seem to be a double fault, but it is that of the Academy and the colleges, not the students. On the one hand, the Academy staff and administration failed to insure that colleges to which Academy graduates were sent were seriously committed to reforming their own educational structures.[1] And, on the other, the colleges to which the Academy students went frequently failed to take advantage of them as resources in improving the accessibility and efficiency of their educational offerings. When only piecemeal attempts at such reform were made, however, it was the Academy graduate and not the larger institution who had the mark of failure on his or her record.

In addition to its impact on those directly involved with it, the Academy exerted a certain amount of tangential influence. A number of other "alternative schools" were begun in Chicago, several of which were inspired by the Academy. Staff and students have acted as informal and formal consultants to several educational experiments, and some reports of the school's operation have appeared in publications of both local and national circulation. In addition, some of the public schools in the West Park area have asked members of the Academy for advice in areas of curriculum development and teaching techniques. Needless to say, Chicago's public schools are much as they were before the Academy was founded, although some Academy programs and suggestions have been tried on a limited basis.[2] But if a major impact of the school on public school instruction is to be found, it may be seen both in the Academy's validation of individualized instruction and in the contribution made to the public image of the dropout. The school's history cuts deeply through the picture of the dropout as characteristically "uneducable."

The school has survived to the present day because it met existing needs. It met a need in the community by offering dropouts a chance to receive a high school education by working in an organization that showed them respect and concern. It met a need for "alternative teachers" by offering a place where they could teach effectively and work toward general educational reform. It met a need for the larger Mission organization by appearing as a visible sign of its presence and a symbol of its success in the West Park area. And it met a need in America by providing foundations with a vital and hopeful experiment to support financially. Thus, the Academy was a place where individuals could come in a variety of ways to advance their alternative careers or to work for reform of the larger society without completely forsaking the conventional rewards of diplomas, salaries, building space, and supportive colleagues.

CONVENTIONAL SCHOOLING:
PROBLEMATIC, CONSEQUENTIAL, AND COMPULSORY

Conventional schooling is, first and foremost, a problem for the student. It exercises a form of comprehensive competition from which there is no effective escape. In school, students win and lose. There may be enrichment programs, new technologies, better teachers, newer buildings, or fewer requirements, but none of these innovations designed to improve individual schools basically changes the power of schooling to discriminate between and among students. Whether it be sifting, sorting, selecting, deselecting, or separating, the schooling system does it—and does it in a comprehensive manner. It should be crystal clear then that no class or collective interests can be improved through "better" schools. The system is designed to select; it will continue to select. The composition of the winners and the losers may change, but their proportions will stay the same.[3]

The system is not only problematic, with winning and losing creating corresponding self-images among students, but it is also consequential. Winning and losing have consequences—not only for one's life within the school, but also for life chances outside the school for the rest of one's life. There are many aspects of life which are problematic, such as the weather, but most are not cumulatively consequential in the manner of schools. With schooling, we have a system that functions to discriminate among the young on the basis of "preparedness" for life, and then insures, through inexorable linkages to adult economic life, that such discrimination persists.

But if these factors go some distance toward describing the common features of conventional schooling, what factors explain the differences? Not only are there important differences among conventional schools, but there are alternative schools such as Mission Academy that seek to change, through their own example, that conventionality itself.

THE VOLUNTARISTIC ALTERNATIVE

One important source of differentiation within and between schools is the choice of an integrating orientation, a choice most clearly seen as consequential when it occurs between the "student" and the "real world." If the student, as a person, is used as the integrating element of a school's offerings, the school may well be structured in terms of what Janowitz has called the "aggregation model."[4] Here there is an attempt to maintain psychodynamic coherence for the student through breaking down separations between home and school (by intervening in his entire life-space) and between work and play (by giving teachers diffuse role prescriptions and emphasizing the development of student-teacher trust) and through organizing subject matter offerings in terms of each student's individual capabilities and interests. In popular discourse, such schools involve "meeting a student where he is at" and working with him or her as a complete person.

On the other hand, schools frequently integrate their offerings through an orientation to professional conceptions of "the real world." The efforts taken under this rubric emphasize the structure of knowledge we have about the real world, and this typically has involved the structure of academic disciplines. In this situation, a high priority is placed on expert staff and sophisticated technology in creating effective patterns of specialized learning. Roles for the staff are functionally specific, and this principle may also be reflected in building design, textbook selection, and the like. Schools integrated in this manner correspond closely to a "specialization" model.

Such orientations, in their ideal typical configurations, have been the target of a great deal of criticism. The "specialization" model is seen to fragment student experience and to assault a coherent sense of the self. The "aggregation" model is seen to allow no private space for the student; when the whole person is treated, all aspects of the person become liable for examination and comment. Such criticisms do not evolve simply from the aggregation or specialization orientation, however, but from the coercive conditions of student involvement. It is because the young *have* to attend schools that these two orientations contain such potential for damaging students. The damage does not flow directly from the structure, but rather from the functioning of such a school in a system of compulsory, problematic, and consequential schooling.

At Mission Academy, schooling was problematic and consequential (though not in the same form as conventional schooling), but it was not compulsory. This was true not only of daily attendance, but also in terms of flexible scheduling, which allowed students to study subjects when they were interested in them. As a result, both the specialized and aggregative aspects of the school were seen largely in their positive terms. Because students could choose whether or not they wanted to work in a highly codified curriculum with the guidance of an expert (as in the programmed units in English grammar), such a specialized program of study was seen as an asset. Because they could choose whether or not to "be friends" with a teacher and discuss their life situation, such relationships were also seen as an asset. Had students been required to do either of these, had they been coerced into such participation against their will, they no doubt would have expressed the same criticisms that are presently voiced in public debate about the corresponding ideal types: too much invention or too much dehumanization and fragmentation.

Though there is much debate as to which of these two models is most effective in educating students and which of them is most humane, my observations of Mission Academy suggest that the heat of the fire is elsewhere. Both highly specialized "subject-coherent" and highly aggregated "student-coherent" schooling may be useful to the aspiring student. Given the choice, students might chose to learn different things in different ways. Given the choice, students might chose to work in different systems for different periods of time. Given the choice, either might be productive. But in a system of comprehensive coercion, both may in fact act as obstacles to learning by invalidating the student's most productive self-image.

With respect to the two models for school organization, Mission Academy appears as an alternative to conventional schools. While the operation of the school did not conflict with the problematic and consequential aspects of American schooling, it did suspend the institution of compulsory attendance and course scheduling. In contrast to conventional schools, the staff and administration of the Academy gave up control over an important part of student experience: designation of the time during which students would engage in the study of a particular subject and the manner in which they would study it. Some control was still exercised indirectly, of course, because not every subject was offered in every way at every time. Students had to choose from among the scheduled offerings if they were to rely on assistance from the teacher. When dealing with the most specialized programs, however (such as the programmed text-books), they were not even constrained by the availability of the teacher but could work on these materials at any time in or outside of school.

There were other dimensions of the school that paralleled this flexibility in scheduling. Not only did students exercise control over what they studied and when they studied it, relative to those in conventional schools, but the membership of the Academy was equally "un-controlled." With some exceptions, most notably the designation of the "not for real" students, the Academy exercised an open admission policy. Anyone who wanted to attend could attend. The contrast can also be made between the Academy and conventional schools with respect to the amount of administrative control exercised over the content of courses, standards of acceptable personal behavior, the content and performance of professional roles, and the kinds of "suitable" work which students could perform. This is not to say that the Academy was a libertarian stronghold, but its operation, when compared to that of conventional schools, granted far more discretion and autonomy to the students and teachers who worked there.

"STUDENTS" AND THE "REAL WORLD": UNRELIABLE CONCEPTS

An explanation for the differences between the Academy and conventional schools involves a complex set of factors. Some of these have already been identified in the discussion of the process of designing the school and its relationship to the social movement for educational reform. In terms of the fundamental rationalization for schooling, however, we might add that such differences point to a disagreement between Mission personnel and conventional school administrators about the nature of the "student" and the nature of the "real world."

In that schools represent the designed contact space between students and the real world, we would expect that the conceptions held of these two elements by school designers and administrators would have some effect on the structure of schools. But here an interesting correlation appears to emerge. For while it seems that the difference in real-world conceptions is reflected in the content and ideology of the school, such differences do not imply a difference in school structure. For example, conceptions of the real world may vary with respect to its acceptability, its need for change, its need for greater cooperation from the population, or its temporary or permanent qualities. Such differences, however, will only affect the content of courses offered and the ideological rationalization for what the school is doing (i.e., its stated purpose). There is no inherent reason for schools inspired by such diverse real-world conceptions as those held by Marxists, the Chicago Board of Education, the Black Panthers, Western Electric, or the Mission to exhibit different structures. The structures of such schools would be rationalized by reference to different conceptions of the real world, but the schools might (and in terms of these examples, sometimes do) look alike. And, more importantly, students in such structurally similar schools would tend to experience them in the same terms, regardless of their differing ideological foundations.

On the other hand, the conception of the student, which may vary independently of real-world conceptions, seems to bear quite heavily on the structure of the school. At the Academy, students were characterized as possessed of natural productive energy. As a result, efforts were made to remove impediments to the students' expression of their own interests and ambitions. This orientation toward students led to individualized scheduling, student-"inspired" course offerings, a general culture of respect and encouragement for student activity, and specialized social situations (such as the Story Workshop) where students were effectively protected in expressing their more personal fantasies and observations—even from the coercion of fellow students.

When students are held to be basically apathetic, bored, or lazy, schools are likely to embrace the system of motivational rewards and punishments characteristic of conventional systems. Without these, it is feared by advocates of the energyless image of students that the young will do nothing in school. Conceiving of students, or at least some of them, as basically destructive has encouraged not only the elaborate and often mystifying systems of tracking, isolation, cooling-out, suspension, and expulsion, but also the perjorative stereotyping of such isolated, suspended, or rejected students.

All this suggests that it is basically the conception of the student that inspires the structure of a school, while it is the conception of the real world from which its ideology is constructed. The structure of a school is the contact point between the administration, the teachers, and the students; it would seem natural for it to be created out of operating conceptions of these groups. The ideology of the school however, serves as a point of contact not between groups within the school, but between the school and the larger society. It makes sense that this articulation of the school's purpose and the rationalizations for its existence should take some inspiration from a conception of that larger world. Such ideology may also be used within the school to rationalize decisions, but this would appear to be rationalization in the popular as well as the sociological sense. Unless the conception of the real world is so comprehensive that it contains as an integral part a conception of student nature, there is no inevitable linkage between the specific reasons for having schools and the kinds of schools we have.

A crucial aspect of this dynamic has been dealt with at length in the present study: the creation of order. At Mission Academy, the teachers and administrators constructing and effectively running the school were seen to pick and choose which aspects of the social movement for educational reform they would emphasize, which aspects of the larger society they would respond to, and which ideological elements would be used in a given situation to explain, integrate, and rationalize the operation of the school. Not only did this process of selection and serial advocacy occur somewhat independently of the social organization of the school—it affected which courses were taught (e.g., Afro-American history, G.E.D. preparation), but not how they were taught (e.g., programmed instruction, noncompulsory attendance)—but the internal order of the school did not necessarily stem from explicit linkages to the larger society. Even though the school was unaccredited by any official agency, students still worked diligently for "credits" within the school. Even though attendance was not compulsory, students still attended. Even though teachers at the school had no educational credentials, the students respected them for what they knew and how they taught. The fact that they hoped to receive an accredited G.E.D. high school diploma for their efforts is no explanation for the creation of the *particular* order of the school.

There are some further implications of this reasoning that should not go unmentioned, for if the structure of contemporary schools is closely tied to the designers' conception of the student, the question remains as to the source of this conception. Does this represent merely the fanciful projection of the design profession, or is it tied to empirical observations of student behavior?

At first glance evidence would seem to suggest that it is only the fanciful projection of those responsible for creating and running schools. Case histories can be cited, the present study included, of the productive energy and ambition of students—not only students in general, it should be added, but those very students who have been identified by the conventional schools as apathetic, lazy, mentally handicapped, or dangerous. There is much literature which takes this dynamic as its focus, the great successes that can be achieved by students who are (conventionally) seen to be difficult, impossible to reach, or undesirable.

And yet this is a bit deceptive. For there are other accounts, not as popular, not as widely read, nor for that matter as widely written, of the apathy, listlessness, and destructive behavior of students in schools. When such accounts reach the public, they are inevitably accounts of the trials of teaching, not the joys. Additional references come to the surface in the form of occupational lore, the classic story of the enthusiastic teacher who loves to teach and thinks that children are marvelous, but who, after a semester or two in a public school, has become disillusioned through daily contact with student hostility, aggressiveness, and lack of cooperation.

Under some circumstances it might be necessary to choose between these two sets of experiences, to suggest that one is really valid and that the other exhibits misrepresentation of the data, lack of understanding and insight, or prejudicial observations. Such a choice is unnecessary here, however, and it also appears foolish, for what seems to be at issue is not just the nature of students as they appear to the world, but their nature as students in the schools created for them. And, it is very likely that both sets of accounts are accurate to some extent. It is also very likely that the student we see as sullen and lazy in a conventional school is also active, curious, and productive in an alternative setting. It is likely that the friendliest, most academically capable and understanding Mission Academy students are also hostile, bored, and frequently insensitive university students. It should come as no real surprise that the kinds of "student nature" which inform the design of schools are largely "student natures" created by those schools.[5]

The same can be said for teachers, and it would follow that the structure of teacher responsibilities in the school grows largely out of the conception of teacher nature that is held by administrators, state legislatures, and so on. This conception is no doubt validated in the same self-fulfilling ways as is that of students, by observation in institutions designed for those kinds of teachers. What is involved, in the case of teachers as well as students, is the construction of social selves. It is a strange and perhaps frightening irony that the machines of construction are not only rationalized by reference to the "naturalness" of their products, but also that they are manned by the cream of the crop.

This structure of authority is maintained, in part, by the conception of schools as institutions of explicit enculturation. As such, they are seen as places where knowledge gleaned from more adult activities in the society is passed on or otherwise transmitted to the young. As long as this general perspective is maintained, schools will be basically conservative in their operation. It seems appropriate, however, in an advanced technological society, to look at schools as not only places where "known facts and skills" are passed on from the old to the young, but also as institutions of specific and diffuse research, where insights of the young can be articulated to the old. At their best they could be places where information is created, not just passed on.

Furthermore, it is only by providing alternatives to mainstream educational forms that individual and collective imaginations can respond intelligently to schooling issues. Without alternatives such as the Academy, both criticism and analysis of conventional school structures would be relatively naive and unsophisticated. The establishment of more experimental schools like Mission Academy (i.e., schools that would be left somewhat to their own devices to work out a program of schooling and education) seems imperative to the increased sophistication of research efforts as well as to the formation of public policy. Social experiments, in this respect, not only provide alternatives for those individuals who are directly involved with them, but they also contribute to the enterprise of social research in its largest sense.

VOLUNTARISTIC SCHOOLING:
EXPERIMENTAL DESIGNS FOR HUMAN DEVELOPMENT

Institutions are characterized by differentials in power and control among their members. Some positions, and some people, have more to say than others about the structure of an organization and its enterprise. In creating and administering these organizations, those with power rely on their own conceptions of "member nature" and create or maintain a structure designed to deal with this presumed nature of the members. Whether or not their perceptions are accurate may be less important to the outcome of the enterprise than their control over the organization. In creating a structure which corresponds to their conceptions of member nature they may indeed create an institution that creates that nature or the appearance of it. At this point, feedback from the members may validate their original conception, giving it even more credence.

In effect this is a poor experimental design. If, in fact, those who were more in control of schools than others wanted to find out something about student nature, they should observe students in a variety of institutional settings. The compulsory nature of American schooling, however, greatly reduces such variety. The consequence of this process in an institution as widespread and comprehensive as universal schooling is that a group of individuals, chosen largely for their occupational credentials as principals, state legislators, board of examiners, and superintendants, through the designing of schools have established and perhaps spuriously validated their own conceptions of student and teacher nature.

Given the large proportion of consequential time that everyone spends in school, this process cannot be dismissed in assessing the development of American nature, citizen nature, or adult nature. This is not to characterize administrators as evil persons, but to suggest the importance of the tasks with which they have been entrusted. It is further directed toward questioning the capacity of any person or group of people to act in the interests of the young, especially when guided primarily by observations of the young in the institutions that have been created for them. There are choices to be made here, and they involve not only questions about what is to be done about and to students, but also the terms by which students will do things for themselves. This suggests that the moral charge of the "crisis in education" literature is well placed. Moral issues and political issues are involved. We should accept, as important data about schools, the testimony of people who have been in them. The issues are more complicated and more profound than simply identifying which schools are best or which schools seem to be more effective in teaching reading. The social construction of selves is also at issue. In exercising choice in this matter, it is only natural that individuals whose lives are implicated by schools work to transform them into places where they can affirm themselves. Questions of better schooling and better teaching will continue to be raised, and they should be considered carefully and thoroughly. They should not be limited to issues of effectiveness, but extended to the general process of developing human beings. This requires that such questions be examined not only by experts in education, but also by those who will work with them and under them: students and teachers.

A final proposition is that there are large areas of agreement about what students should learn, even among students. It seems, for example, that everyone would like to learn how to read. People may differ over how they want to learn, or what they want to read, but that should be their choice. Everyone seems to want to know more about something, even though they may differ about what that something is, or about how they want to find it out. But this type of difference is natural, and when it occurs among a faculty at a prestigious university it is protected by the principle of academic freedom. When it occurs among citizens of America, it is protected not only in principle but through legal guarantees of civil rights. Engaged in compulsory schooling, a student is effectively denied these rights for fear that he or she will not learn the correct things in the proper way.

The importance of student choice in these matters cannot be stressed enough, either in terms of the productive energy it releases, the self-concept it engenders, or the improvement it occasions in academic achievement. It seems that in conventional schools it is so important that students only learn the right things in the right way that we are prepared to have them do that or not learn at all. It is so important that students read the right things and learn to read them in the right way that we would rather have them not learn to read at all than give them their head.

Schooling can be an opportunity of great value, and as such it should not be denied to anyone who wants it. The same can be said for museums, libraries, parks, work, wilderness areas, voluntary associations, and other important institutions. These should be supported; they are the fabric of many civic lives. We should grant the same status to schools, and at the same

time break the pernicious linkage between schooling and economic opportunities. Let there be schools, and let those go who want to when they want
to.

Someone, on their own, when faced with an attractive library and some
leisure time, and knowing how to read, might read Silas Marner one year,
Julius Caesar the next, and Hamlet the year after that. Someone might study
South America at the age of 10, Canada at 11, and U.S. government at 12.
But why should that someone, in the company of everyone else his or her
age, have to?

13

Priorities in School Reform

I began this book with anecdotal references to the lives of both misfits and missionaries and with a brief description of how they related to each other at Mission Academy. In subsequent chapters I have tried to describe these encounters as a general social phenomenon, one in which the misfit/ missionary relationship generated a characteristic set of rewards, costs, and structural ambiguities. It now seems appropriate to examine the relationship between the missionary/misfit pair of reciprocal roles I observed at the Academy and the general issues of contemporary educational reform.

A central theme in such an analysis is the manner in which missionaries— the kind Becker has termed "moral entrepreneurs"—translate marginal status in the conventional order into dominant status in a reformed order. This is a process in which their own "mis-fit" comes to be perceived as a moral "fit." The change of status begs for confirmation, however, and the work of saving other kinds of misfits provides just that. In taking rejects of the dominant order and improving their lot, the misfit-cum-missionary can generate social approval for the status translation. The role of the misfit is thus both the foil by which the missionary defines his or her task and the raw material to be worked, educated, or polished into a socially valued product. It is a process that manufactures not only new generations of social persons, but also legitimation of the missionary endeavor.

It is difficult to write about these matters without appearing to take sides, and yet that is just what I am trying to do. The words "missionary" and "misfit" are so loaded with conventional meanings that they are unlikely terms for dispassionate analysis. I have stayed with them, however, with a hope both of expanding our conception of what they might imply and of neutralizing some of their more popular agency. Clearly there is nothing good about being a missionary, nor is there anything bad about being a misfit. And,

I would argue, it is just as clear that there is nothing intrinsically bad about being a missionary nor intrinsically good about being a misfit. taken together, these are social and cultural roles that have important reciprocal connections, but their value and meaning cannot be assessed apart from the manner in which they are performed, experienced, and grounded in other institutional contexts. It is as if they were elements of a language, neutral and symbolic forms we charge with value with every word we utter.

In this case the language is social reform. Misfits and missionaries can be seen as one aspect of this language, a pair of inert roles that we fill with value as we take them on as part of our own identifies or those of others. The ideologies and practice in which these associations take place give life to what are otherwise no more than tools of social analysis.

These ideological and practical coefficients of the misfit/missionary roles, however, are not neutral, nor are the human events they reflect. Here it is also difficult not to take sides, but for good reason: at issue is the definition of the social world and the particular order associated with it. I will argue that here we should let the questions of status translation fall away in order to more clearly reveal the ideological and practical concerns of social reform. In effect, so what if a missionary participates in the translation of a status system? So what if such translations require the confirmation of other "improved" misfits? The important political questions involve the goals, ideology, and practice of the missionary effort itself. Are they life-serving and liberating or are they inhumane and oppressive? And for whom? Missionaries will have their misfits—let us accept that as no more than interesting—but let us ask how they are treated. Under what conditions do they live and what is their experience? These questions have answers that are more than merely interesting, for they can form the basis for our political and moral orientation.

In order to realistically evaluate a missionary endeavor, we must become familiar with its goals and practice. Similarly, we cannot judge "educational reform" without learning what it is that is being reformed. When all we know of a school is that it is "alternative," we know nothing.

The importance of these matters to current concerns about changing the schools should be clear. The missionaries and misfits of the schooling business are neither good nor bad because they are missionaries or misfits. In addition, we would be exercising a powerful ignorance to insist that what is really at issue, for all missionaries and their reform movements, is an effort at status translation (e.g. from "conventional school dropouts" to "alternative school graduates"). While this may be one of the things at issue, it is hardly the only thing to be considered, nor is status a more salient fact of missionary life than of the lives of nonmissionaries who cast their lot—whether in cowardice or courage does not really matter here—with the status quo. When we examine schooling practice, we find that some alternative schools are certainly more humane and responsive to students than most conventional schools; some clearly are not. The time has passed—if it ever was—when the good guys and the bad guys were so easy to tell apart.

In the previous chapter I have argued for voluntaristic reform of conventional schools, a change I feel would improve the lives of those who spend time in them. This kind of transformation can be begun by collective associations committed to humane, liberating, or student-centered education, but it will not be realized out of dedication to these terms alone. Schooling always involves important transactions between different and frequently disparate social groups, and the calls for student-centered schools typically are made just as loudly by nonstudents (parents, teachers, reformists, and others) as they are by students. At its worst, the "reform" could result in no more than the use of liberation rhetoric to rationalize what is currently going on.

We can hope and work for something better than the worst, however, and I suggest that we do. Students are deeply affected by schooling, and we ought to design institutional mechanisms that guarantee their participation—both as a group and as individuals—in the schooling business. But they are not the only group affected, and we would also do well to define appropriate connections between students and these others. It may be true that students ought to take charge of their own education. When they ask us to leave them alone, we ought to respect their request. Pushing them together and walking away, however, is another matter. No matter how fancy our ideology or reform strategy, "freeing the students" will have to be their own business.

There is a very fine line, then, to guide us in voluntaristic reform, and we should begin not so much by enforcing "new age" school practices as by ceasing to enforce the institutional arrangements that keep students disenfranchised and debilitated. It is not so much that there are limits to voluntaristic schooling, but that individuals have their own agendas for growth. Such growth should no more be legislated than are morality or religion. This should not keep us, however, from finding institutional obstacles to it and seeing that they are removed. While some schools are making room for individualized instruction, in one form or another, the individualization of learning and growth itself awaits more imagination and flexibility in designing and running schools than we have seen so far.

A careful examination of those affected by schools has led me to broaden the kinds of concerns I have for students to include teachers, parents, and administrators. While these groups typically have been more successful than students in making an impact on how the schools are run, this has frequently occurred through coercion, ad hoc organizations, subterfuge, and sporadic explosions of general ill will. In part this is to be expected; schools are highly charged social arenas and the scene of great symbolic conflicts. On the other hand, much of the turmoil in schools is a manifestation of the lack of a well-defined political process, one which would connect all who have a stake in schools with each other.

At Mission Academy, the lack of this process was clearly in evidence. While rhetoric stressed the "voluntaristic" dimensions of student participation and a "student-centered" school, no significant institutional provisions were made for students to take part in regulating the affairs of the Academy. Similarly, the teachers at the Academy were encouraged by the administration to be active in school affairs, but they were excluded from participation on the governing board. In the absence of formal mechanisms for sharing power, the almost daily crises took on a surrogate function. What formal processes were ill-designed to deal with in routine meetings—the relationship between students, teachers, and administrators—was openly contested in erratic encounters in the halls of the school.

The argument I am making in favor of voluntaristic schooling for students, then, is part of a more general argument to be made about schooling itself. There are features of schools that can be designed by outsiders, and there are those that require participation by insiders, those affected by schooling itself. Features appropriate to extrinsic design—based on political and moral concerns—are the formal connections and relationships among the groups involved. Features that await activation of these relationships in collective processes include the details of schooling practice and the shared understanding in which the school participates.

All this has pointed to a need for a new kind of educational process, not so much one that redefines the classroom—although that might follow—but one that redefines the school. Such a process will have to involve all those who have a legitimate stake in the practice of schooling—students, teachers, administrators, and the community of parents and others in which the school is found. It will have to be a process in which "reform" and "conventional" have no meaning, one in which the only concern is to develop a reasonable way for each group to meet its own needs while guaranteeing the rights and resources for others to do the same. This educational process—lacking at crucial times at Mission Academy—could become the guarantee of a democratic, stable, and constructive educational system. By designing this process to be inclusive of those most affected, we can make schools work as agencies of human liberation and humane learning.

These are consequences. When we have done this—when we have found ways of encouraging those in schools to take responsibility for them—we will have taken a major step toward encouraging individuals to take responsibility for what they learn. While some may see this as a dangerous direction in which to move, I find it quite to the contrary. Compared to the generations of students who have become adults after having schooling done to them—those for whom learning is but one of the many dimensions of experience they have surrendered to external authorities—a generation or more of self-possessed and self-directed students seems to be a supremely safe bet.

Were such a generation to be birthed, future historians and other social scientists will no doubt be able to identify the misfit and missionary elements of the social movement that conceived it. Such elements, of course, are with us now. In calling for the broadening of educational responsibility and process to include those most affected by schools, I am exercising my own missionary inclinations. I want schools changed, and I want them changed in certain ways. And, while Mission Academy is not my idea of the perfect school, it certainly demonstrates that some of the reasons people have for *not* reforming schools are untenable.

If this description of the Academy has made it easier for people to think about more humane and liberating educational processes, then I will consider the political objectives for this book to have been achieved. What will remain, for all of us who are so persuaded, is to insure that such thinking makes its way into the very fabric of the schools and that the schools with which we are familiar become all that, indeed, they could be. This is hardly a thankless task, but it seems to have always just begun.

Implications

A number of things have emerged as I completed the research described in this book. In one way or another, these are conclusions, and I would like to identify them. No effort will be made to argue for their value or validity; if it is not apparent in the preceding pages, it would require another book at the very least. I have reached conclusions about the following topics.

SCHOOLS

(1) There is a complex connection between student self-image, the definition of the academic task, and academic performance. When the student sees both himself and the task in positive terms (terms free of previous or anticipated failures) academic performance is greatly enhanced.

(2) Teachers can actually learn how to teach effectively if they are involved in responsive and sympathetic collective processes.

(3) Connections between schooling and cultural roles (e.g., student, teacher, administrator) or economic structure (i.e., more years in school are seen to lead to greater lifetime earnings) are such that attendance does not have to be made compulsory in order to insure that many if not most people would go to school.

(4) "Community control" is too simplified a term to describe a model for the accountability of schools. "Community" may involve residents, participants, cultural groupings, or many other groups.

(5) Cooperative authority in a school is not the automatic result of a dissolution of the conventional order. Rather, it must be provided for, organizationally, in much the same way that conventional authority is now.

(6) The roles of student, teacher, and administrator are part of a cultural reality and are not generated by organizational structure alone.

(7) Conflict between students and staff may be more effective in encouraging student organization and responsibility than direct solicitation and encouragement.

ORGANIZATIONS

(1) Organizational roles may be cultural or culturally familiar (e.g., student, teacher, administrator, supervisor), and attempts to redefine them

may require or imply cultural disorganization.

(2) Organizational goals are not the core of an organization, but rather are symbolic resources of individuals whose lives come together to create or maintain the organization.

(3) Organizational goals may be contradictory, mutually exclusive, and complex; this provides an adaptive capability of the organization to meet complex demands of its environment, constituency, and so on. Integration of these goals may involve several characters rather than a holistic, exhaustive identity.

(4) Individuals can maintain involvement in an organization even though its de facto operation is in contradiction to its professed ideals.

(5) A reasonable metaphor for the authority structure of an organization is that of language, for in addition to "official" authority, there develops a rich set of manipulations, translations, and embellishments by which individuals make the official system personal.

SOCIAL THEORY

(1) Although social context is an important element in understanding behavior, it is important to identify the personal and cultural elements that individuals bring to the situation at hand.

(2) In order for social theory to be explanatory, it must address the question of personal reward. Such theory can suggest that much of what people think and do is confused, but it must identify a structure of human motivation.

(3) Common language may be the most appropriate vehicle for articulating existential social theory, and it is an important strategy for grounding such theory in the relevant cultural-historical moment.

(4) The relationships among beliefs, values, and behavior are much more complex than has been suggested to date. What people say, what they do, what they think, and what they feel are integrated in existential careers, multiple realities, and complex identities. In studying these, scientists must move beyond the study of sociology to the study of human lives.

(5) Efforts at social reform and social experimentation are important inputs to the imagination of theorists as well as a convenience or service to actual participants.

SOCIAL REFORM

(1) Reform efforts, to be effective, must address the connections among personal experience, social institutions, and the prevailing culture.

(2) Individual and popular agency can be a creative and effective power in bringing about social reform. The limitations of experience and imagination that accompany such efforts can be remedied through ideology, exemplary careers, and an open and sharing community in which personal information is exchanged.

(3) Ambiguities of authority—stemming from personal, institutional, and cultural traditions—are such that consensus does not work by itself but relies on a defined process. These ambiguities are such that reform cannot be successfully based on ideologies alone but must be responsive to the situation at hand.

(4) Social reform depends on an aggressive social posture. It is not enough to be fair, make space and withdraw from conventional institutions. Alternative structures and patterns must be developed to contradict the status quo.

(5) Short-lived, complex, and compromised programs for social reform can make fundamental changes in the lives of individuals and particular social settings, even if they do not deliver us all into a new social order.

(6) Fatalism, naive surprise, and other romantic attachments to the "failure" of past reforms function to keep us ignorant and inattentive to possibilities for reform in the present.

(7) Social reform is similar to public art in its capacity to enrich and diversify the social landscape. As a national resource, reform efforts can nourish individual and collective imaginations as well as create a hedge against social totalitarianism.

(8) Individually and collectively, we create the social worlds in which we live. Every day we construct anew our participation in the schools, homes, prisons, cities, jobs, friendships, and even the news with which we surround ourselves. Within the context of politics, we have indeed designed our lot as well as chosen it.

Notes

CHAPTER 1

1. In order to make the identity of my informants and co-participants less accessible to the general public, as well as to grant them some measure of privacy, I have changed the names of individuals and organizations. Those who would like to replicate my study may write to me to negotiate access to the real situations in which I did my work.

2. Sherrif, the public high school nearest the Academy, had admitted 1,400 freshmen in 1963; of those, 480 graduated in 1967. The average reading skills of those who did graduate were equivalent to the seventh-grade level according to nationally standardized tests.

3. The ecumenical organization of churches was formed in the West Park area of Chicago as a response to lingering urban crises. Called, "The Mission" (or simply "Mission"), it embarked on a number of programs designed to improve the quality of urban life in the surrounding communities. These included a program for teenagers in the community, summer programs for school-age children, a housing program, the sponsorship of an employment center, a legal aid service, a precollege counseling program, an economic development corporation, and an experimental secondary school known as Mission Academy.

Chicago's other inner-city high schools had problems comparable to Sherrif's, but the dropout population in these schools was about three times the national average, as the following figures show:

Percent of high school dropouts among persons 14 to 24 years old, by race and sex: United States, 1967 and 1974

Age	1967				1974			
	Black		White		Black		White	
	Male	Female	Male	Female	Male	Female	Male	Female
1	2	3	4	5	6	7	8	9
Total, 14 to 24 years old	23.9	21.8	11.6	13.1	16.3	18.1	11.0	11.0
14 and 15 years old	3.5	4.0	1.5	1.4	3.9	2.1	1.8	1.9
16 and 17 years old	11.7	14.6	7.0	9.4	8.3	12.6	9.4	9.1
18 and 19 years old	30.6	22.0	15.4	16.3	26.9	20.2	17.4	13.9
20 to 24 years old	42.6	26.1	18.8	19.0	23.6	27.7	13.6	14.5

NOTE: Dropouts are persons who are not enrolled in school and who are not high school graduates.

SOURCES: U.S. Department of Commerce, Bureau of the Census, **Current Population Reports,** Series P—23, No. 46, and Series P—20, No. 278.

By 1974, it appears that—with the exception of white males—dramatic gains have been made in reducing the percentage of school dropouts among persons 14 to 24 years old. This is slightly deceptive, however, and may only indicate that persons stay in school longer before dropping out or failing to graduate. The decrease in "dropouts" has not been reflected by an increased percentage of high school graduates. As the following table indicates, the total number of such graduates has increased steadily during the past

Number of high school graduates compared with population 17 years of age:
United States, 1869-1870 to 1973-1974

School year	Population 17 years old[1]	High school graduates[2]			Number graduated per 100 persons 17 years of age	School year	Population 17 years old[1]	High school graduates[2]			Number graduated per 100 persons 17 years of age
		Total	Boys	Girls				Total	Boys	Girls	
1	2	3	4	5	6	1	2	3	4	5	6
1869-1870	815,000	16,000	7,064	8,936	2.0	1949-1950	2,034,450	1,199,700	570,700	629,000	59.0
1879-1880	946,026	23,634	10,605	13,029	2.5	1951-1952	2,040,800	1,196,500	569,200	627,300	58.6
1889-1890	1,259,177	43,731	18,549	25,182	3.5	1953-1954	2,128,600	1,276,100	612,500	663,600	60.0
1899-1900	1,489,146	94,883	38,075	56,808	6.2	1955-1956	2,270,000	1,414,800	679,500	735,300	62.3
1909-1910	1,786,240	156,429	63,676	92,753	8.8	1957-1958	2,324,000	1,505,900	725,500	780,400	64.8
1919-1920	1,855,173	311,266	123,684	187,582	16.8	1959-1960	2,862,005	1,864,000	898,000	966,000	65.1
1929-1930	2,295,822	666,904	300,376	366,528	29.0	1961-1962	2,768,000	1,925,000	941,000	984,000	69.5
1939-1940	2,403,074	1,221,475	578,718	642,757	50.8	1963-1964	3,001,000	2,290,000	1,121,000	1,169,000	76.3
1941-1942	2,425,574	1,242,375	576,717	665,658	51.3	1965-1966	3,515,000	2,632,000	1,308,000	1,324,000	74.9
1943-1944	2,410,389	1,019,233	423,971	595,262	42.3	1967-1968	3,521,000	2,702,000	1,341,000	1,361,000	76.7
1945-1946	2,254,738	1,080,033	466,926	613,107	47.9	1969-1970	3,825,343	2,896,000	1,433,000	1,463,000	75.7
1947-1948	2,202,927	1,189,909	562,863	627,046	54.0	1971-1972	3,957,000	3,006,000	1,490,000	1,516,000	76.0
						1973-1974	4,096,000	3,069,000	1,512,000	1,557,000	74.9

1. Data from Bureau of the Census
2. Includes graduates of public and nonpublic schools
NOTE: Beginning in 1959-1960, includes Alaska and Hawaii

SOURCES: U.S. Department of Health, Education, and Welfare, National Center for Education Statistics, Statistics of State School Systems; Statistics of Public Elementary and Secondary Day Schools, Fall 1974; Statistics of Nonpublic Elementary and Secondary Schools; and unpublished data.

100 years or so, but the number per 100 persons 17 years of age has done no more than bounce around a bit in the last decade.

4. For a more complete description of my research experience and methods of study, please see "Appendix: Field Research as a Full Participant."

5. George Dennison makes a similar point in connection with the "First Street School," suggesting that the cost per child there was about the same as the $850 annual operating cost per pupil in the public schools. The economics of these "alternative" schools are important to an evaluation of their impact. They are not necessarily more expensive than conventional education. Therefore, decisions to pursue more conventional education must be seen as expressions of distinctive educational policies and not simply as efforts to economize.

6. Requirements for Level One diplomas included completion of the following classes: basic math, basic English, Story Workshop, and Afro-American history. In order to receive a Level Two diploma, students had course requirements in addition to those for Level One, and a Level Three diploma indicated completion of courses in addition to those required for Level Two. "Story Workshop" is a method of teaching English developed by John Schultz. It emphasizes various word games, memory exercises, "storytelling experiences," and writing exercises, all guided by a director. The director works to engage all students in these proceedings, and this collective aspect of the method is essential to its success.

These conditions for the awarding of Academy diplomas were put into effect in April 1968. Previous to this date, the Academy awarded only one form of diploma, and it was awarded to students who had completed the equivalent of four full years of high school course work. Provisions for awarding three levels of diplomas were made when it was noted that very few students would receive recognition for their work during the year at the graduation ceremony in May 1968. At this ceremony, thirty-three Academy students received diplomas indicating completion of one of the three levels. Under the old provisions, only four of these students would have received a diploma.

The cumulative nature of this process was greatly preferred to the process of "tracking" that was in evidence in conventional schools. The fact that cumulative records can provide credentials that are functionally equivalent to those provided by tracking has been pointed out by Robert Dreeben: "There is no necessary reason ... why recruitment to college and to post-high school employment cannot be tied to the cumulative achievement records of pupils who have spent their high school years in heterogeneous classrooms rather than in the relatively more homogeneous ones comprising the various tracks." My indebtedness to Dreeben's work extends far beyond this specific reference.

7. These titles correspond roughly to the significance the administration attached to the school's development. The demonstration phase was intended to test and document the practices developed during the experimental phase; the Mission administration contended that only through such documentation would significant change be brought about in existing educational systems. These titles indicate that two major goals were set for the Academy: assisting high school dropouts in the West Park community and integrating the successes of this assistance into a program of general educational reform.

CHAPTER 2

1. It might be noted, for example, that Richard Speck, when accused of brutally murdering eight women, had bail set at $115,000.

2. The excessive bails set for these six individuals effectively kept four of them in jail from April 1968 until November 1968. When the trial itself was held, the case was dropped because of lack of sufficient evidence. Similar proceedings were not uncommon with respect to Academy students and others in the community, but this case had greater significance because of the importance of the individuals to the political life of the West Park area.

3. The new advisory committee for the Academy was considered temporary, to be replaced at some time in the future by a committee whose membership included some students and parents.

CHAPTER 3

1. Buildings have a lot to do with what goes on in schools, and connections between the physical plant and social behavior have not always received the attention they deserve.

2. Although she made no general statements to the effect, in specific situations Nancy admonished students for engaging in petting because of the threat it posed to the survival of the Academy.

3. Cockey showed up at the talent show after having had several drinks, and he acted rather tipsy. The students at the door were outraged. "What do you think this is?" they asked indignantly. "How come you come to our show drunk?" Cockey replied in a rather flip tone of voice, "Well, you come to my classes stoned all the time, so I thought I'd come to your talent show drunk." The students did not take this lightly, and they accused Cockey of being very disrespectful.

4. Rev. Keen in particular was singled out by the students and staff as the source of much of the pressure to "tighten up" the operation of the school. In fact, he told me on a number of occasions that he wished he had been an engineer instead of a pastor. He expressed his great admiration of "perfectly running machinery" and took me on a tour of his church to show me the work he had completed there. In addition to refurbishing the interior, he had installed an elaborate burglar alarm system and a central console for monitoring the lighting and sound amplification. He said, "I like to think of a building as a ship, where everything ought to be in its place and the whole thing just runs real smoothly."

5. My own work draws deeply on Erving Goffman's vision of social organization as a meaningful construction of human beings.

6. My most general orientation toward social analysis has been enriched by the work of those dealing with "semiotics" and the "communication model of society."

CHAPTER 4

1. The pastor of a local church reported that his entire congregation went from all white to all black in one week. The changing of residences by the congregation of this church was a gradual and continuing process, but at one point, the white members of the congregation voted to leave this particular church and attend other churches that were closer to their new residences. At the same time, black residents from the immediate area decided to attend the church. The mechanism by which they made this decision was not revealed to me.

2. During the pilot phase, all Academy staff members were white. For the experimental phase, three were black and six were white, and the demonstration phase had four black and four white staff members.

3. For example, Neal Amidei reports:

"Do you know what a hard-core hustler wants?" asks [Rev. Keen.] "I do. I've talked to thousands of them. And I swear that while he's running dope, or lifting a radio, or doing anything else that'll keep money in his pocket, all he wants are the good things that a middle class existence can bring. And that's what every Negro is asking for when he talks black power."

The [Mission] people talk it with the best. They wear the buttons the police won't let the students wear, they make the fist, they say "Black Power" instead of "hello" to the militants. "All we're talking about is community self-determination, and an end to the frustrations that come with outside white control of business and politics."

Some of these comments seem a bit romanticized in retrospect, but their major significance lies in the presumptions of leadership by the white members of Mission in the development of black consciousness.

4. Amedei also reports: "Black Power is a matter-of-fact necessity to many of the people of [West Park], and all of the leaders of [Mission]. Everybody wants it, no one is afraid of it, and not one of them interprets it to mean violence."

5. In fact, the Mission organization, in its policy of explicit integration, provided a rationale for the continued involvement of whites in programs designed to organize blacks to promote their self-interests. Although this integration did not necessarily imply that such programs would be dominated by whites, their de facto domination was more easily maintained in an organization that emphasized "integration" and "racial harmony" as one of its goals than it would have been in an organization that sought only to achieve equality of opportunity for blacks.

6. In fact, they were frequently congratulated and complimented for the personal sacrifices they appeared to be making in order to help disadvantaged blacks achieve a sense of dignity.

7. Although the Academy added to the number of options (institutional) young blacks had in the West Park area, the additional options that they provided were largely white and controlled by whites.

8. The number of students enrolled in the school had risen from forty during the pilot phase, to 140 during the experimental phase, to over 250 during the demonstration phase. In addition, the percentage of the total student body that was female increased from sixteen percent, to twenty-one percent, to over thirty percent. As Table 2 indicates, the preparedness of students entering the Academy also improved. According to California Test Bureau exams reading levels went from 6.37 to 7.75, math levels from 6.20 to 7.29, and language levels from 5.95 to 7.40.

CHAPTER 5

1. The classic examination of schools from this perspective is Bidwell's comprehen-

sive (if tedious) article. Mission Academy, however, was very much a school without being very much of a formal organization. Of the eight characteristics of the bureaucratic form of organization that Blau has excerpted from Weber, the Academy exhibited none. In fact the only aspect of correspondence between the school and this ideal type is that personnel were placed by appointment rather than election.

2. In the early stages of my analysis of the Academy, Philip Selznik's work was of immense assistance to me. It is from him that I have borrowed the concept of "organizational character" as well as a general concern for questions of organizational integration.

3. It is in this sense that goals are "reflexive" and properties of the social situation in which they occur. They are both goals "of individuals" for the organization and "goals of the organization." The more popular practice of identifying the goals of an organization as those of its administrators is inappropriate to this kind of analysis. As my efforts are to describe the manner in which goals emerged as well as their function in making activity meaningful, this reflexive approach seems essential.

4. The dropout rate at Sherrif High School, the major public high school in the area, was about sixty percent. That is, sixty percent of those who entered the school as freshmen had dropped out before graduating. Rev. Keen's favorite analogy for describing the absurdity of the situation was, "Can you imagine General Motors allowing sixty percent of its cars to come off the line and not work, year after year?"

5. Pud was the tacit leader of the old gang and one of the students who had done little academic work in the Academy. Lamont was a new student from a different neighborhood than that of the Academy, and he had shown exceptional academic capabilities, having progressed more quickly than any of the other students in the school. Lamont was challenged a number of times by Pud to fight, but was restrained from doing so by instructors who were present. However, after lunch, Pud (and some members of what was now only an informal gang) waited for Lamont, attacked him, beat him, and burned his hat. Lamont left and indicated that he was going to get a gun and come back. During the weekend a number of attempts were made to resolve the conflict, all unsuccessfully. Lamont called me on the phone and asked me to come with him to find Pud, as he (Lamont) had a gun and wanted to kill him. I refused but arranged a supposedly "weaponless" meeting between Pud and Lamont for the following Monday morning. In fact, the meeting was not "weaponless"; neither was it productive.

6. At Mission Academy this we-ness was carefully nurtured by the staff and administration through constant references to the difference between the public schools and the Academy. Students were told, in effect: "We all understand how terrible Sherrif High School is; we understand why you dropped out, and we want to give all the other students in Sherrif the same kind of good education that you can now get here at Mission."

7. I told Rider that I was upset by the manner in which Rev. Keen imposed his aesthetic judgments on the staff and students. My remarks were precipitated by Rev. Keen's refusal to allow student paintings to be hung in the Academy lobby. I felt that hanging student paintings in the lobby would grant them much needed recognition.

8. Rev. Keen remarked once, "The only organization worth a damn in this community is [Mission]. All these other guys are just a bunch of goof-offs. This community needs [Mission] a lot more than it knows."

9. The corollary of this position had its own validity. Once, in a fit of rage and frustration at Call Strow, Rev. Keen commented to Nancy and me, "Well, I'll be damned if I'm going to raise any money so that monkey can run this school."

10. This is not to say that Nancy Sheen and Rev. Keen were not committed to

educational reform and broader social change; their commitment predated the Academy, and, in fact, was not dependent for continued expression on the school's continued operation.

11. Previous to his principalship, Call Strow had been a probation officer, and some of his parolees were students at the Academy. However, this had prompted no more than four or five visits to the school before he was hired as principal.

12. Call Strow was somewhat of an exception to this general rule, and this can be in part explained by two aspects of his life situation: first, he shared a very rich artistic, intellectual, and political life with members of the black community of the city, and this freed him from the total involvement in the Academy that most of the other staff experienced; and, second, his own evaluation of his life chances was such that, in any given year, he assumed he would either make more money than he had in the previous year or he would need less. Consequently, his imagination was somewhat less fettered by "making it" at the Academy than was the case with the rest of us.

13. The caricature of this model is that of a group of students and teachers sitting around all year long deciding what it is that they are going to learn. In fact, this did not occur at the Academy. However, a strong emphasis on student involvement in the school did disrupt the performance of the Academy's technology as it was then developed. Raising the question of what ought to be learned did take attention away from what had been prepared to be taught.

14. The exception to this was that after a number of Academy students had graduated and were attending college, parents of students were willing to trust the Acadmey's methods implicitly. By admiring the products of the Academy's technology, they were convinced of the appropriateness of its process.

15. For example, in his defense, Call Strow characterized the Academy as a "community school." His supporters, numerous black professionals and community organizers, took their cue from this statement and defined their constituency as the "Black Community." When pushed to reveal his place of private residence, one supporter remarked, "Baby, there is but *one* Black community." Simultaneous to these developments, Rev. Keen characterized the school as a Mission educational research project. This provided him with the opportunity to call upon Mission for support. The expulsion of sixteen students in April 1968 was accomplished by adhering to the "educational research" model of the school. This action could not have been taken within the framework of any of the other three models.

CHAPTER 6

1. Although these general categories suggest a summary of socioeconomic differentials of a national or citywide character, those at the Academy were also sensitive to more specialized authority differentials. Popular discourse often identifies the "haves" as the rich and powerful and the "have nots" as poor and weak. A more appropriate metaphor, however, may be the "imperatively coordinated association" described by Ralf Dahrendorf. That the "have" and "have not" terms were relatively determined is exhibited in the manner in which teachers were classified by Academy personnel. In relation to the students they taught, conventional school teachers were considered to be members of the "haves" and all "have"-oriented character elements were attributed to them. With respect to school administrators, however, these teachers were considered to be "have nots" and were seen to possess "have not" character structure.

2. This is not to suggest that Mission administrators made none of these speeches themselves or were unwilling to use "heartfelt" techniques to make their point, but only that these efforts on their part declined throughout the Academy's history. Accompany-

ing this decline, there was an increase in the amount of attention they gave to conventional educators in high places.

Early in the school's development, however, Rev. Keen and Nancy Sheen showed both persistence and virtuosity in rousing the grass roots population. In the fall of 1967, for example, local residents were organized to protest the deteriorating condition of curbs and gutters in the West Park area. As part of their protests, an evening rally was held in the yard of Rev. Keen's church. At this event, Rev. Keen not only gave a stirring speech, but then led the procession with a flaming torch as it made its way to the local aldermanic offices several blocks away. The drama of this event not only captured the attention of the community residents, but also prompted the Chicago police department to dispatch several vans of riot police to the scene of the "incident."

3. I prepared this document as part of my official duties as "Curriculum and Research Coordinator," a position to which I had been appointed during the summer months. My first task in this new position was to "write up a description of the curriculum." The title of the completed document was "[Mission] Academy: This Is a Tuned-In, Turned-On, Brand-Now School for Drop-Outs, and This Is How."

4. Emphasis on adaptation to the "American way" was in evidence not only in the remarks of the director and associate director, but also in the decor of the organization's building. As my notes indicate: "The AIET director had patriotically decorated the outer office of his large suite with a white marble statue of George Washington, nude except for a white marble fig-leaf over his genitalia and a red, white and (yes) blue American flag draped suggestively over his shoulder. Equal deliberation and love of country was evidenced in the office conference room, where two large paintings depicted the passage of the Manpower Defense Training Act, and the Guaranteed Minimum Wage. These paintings, done by the director himself, showed a facsimile of the two bills, jutting up behind a clump of white, black and yellow fists of very powerful proportions. It was incredible."

5. This admiration went beyond simple statements, and Rev. Keen purchased a copy of the Manpower Defense Training Act painting, replete with the colored fists, had it framed, and hung it in his office in the Mission building. He spoke of it admiringly, indicating that if he was an artist rather than a pastor, he would want to paint like that.

6. Although he did not state that students were discouraged from continuing their education past the eighth grade level, the director of the AIET program stated that they had no provisions for aiding students who wished to do this, nor did they intend to establish any.

7. A similar meeting held at a large West Side theater was attended by 600 to 700 students from around the city.

8. Although students were not dismissed for what was at the time considered to be their "revolutionary posture," the Academy provided few opportunities for engaging the "unacademic" or "unadapted" student. If the only recourse for students who desired such opportunities was to disrupt the proceedings of the school that they found most debilitating (i.e., the normal well-behaved student role), then such disruption can be seen to reflect the inadequacy of political options with which the school provided the students.

9. Among these references are the following: "The Academy is now seeking to create closer communication between the public schools and the program at the Academy, to share what we are learning in terms of tools and approaches" [Nancy Sheen]. "[Mission] is determined that this important demonstration of methods and approaches which work when our SYSTEM has failed not stop now when the idea has been tested and is now ready for a larger application and effectiveness" [Nancy Sheen].

"It will take several years to find out if there is justifiable merit and success in the programmed approach for inner-city education, and in the other innovative aspects of the Academy. We must have the results of several years before any convincing evidence can be obtained, and before significant influence upon the School System and other inner-city projects will be possible" [Nancy Sheen]. "Nancy thinks of [Mission] Academy as a catalyst, a framework for action, and a pilot model of a new type of inner-city education that hopefully can be transplanted to other city communities and exported to cities across the nation. . . . 'We want to develop a pattern and some new tools,' she said, 'and then get out of the education business' " [Neil Amidei]. "We need to continue to *prove* (without a doubt) that there are more effective and efficient means of educating the youth of the inner city for meaningful participation in life" [Nancy Sheen]. In the fall of 1968, when I suggested a change in the curriculum that would place more emphasis on the arts, I was told by Nancy Sheen and Rev. Keen: "We can't afford to experiment now. This year we really have to demonstrate and prove that what we do here really works, before the [public] school system will take our advice."

10. Thus they found very attractive Edward Banfield's accounts of Chicago politics. In fact, I had loaned my copy of his book to Rev. Keen. After reading it, he told me, "This is really great. It really shows you what a political leader is, just a broker between interest groups," and he further commented that he was going to recommend the book to everyone in the Mission organization.

This was not the only book that was read by Rev. Keen and Nancy Sheen and universally recommended. Another that had a similar career was George Leonard's *Education and Ecstasy*, a work that nourished the Mission administrators' efforts to change schools by "getting the ear of those in power." When I asked Rev. Keen what he thought of Leonard's book, he told me, "I thought it was just great, and we're sending copies to every member of the Chicago Board of Education, and one to Redmond [the Superintendent of Schools]."

11. Nancy Sheen and Rev. Keen expressed real enthusiasm for Richard Hauser, from the Center for Group Studies, London, England, and his writings. Hauser, a social engineer, has prepared a scheme for determining roles and missions for organizations, which has as its basic tenet: "Be conciliatory towards individuals, and aggressive towards conditions." After taking a seminar from him for ten days at the Urban Training Center, Nancy and Rev. Keen began teaching his material at suburban churches and within the Mission organization. However, these efforts did not succeed in establishing a clear mission for the Academy, in spite of the energy and enthusiasm which were brought to bear.

CHAPTER 7

1. This distinction can be illuminated with the following model: The teacher-student role relationship can be viewed as an information system in which the teacher is the encoder of messages and the student is the decoder. In this model, a distinction can be made between latent and manifest encoding and latent and manifest decoding. The concern here will be primarily with manifest encoding and manifest decoding. The latent processes inherent in this relationship will be considered in other appropriate chapters.

2. At registration, each student was given the California Test Bureau's TABE (Test of Adult Basic Education) exam. This provided a pretest of all students in the three areas of language, reading, and arithmetic. A variant form of this exam was also administered to all students in January 1968, and the arithmetic section was administered to students when they had completed the basic math class. This provided the post-test from which the achievement levels of improvement were determined.

It should be remembered that attendance at the Academy was not compulsory, and it was irregular to say the least. Forty percent of the students enrolled attended less than three days a week. No student attended his math class every day for the twelve week period, and if a student came three times a week, he or she was considered to attend regularly.

3. The improvement in grade levels of achievement during the twelve week period referred to above was characteristic of the operation of the Academy after that period of time. At no subsequent time, however, were all students tested on the mathematics section of the TABE. Rather, the Academy continued its policy of administering the exam to new students as part of their registration process and then administering it again when they had completed the work for the basic math course.

In addition, the improvement did not continue indefinitely for each student. The TABE exam did not measure student performance above the twelfth grade level, and, as a rule, students would not take the exam again after they had taken it in conjunction with completing the basic math course.

4. Each of the four science books was a different color, and each was about a different subject. Students organized the course around the colors, saying to new students, "You got to do the yellow one first, then the green," or "I already finished the yellow one; when do I get my credit?" This indicates that their concern was with a unit of analysis, not with proper organization of the subject matter. The students were asking for a clear sense of organization, not a good conceptual framework.

5. With a few exceptions (to be examined in the section on "experiential classes"), when class discussions did occur at the Academy, they did so in a relatively spontaneous manner; on some occasions, teachers were able to direct them after they were under way. For example: one day in March 1968, Hal, the science teacher, brought ten laboratory white and black mice into the science room. The students crowded around, leaving their books at their desks. They picked up the mice, stroked them, occasionally screamed and laughed, and asked a great many questions. Hal was able to guide their discussion, and in the process the students learned a great deal about genetic processes, mice, and bodily functions. Several days later, when Hal attempted to initiate another such discussion, students would not cooperate. As one student remarked, "Why you got to ask us all them silly questions? I thought you were a teacher. You're supposed to tell us things, not play with our minds."

6. In describing his class to me, Marcel commented: "Shit man, I don't know what's going on in there from one day to the next. I just show up and say, 'O.K., what do you want to learn about today?' and one of the students will say, 'Chemistry.' Then I say, 'Well, I don't know anything about chemistry; is there anyone here who does?' and some student will say 'yes', and we get to talking about it, looking things up in books, and all that. Thank god someone always says 'yes'."

7. This was similar to the "Sharper Minds" approach, but it differed in that in the "Observation and Inquiry" course there was no real control of the interaction among students, and the experimental situation was physically present rather than just invoked through reading a paragraph.

8. This process spawned some rather ironic events. On two or three occasions, a student fell asleep in my classes, and the rest of us would discuss him, the reasons for his sleeping, the nature of dreams, and so on. Upon awakening, the student would actively join in.

CHAPTER 8

1. This example is representative of the male focus of such anti-dropout literature.

Although it is popularly understood that high school is important for both males and females, there is no anti-dropout propaganda, to the best of my knowledge, that is addressed to women. 2. This notion is not new, although it has a certain contemporary impact. In 1932, Willard Waller wrote much the same in a sound, comprehensive analysis of the sociology of education. The interesting aspect of this proposition about schools is that it has been received as newsworthy. Although it corresponds to the facts of schooling with which most people are familiar, it is disjunctive with their "schooling experience." This suggests an underlying conflict between the values of "equality" and achievement." On the one hand there is some recognition that social class begets social class through the agency of individual families (e.g., marriage is endogamous with respect to class). On the other hand, there must be, for anyone to be surprised by the school's lack of intervention in this class structure, a belief in some other factor that is distributed irrespective of class and that, at least implicitly, is not hereditary. It appears that until recently many Americans felt that "intelligence" was such a factor, distributed randomly throughout the population, regardless of race, creed, social class, ethnicity, and so on. Therefore, it was assumed schools selected and promoted individuals in terms of ability which means academic achievement which means intelligence, and this process cut across the emphasis on social class itself. Perhaps as a result of belief in this peculiar variable, "intelligence," there developed such an outrage at the appearance of an article by Arthur Jensen. To suggest that this thing called "intelligence" (which was the keystone of the assumed "opportunity" offered by schools) was hereditary and pooled by endogamous marriage practices was heretical.

More generally, schools are seen, in the "opportunity" conception, to select out for some variable other than class, even though that variable itself may not be well specified. If "intelligence" receives a bad name (that is, if it becomes as "tainted" with social class and ethnic variables as has "achievement levels") another term will no doubt be coined or co-opted to take its place: for example, "creativity", "imagination", or "attitude." The lesson of all this is that if Americans wish to have an egalitarian society, they cannot establish contingencies of achievement in terms of any of these variables but must reward individuals for the simple fact of their being citizens of the social order.

3. Figures from November 1968 indicate that sixty-six percent of the students enrolled in the Academy came from the five nearest public high schools.

4. In November, 1967, seventy-nine percent of the student body was male and twenty-one percent was female. In November 1968, sixty-nine percent was male and thirty-one percent was female. There was only one white student in the school, and she graduated in June 1968.

5. The average age in November 1967 was 18.4 years; in November 1968 it was 18.1.

6. In fact, an accounting of this statistic in January 1968 showed that only one student out of thirty-eight had completed three year-long high school courses; the other thirty-seven had completed much less.

7. All of these statistics are for the day school, which was by far the most important aspect of the Academy's operation. Students enrolled in the night school were older (average age 20.8, range 16 to 41), and they had been out of school longer (average of 46.2 months) than those in the day school. Both day and night school students, however, showed a considerable range for the number of months out of school before coming to the Academy. For the day school, the range was 0 to 132 months; for the night school it was 0 to 292. In addition, there was a higher percentage of women (forty-two percent) and of married students in the night school.

8. At various times, there were from fifteen to twenty students who fell into this category.

9. For example, a white couple bringing Mose to the Academy were referred to the school by a mental health worker. Sarah was referred to the Academy by counselors of her Upward Bound program. In this respect, the Academy served as a "catch-all" for referrals from many other kinds of agencies.

10. Educationally, the average father of an Academy student had about nine years of school, the average mother about ten. About half of the students came from families in which the parents were separated, although this was never the news at Mission that it is in more middle-class settings. The accounting of these statistics was difficult, however, and based primarily on responses to registration questionaires administered to students. Some items were rarely completed, especially those on the back of the form. With sixty-five of the 113 registering students responding, forty-eight percent had parents who were living together. Only twenty-seven students indicated the number of years of their mother's education, the average of which was 10.2. For their fathers, only thirteen students responded, and the average was 8.8. One-fourth (sixteen of the sixty-four students responding) of the students indicated that no member of their family had completed high school.

11. The scores of both male and female students were about one-half grade level higher in the reading section than they were for the mathematics section, and female scores slightly exceeded those of male students on the language portion of the exam. At the Academy, we assumed that these ability levels were higher than they might have been had students not gone to school at all, but that is an empirical question yet to be answered.

12. Apparently, there was no question as to the fact of the killing. However, in order to convict someone accused of a third-degree murder, it must be shown that their actions were clearly premeditated. A contemporaneous magazine article by Amidei contained the following reference to the trial: " 'It was a case of self-defense,' says [Nancy], who spent days at the court, and obtained a professor from John Marshall Law School to defend the boy."

13. When Lamont visited his former principal at Derrick High School and told him of these achievements, the principal remarked, "Well, you are the *best* student I've ever kicked out of Derrick."

14. At that university, approximately fifty of the 16,000 students were black.

15. Although Walter was not the only one singled out for abuse, he was the student most visibly and consistently treated in this manner. Lamont was particularly incensed by Walter's continual deference and obeisance and on one occasion physically beat him in an attempt to get Walter to strike back. Lamont also told me about how he got fired from a well-paying factory job. One day on a lunch break, his supervisor told Lamont that he loved him and asked him if they could live together. I asked Lamont how he replied to that, and he said, "Hell, I fired on the dude, hit him right in the fucking mouth. What else could I do?"

16. One exception to this was the award, made at the Academy's graduation, for the "most progress made" during the year. But even here, it was "progress" and not achievement or ranking that was being affirmed.

CHAPTER 9

1. This was a person whom they felt would be totally unacceptable as a teacher at the Academy. Nancy reported that he came to see them drunk, disheveled, and acted like a madman. This candidate, it turned out, was known to Call Strow, and when I

related to him Nancy's remarks, he howled with laughter. "They're right," Call Strow said, "he's probably the weirdest, craziest mother-fucker I know."

2. It seems likely that other criteria were active in selecting and not selecting staff members at the school, but these frequently involved such personalistic judgments that they were not accessible to me.

3. In this case, "basic" frequently meant having studied the subject or some advanced form of it in college or within the framework of previous employment.

4. The term "maladjusted" is not used here in a pejorative sense. In fact, my own prejudice is to recognize "adjustment" to the conventional social order as a dangerous malady. The staff sought to correct the "maladjustment" by changing the social order, not just by changing themselves.

5. Some of the rewards offered to the staff for their participation in the Academy were quite conventional. During the pilot and experimental phases, an attempt was made to pay staff members salaries equal to the minimum paid to public school teachers in Chicago. During the experimental phase, this attempt fell about ten percent short of its intended mark, and a raise in public school salaries the following year increased the disparity to about fifteen percent. In a comparison with public school benefits, Academy teachers suffered not only smaller salaries, but also a lack of "fringe benefits." The Academy was incorporated as a small nonprofit corporation, and it did not pay premiums for unemployment compensation and disability benefits, nor did it offer a staff health plan. Staff members did not sign contracts and had very limited avenues for legal redress with the Mission administration.

6. Don Flournoy describes how a group of college teachers have made and used a "second chance" at teaching.

CHAPTER 10

1. In Herndon's classes, he was playing with a distinction between kinds of social order, one that is similar to a distinction Lemert has made between "passive" and "active" social control.

2. All forty students at the meeting were black, with one exception. "Sister" referred to "soul sister" or black female; "brother" referred to "soul brother" or black male.

3. This rule was "recommended" by Nancy Sheen, principal of the Academy; all other rules were suggested and recommended by the students themselves.

4. On one occasion however a student who had been harassing me struck a cigarette out of my mouth with a rolled up newspaper. I flushed with anger and literally threw him out of the room and into the adjoining hall. Other students were not surprised or disapproving of what I had done; in fact, they suggested that I should act that way more often. This would indicate that the avoidance of direct, interpersonal authoritarian behavior which was characteristic of the teachers in the school was not accurately based on student opinions of such behavior.

5. "Wrong ideas" to this woman were contained in the writings of Black Power advocates and often involved the use of conventionally determined "obscene expressions."

6. On two occasions I was stopped and frisked by local policemen while waiting for a bus at a nearby bus stop. On the second occasion, they launched into a torrent of derogatory remarks about the school. The three policemen who detained me the second time indicated a rather thorough knowledge of who I was, where I lived, where I had gone to college, and where the school was located. None of them had been present at the first incident. This suggests that there may well have been a police file on the Academy,

its students, and its teachers. Such a file was never used in prosecuting the Academy as an organization, but it might have been used against individual students.

CHAPTER 11

1. The importance of this ideal should not be underestimated. Even though events might appear to contradict claims that this ideal was realized in the Academy, this was not the experience of staff, students, and the administrators. They acted on their perceptions of the school, and they frequently perceived it as a cooperative endeavor.

2. A number of incidents illustrating this fact have already been described: the expulsion of students for being "not for real"; the incidents surrounding the "danger list" of December 18, 1967; the conflict over use of the rooms in the new building; the efforts of the Mission administration to restrict access to the building itself by limiting to one person the number of Academy staff who could legitimately possess keys. An additional example of "non-cooperation" was the planning of a conference sponsored by Mission in the fall of 1968 which was entitled "Crisis in Education." The conference, originally designed to be sponsored by the Academy, was actually planned without any participation from Academy personnel. Nancy Sheen drew up the list of proposed participants without any consultation with Call Strow, who was then principal of the Academy. When he confronted her with accusations that she had acted in an unethical manner, she replied, "Well, I just treated the Academy as if it was any of the other schools which have been invited to attend."

3. At times these exchanges could be compromising. On one occasion, Rennard was in jail and a friend was collecting money for his release on bail. Nancy agreed to contribute $50, but only if she was given a security deposit. Rennard's friend brought her an expensive AM-FM table radio in excellent condition, and she handed over the money. After Rennard was out of jail, he stole the radio from Nancy's office, insisting that it was really his and not hers because he had stolen it in the first place. Nancy threatened to call the police, but withdrew as she recognized the hollowness of the threat. In order to charge Rennard with theft, she would have to admit possession of the stolen radio herself.

4. Rev. Keen often suggested putting the Academy on a strict money basis, whereby students would be rewarded with money for doing well. The staff found this to be totally unacceptable.

CHAPTER 12

1. In some sense the Academy had "heated up" students—in terms of their ambitions, confidence, and abilities—to the point where a normal college scene would effectively "cool them out." Burton Clark has described how student aspirations were deliberately lowered by administrators in one community college, and L. Steven Zwerling has described another community college where student aspirations were deliberately raised. Pygmalion is to be found not only in the classroom, but also in the whole of American schooling.

2. In 1971 for example, the Chicago Board of Education funded a program to introduce the Story Workshop techniques to groups of interested public high school teachers, a consequence not only of the success of the workshop at Mission Academy, but also of its similar success at Columbia College.

3. While this should be clear to anyone who casts more than a passing glance at schools, the rhetoric and ideology of "equal opportunity" have kept many proponents of educational reform uninformed about the manner in which the school system functions in the larger society. Analysis of this "winning and losing" dynamic has been

clearly stated, in spite of the lack of attention it receives, by James Herndon, Everett Reimer (who has discussed "winners and losers" as international dimensions of national educational systems), and Morris Janowitz, who has written that, "The American school system is adapted to facilitating the mobility of individuals rather than dealing with problems of group mobility. . . . Again, it needs to be stated that group mobility depends, of course, on fundamental social change, such as the introduction of the negative income tax and the elimination of outmoded systems of social welfare."

4. The terms "aggregation" and "specialization" are those of Morris Janowitz. The explication of these two models as "student-coherent" and "knowledge-coherent" is my own, however, and does not accurately represent Janowitz's remarks on the issue.

5. There is already a sizable body of literature on what might be called the "institutional self," a distinctive configuration of behavior, identity, and feeling which develops as a response to institutional settings.

Appendix

Research as a Full Participant

In the fall of 1967 I was hired to teach mathematics, physical science, social science, and art at Mission Academy. I took the position at the school in part because I wanted to reform conventional educational systems, an objective which the administration of the school identified as their own. In addition, I looked forward to "making like a sociologist" in an environment other than that of graduate school course work.

For eighteen months I was actively involved in the school and the welfare of its students and teachers. In addition to the teaching for which I was initially hired, I took on the responsibilities of Research and Curriculum Coordinator in September of 1968. Throughout my stay at the Academy I sought to record, report on, document, and describe its operation.

These efforts were not always encouraged by the administrators of the school, and on several occasions they requested that I curtail my "research and analysis" and devote a greater portion of my time to teaching. On two occasions I was told explicitly by students not to write anything about anyone who went to the Academy. Although my fellow teachers were more encouraging, they usually attempted to impress on me the practical limitations of my research, and two of them suggested that the Academy would operate better if its de facto structure were not public knowledge.

The climate in which I was doing research was not a simple one, as this should indicate, and yet most of the time I was accepted or tolerated as a researcher by most of the people. The fact that some of the people some of the time asked me not to continue was seen by me as an obstacle to research rather than a general censure by those whom I was studying.

My research at the school was cut short, however, when I was fired for protesting, in my own way, the firing of Call Strow. This abrupt end to my stay at the Academy came as a surprise, and it kept me from finding answers to some of the questions I was asking about the school. On the other hand, it put me in touch with elements of the Academy's operation that otherwise I might have easily overlooked. In completing my analysis of the school, my goals were much more than academic; I needed to know, for my personal peace of mind, how this place operated. The following account should provide an introduction to the matter, and I think it illustrates both the assets and liabilities of doing research as a full, bona fide participant.

When the Mission Council, or at least part of it, voted to fire Call Strow, I was outraged. In addition to my feeling for the good influence he had on the Academy, he was a good friend and delightful colleague. His loss from the school was made all the more disturbing to me by the unfairness and deception that surrounded the vote to fire him.

Late one night I received a call from one of the Mission pastors telling me that Call had been fired. I quickly called Cockey, Rider, and others to tell them. We were all incredulous, as the Council had recently given him a strong vote of confidence. All of us felt that something should be done, but we were unclear about what to do.

The next morning, when the teachers arrived at the Academy, we found it locked; after an argument with Nave Sheen, he let us in. Meeting as a staff we drafted a statement protesting Call's firing and demanding that any hearing at which our attendance was requested would be open to other staff members as well. We felt that the issue involved us as a group, and we wanted to be dealt with as a group. The Mission administrators took our statement under advisement, guaranteed our right to open meetings, and the business of the Academy continued much as usual.

In working to reinstate Call as principal, however, some of us took our case beyond the Academy itself, and this greatly displeased the Mission administrators. Cockey and Marcel appeared on a Chicago radio station, speaking in defense of Call and accusing the larger Mission organization of being racially insensitive and dictatorial. An article sympathetic to Call also appeared in a small underground newspaper published by some friends of Theodore.

What seemed to upset the Mission administrators the most, however, was a letter that Cockey and I surreptitiously placed in copies of Theodore's Afro-American history text the day before it was to be bound. This letter, which appeared as a supplement to the first chapter, described the firing of Call Strow and criticized the Mission Council, Nancy Sheen, and Rev. Keen for what they had done. It would be fair to say that our letter described them as hypocritical and self-serving.

The unknowing administrators bound the letter into the book and began sending copies to selected places around the country. When they finally noticed our special "supplement," they had already sent several dozen of the books on their way.

This book was controversial in its own right. Theodore wanted to give copies to his Academy students who, he felt, had assisted him in preparing it. He also wanted any money received from the sale of the book to go toward college scholarships for Academy graduates. Nancy Sheen and Rev. Keen, however, wanted to use the books for public relations efforts. While several of the staff argued for Theodore's position, Nancy and Rev. Keen locked the books in the safe deposit vault, a handy leftover from the building's former tenant (a bank).

All this was taking place during the week before and after Call was fired. While the distress of teachers at these events was accumulating, someone noticed the letter. This discovery was made public at a Mission Council meeting to which Academy staff had been invited, and one of the Mission administrators demanded to know who had written it. I spoke up and said that I had written it and that I wanted to discuss its contents. Even in the face of this explicit admission, members of the Council continued to ask,

"Who could have written this?" No one acknowledged my willingness to discuss the letter, and the whole business only came to an end when, amidst a great deal of yelling and screaming among the Council members, one elderly woman rose from her chair and said:

> Quiet! Quiet! Now, you know we are all Christian people. And, as Cristian people, you know that we learn to recognize the devil when we see him! And, as Christian people, you know that when we see the devil, we have to get rid of him!

Her remarks were punctuated by a great deal of hand-clapping (particularly by white Mission administrators) and sporadic shouts of "yeah," "you tell him," and "amen"; and they were followed by a motion that three of us (Cockey, Marcel, and myself) be asked to meet with the Mission Personnel Committee to determine our future status with the school.

While we agreed to meet with the Personnel Committee at the proper time, we insisted that our earlier agreement, which would allow other teachers to be present at such a meeting, be recognized. This the Personnel Committee refused to do. Meeting in closed session, without any of the staff present, the committee voted to fire Cockey and me. At the news of this action, two additional staff members resigned. Two days later I received a letter indicating that my subsequent presence in the Mission building would be considered "hostile trespass."

•Although I maintain personal relationships with friends and coworkers at the Academy, I have not visited the school since. I doubt the injunction of hostile trespass is still in effect, but few of my aquaintances remain there. The students I knew have left, as have most of the teachers. At last word, Nancy Sheen was still working hard in the Mission organization, and Marcel was the principal. I wish them all well. I'm sure that time has taken the punch out of some of the conflicts that surrounded my own departure from the Academy. For that I should be grateful, and yet I am a little sad. In some respects, they were the life of the school.

As an observer, I could record and describe many organizational features of the Academy. It was as a full participant, however—as I was in the events surrounding my being fired from the Academy—that the "life of the school" was made most accessible to me. Some might argue that concern with something as ephemeral as "the life" of an enterprise is beside the point, that this is an inappropriate object of empirical investigation. I contend, however, that the ultimate goal of science is no less than the exploration and understanding of the universe; no matter where we might begin our inquiry, we are led to important questions about existence, reality, meaning, and the lives we might live. In social science, the subjects of our study are no less complex than we are, and to understand what they do and why, we must pay attention to all those features of our human condition that bring inspiration, sorrow, passion, and despair to our own lives. Within an outline of what it is that people do, I argue, the "life of the situation" is precisely the question social scientists ought to investigate. Following are a few notes about my understanding of this process at Mission Academy.

MAKING SENSE OF THE FIELD:
PERSONAL AND EXTRAPERSONAL VALIDITY

As a social scientist I tried to understand the social world I was part of at Mission Academy. This goal of "understanding" in social research has been dealt with at length lately (e.g., by Truzzi, Glaser and Strauss [1965], and Psathas), but my own conceptualization of it may be useful to the reader in "understanding" what I have done.

Three kinds of understanding are real to me: the satisfaction of personal curiosity; the familiarity needed to successfully negotiate the social world at issue; and the logical and analytical coherence required to communicate about what I observed to others.

I am curious about social phenomena. I care about how it is that people make sense out of their lives; how institutions are designed; the manner in which goals and ideals are realized, transformed, or abandoned; and the rich variety of social and cultural forms. I want to know about these things, and I enjoy deep personal reward when I feel I am familiar with the life manifest in social situations. I doubt this distinguishes me from others. I see it rather as a crucial point of connection between the reader and the researcher.

Research in this book represents personal understanding that has been put to two tests, two trials of evidence. In the first place, my full involvement placed constant demands on my understanding of Mission Academy. As a member, the success or failure of my efforts to negotiate the social structure were in part determined by how well I understood it.[1] I assume there to be a social reality that is distinct from my personality. I am less interested in whether this reality is inside or outside my self than I am in the pattern of incongruities that exists between my states of "feeling I understood" and reactions and behavior of others that indicated to me that I did not. In this way, whatever I thought to be true of the situation was constantly tested as I tried to take care of myself in it. Some ideas I had about Mission Academy were not validated in everyday efforts to make my way around the place, and some were, thus refining my cognitive model.[2]

In the continuing debate about different research methods, this trial by fire points to an asset of participant observation in which the observer participates as a bona fide member. Such membership provides "predictive" tests of hypotheses that those at greater remove will never know.

The second test of my personal understanding was that presented in communicating my observations and experiences to others. I assume that such communication requires a coherence of observation and analysis, a comment in itself on my own construction of social reality. In this case, the work of translation from my personal voice to that of someone else required the intermediate expression in some shared, and as such, more abstract language.³ The refinement of my explanatory model of Mission Academy that this interpersonal communication engendered was not a simple matter. The increased validity of my analysis that it provided, however, may be irrespective of the "others" to whom I was communicating.

I found that my "translations" were addressed to several audiences, each with a distinctive language: professional sociologists; educational reformers; the subjects of my study; and the literate public. Thus I tried to take my personal understanding and cast it in terms familiar to my colleagues in sociology. I used at times a sociological vocabulary and relied on a tradition of literature and research to make the appropriate connections.

And yet I tried to stay within the bounds of literate English, avoiding the temptation to translate into exclusively sociological terms when the sense of the matter could be just as easily communicated in more common expressions. I tried to speak to the subjects of my study as well, not only in respecting their versions of the place as the social reality in which they acted, but also in staying as close as possible in my analysis to events and patterns of behavior that had some salience to those who worked at the Academy. And through all this I tried to present a picture of the school's operation that has logical and analytical coherence, an effort to work over my observations and experience into mutually exclusive and exhaustive categories and to organize them into meaningful relations.

The book is oriented toward all these concerns, both in research and in writing. My research methods were inspired by the same groups for whom I wrote: sociologists, reformers, my subjects, and the literate public. And I found out things about the Academy that allowed me to survive there as a member, to satisfy my curiosity, and to act as a representative of one or more of these presumptive audiences. At times I was a sociologist and acted like one. At other times, I was a literate citizen or a social analyst. And there were occasions when I was only a member-subject, my actions and being integrated only through the immediate, real-time, live consequences of my behavior at the school. Thus my interests and efforts exhibited a constant fluctuation in and out of these identity orientations, each of them contributing something of value to the overall effort of understanding the social structure and process of Mission Academy.⁴

In all of this I have been well served by my memory of life at the school—memory supplemented by notes, copies of letters, documents, and informal interviews, but memory all the same. I did not take very systematic or regular field notes, nor did I conduct many formal or comparable interviews. I wrote lengthy accounts of events which interested me at the time, and I talked with other members of the school when there was something I wanted to learn from them, tell to them, or share with them. And I collected literally hundreds of documents, ranging from official publications of or about the Academy to handwritten memos and dittoed notes of curriculum meetings. These more "informal" documents have been impossible to footnote or put in bibliographical form, and some of them may exist only in my personal collection.

BIAS AND POINT OF VIEW

In a well-known address as President of the Society for the Study of Social Problems, Howard Becker observed that when social scientists accept official and superordinate statements as valid descriptions of social life it is usually seen as an expression of simple respect and value neutrality. When the statements of subordinates are accepted as valid, however, researchers are typically accused of partisan involvement. I share much of Becker's analysis, and I think the reader has a right to know whose side I am on.

For the last ten years, I have participated in activities aimed at making this country less racist, sexist, and economically exploitative than it is. Genetic and economic privilege within the structure of American society enrage me, and I set myself clearly against the dehumanizing effects of many organizations and social institutions. In general terms I advocate civil liberties, socialist or cooperative economic arrangements, and human potential.

My sympathies are usually with the "lower" person or group in any authority relationship, but I offer no comfort to those who enjoy their status as victims. Individuals I respect more than groups, groups more than institutions, and institutions more than the larger social order. I am perfectly comfortable demonstrating with students against inhumane teachers, as well as with teachers against oppressive administrators. Upon occasion, I will even show my support for school administrators in a conflict with the state legislature.

I am sure that my prejudices have emerged time and time again in the pattern of what I have noticed and commented upon. I did not deliberately work them in, but I could not keep them out. They are the elements of my particular intelligence, and they stand as the products of my civic imagination. For example, a reader of an earlier version of this manuscript said that I seemed innocent or naive in my contention that organizations and institutions owe things to individuals. I admit to an innocence and naivete here, but none greater than that of the person who thinks that individuals owe things to organizations. I happen to think that social structures and organizations exist in order to make life possible for human beings; when they no longer serve that function, they ought to be dismantled or detoxified. That is my politics. I consider those who think otherwise to be wrong-headed and in need of a change of consciousness at the very least.

I submit that this does not make the book anything more or less than other studies of the social order. However, I do acknowledge the importance of personal contributions to this kind of sociological analysis. Furthermore, I feel that social scientists have a deep responsibility to explicitly reveal their sympathies to the reader. Like it or not, the sympathies are there, and to suggest that we can be at the same time familiar with social realities, detached from their implications, and still desirous of writing about them is wholly naive. Books neither write themselves nor are they written by unsocialized and uninvolved creatures.

Does this mean the book is biased? If by "biased" we mean untrue or distorted, then I would say no, it is not biased. But if we are asking, "Does this book show things from a certain point of view?" then I would answer yes, most assuredly, and I would add that this is the only way we ever see anything. While this account is not the only one to be made of it all, I present it as the best I can give, the one which goes farthest toward describing and explaining how a building, a group of individuals, and some ideas came to be Mission Academy.[5]

I have relied in my presentation on a complex narrative, one which is reliable and yet subjective, removed but personally revealing, informed and still innocent of much. I had to acknowledge what my subjects thought of themselves and each other, as well as the form of my agreement or disagreement with these appraisals. I also had to show how their impressions of the larger social world, accurate or not, influenced what they did at the Academy. And I tried, though I think with less success, to trace the natural history of these impressions and to assess the degree to which they were accurate, true or well-founded.

The result is not a simple account, and there are numerous opportunities for the reader to fall away from the multiple realities I have tried to examine. I hope they are not too tempting, for I have nothing simple in mind—no villans, no heroes, no easy solutions to bad schooling. My sympathies should be clear; I hope they are a useful context for my commentary.

NOTES TO APPENDIX

1. Informative publications dealing with this interaction have been presented by Roy Turner (especially Part Two and Part Three), Barney Glaser and Anselm Strauss [1964], Mathew Speier, and Severyn Bruyn in William Filstead.

2. The problems of the participant-observer have been discussed by Harold Garfinkel, Howard S. Becker, and Norman K. Denzin.

3. C.W. Mills makes a nice distinction between the "context of discovery" and the "context of presentation," and this clearly applied to my own work: "You will get new ideas as you work in the context of presentation. In short, it will become a new context of discovery, different from the original one, on a higher level I think, because more socially objective." I urge anyone interested in "doing social research" to look closely at the appendix (entitled, "On Intellectual Craftsmanship") to Mills' book. It is a highly informative, candid, and revealing account of the connections between "being" a social scientist and "doing" social research.

4. For readers interested in the complexities of these issues, I recommend the work of Leonard Schatzman and Anselm L. Strauss, John Lofland, John O'Neill, M. Patricia Golden, and George Lewis.

5. I hope that my own narrative achieves some of the effect that Mills describes so well in his appendix, "On Intellectual Craftsmanship," to *The Sociological Imagination.* He writes, "One way [of presenting the work of social science] results from the idea that he [the writer] is a man who may shout, whisper, or chuckle—but who is always there. It is also clear what sort of man he is: whether confident or neurotic, direct or involuted, he *is* a center of experience and reasoning; now he has found out something, and he is

telling us about it, and how he found it out."

I owe a great but indirect debt to this work by Mills. I have not been influenced by it in what I have done, for I only read it after having written the body of this book. On the other hand, reading his analysis and account of the sociological enterprise has given me the courage to, in effect, "come out of the closet." Finding in his writing to be such a clear and sensible confirmation of my own concerns has made it possible for me to "be" a sociologist. In some sense he is the colleague for whom I was always writing, without knowing it; his work has made it possible for me to publicly affirm my own.

References and Further Readings

1. Schooling and School Reform

AMIDEI, N. (1967) "Second chance in a 'classic' ghetto." Chicagoland and FM Guide (September): 37.

――― (1969) "Architecture and education." Harvard Educational Review 34.

ASHTON-WARNER, S. (1963) *Teacher*. New York: Simon & Schuster.

BARTON, A. (1970) "The hard-soft school," and "Soft boxes in hard schools," pp. 183-208 in S. Repo (ed.) *This Book Is About Schools*. New York: Vintage.

BECKER, H.S. (ed.) 1970) *Campus Power Struggle*. Chicago: Aldine.

BIDWELL, C. (1965) "The school as a formal organization," in J.G. March (ed.) *Handbook of Organizations*. Chicago: Rand McNally.

――― (1970) "Students and schools: Some observations on client trust in client-serving organizations," in W. Rosengren and M. Lefton (eds.) *Organizations and Clients: Essays in the Sociology of Service*. Columbus: Merrill.

BREMER, J. and M. MOSCHZISKER (1971) *The School Without Walls*. New York: Holt, Rinehart & Winston.

CICOUREL, A. V. and J. I. KITSUSE (1968) "The social organization of the high school and deviant adolescent careers," in E. Rubington and M. S. Weinberg (eds.) *Deviance: The Interactionist Perspective*. London: Crowell Collier Macmillan.

CLARK, B. (1960) *The Open Door College*. New York: McGraw-Hill.

――― (1962) *Educating the Expert Society*. San Francisco: Chandler.

COTTLE, T. J. (1971) *Time's Children*. Boston: Little, Brown.

DENNISON, G. (1969) *The Lives of Children*. New York: Random House.

DREEBEN, R. (1968) *On What Is Learned in School*. Reading, Mass.: Addison-Wesley.

FARBER, J. (1969) *The Student as Nigger*. New York: Contact.

FENNESSEY, J. and M. S. McDILL (1971) "Elementary school as a social system," pp. 262-268 in *Encyclopedia of Education*, Volume 8. New York: Macmillan and Free Press.

FLUORNOY, D. (ed.) (1972) *The New Teachers*. San Francisco: Chandler.

FREIRE, P. (1973) *Pedagogy of the Oppressed*. New York: Seabury.

GROSS, R. and B. GROSS (eds.) (1969) *Radical School Reform*. New York: Simon & Schuster.

HALL, D. J. (1971) "A case for teacher continuity in inner-city schools." School Review 80 (November): 27-49.

HENTOFF, N. (1966) *Our Children Are Dying*. New York: Viking.

HERNDON, J. (1968) *The Way It Spozed To Be*. New York: Bantam.

――― (1972) *How To Survive in Your Native Land*. New York: Bantam.

HOLT, J. (1966) *How Children Fail*. New York: Pitman.

――― (1967) *How Children Learn*. New York: Pitman.

ILLICH, I. (1970) *Deschooling Society*. New York: Harper & Row.

JANOWITZ, M. (1969) *Institution Building in Urban Education*. Hartford, Conn.: Russell Sage.

JENSEN, A. (1969) "How much can we boost IQ and scholastic achievement?" Harvard Educational Review 39 (Winter): 1-123.

KOHL, H. (1968) *Thirty-Six Children*. New York: Signet.

KOZOL, J. (1968) *Death at an Early Age.* New York: Bantam.

LEHMAN, C. (1967) "The physical plant," pp. 266-282 in P. H. Rossi and B. Biddle (eds.) *The New Media and Education.* Garden City, N.Y.: Doubleday Anchor.

LEONARD, G. (1968) *Education and Ecstasy.* New York: Delacorte.

NEILL, A. S. (1960) *Summerhill.* New York: Hart.

POSTMAN, N. and C. WEINGARTNER (1969) *Teaching as a Subversive Acitvity.* New York: Delacrote.

PRATT, C. (1948) *I Learn from Caroline.* New York: Simon & Schuster.

RAFFERTY, M. (1965) "The cult of the slob," in F. R. Smith and R. B. McQuigg (eds.) *Secondary Schools Today: Readings for Educators.* Boston: Houghton Mifflin.

REIMER, E. (1971) *School Is Dead.* Harmondsworth, Eng.: Penguin.

REPO, S. (ed.) (1970) *This Book Is About Schools.* New York: Vintage.

RYAN, K. (ed.) (1970) *Don't Smile Until Christmas: Accounts of the First Year of Teaching.* Chicago: University of Chicago Press.

SILBERMAN, C. E. (1971) *Crisis in the Classroom.* New York: Vintage.

WAGNER, J. (1971) "Model building," pp. 65-70 in D. Fluornoy (ed.) *The New Teachers.* San Francisco: Jossey-Bass.

——— (1971) "Education and 'Black' education: Some remarks on cultural relevance." School Review 80 (August): 591-602.

WALLER, W. (1932) *The Sociology of Teaching.* New York: John Wiley.

——— (1968) "Where dropouts tune in." Saturday Review (December 21): 54.

——— (1968) "Where failures make the grade: Two schools for dropouts." Carnegie Quarterly 16 (Fall): 1-5.

ZWERLING, L.S. (1976) *Second Best: The Crisis of the Community College.* New York: McGraw-Hill.

2. Social Theory

BANFIELD, E. C. (1961) *Political Influence.* New York: Free Press.

BARTHES, R. (1970) *Elements of Semiology.* Boston: Beacon.

BECKER, H. S. (1963) *Outsiders: Studies in the Sociology of Deviance.* New York: Free Press.

——— (1967) "Whose side are we on?" Social Problems 14 (Winter): 239-247.

BLAU, P. (1955) *The Dynamics of Bureaucracy.* Chicago: University of Chicago Press.

COHEN, A. (1966) *Deviance and Control.* Englewood Cliffs, N.J.: Prentice-Hall.

COLE, S. and R. LEJEUNE (1972) "Illness and the legitimation of failure." American Sociological Review 37 (June): 347-356.

DAHRENDORF, R. (1959) *Class and Class Conflict in Industrial Society.* Stanford: University Press.

DORNBUSH, S. M. (1955) "The military academy as an assimilating institution." Social Forces 33 (May): 316-321.

DREITZEL, H. P. (ed.) (1970) *Recent Sociology No. 2.* New York: Macmillan.

FLACKS, R. (1971) *Youth and Social Change.* Chicago: Markham.

GEERTZ, C. (1974) "Deep play: Notes on the Balinese cockfight," in C. Geertz (ed.) *Myth, Symbol and Culture.* New York: W. W. Norton.

GLASER, B. and A. STRAUSS (1964) "Awareness contexts and social interaction." American Sociological Review 29 (October): 669-679.

GOFFMAN, E. (1961) *Asylums.* Garden City, N.Y.: Doubleday Anchor.

GUSFIELD, J. R. (1963) *Symbolic Crusade.* Urbana: University of Illinois Press.

HABERMAS, J. (1970) "Toward a theory of communicative competence," pp. 115-148 in H. P. Dreitzel (ed.) *Recent Sociology No. 2.* New York: Macmillan.

JANOWITZ, M. (1976) *Social Control of the Welfare State.* New York: Elsevier.

LEMERT, E. (1967) *Human Deviance, Social Problems, and Social Control.* Englewood Cliffs, N.J.: Prentice-Hall.
LIEBOW, E. (1967) *Tally's Corner.* Boston: Little, Brown.
LYMAN, S. and M. A. SCOTT (1970) *A Sociology of the Absurd.* New York: Appleton-Century-Crofts.
MANNING, P. K. (1972) "Locks and keys: An essay on privacy," pp. 82-94 in J. Henslin (ed.) *Down to Earth Sociology.* New York: Free Press.
MILLS, C. W. (1959) *The Sociological Imagination.* New York: Oxford University Press.
MOORE, W. E. (1963) *Social Change.* Englewood Cliffs, N.J.: Prentice-Hall.
MUELLER, C. (1970) "Notes on the repression of communicative behavior," pp. 101-113 in H. P. Dreitzel (ed.) *Recent Sociology No. 2.* New York: Macmillan.
PARSONS, T. (1964) *The Social System.* New York: Free Press.
PERROW, C. (1967) "A framework for the comparative analysis of organizations." American Journal of Sociology 71: 194-208.
SELZNICK, P. (1957) *Leadership in Administration.* Evanston, Ill: Row, Peterson.
SHAPIRO, J. (1970) "One-dimensionality: The universal semiotic of technological experience," in P. Breines (ed.) *Critical Interruptions.* New York: Herder & Herder.
SLATER, P. (1970) *The Pursuit of Loneliness.* Boston: Beacon.
SUTTLES, G. D. (1968) *The Social Order of the Slum.* Chicago: University of Chicago Press.
——— (1972) *The Social Construction of Communities.* Chicago: University of Chicago Press.
WOLFE, T. (1970) *Radical Chic and Mau-mauing the Flak Catchers.* New York: Farrar, Strauss & Giroux.
YABLONSKY, L. (1959) "The delinquent gang as a near-group." Social Problems 7: 108-117.

3. Research Methods
BECKER, H. S. (1958) "Problems of inference and proof in participation observation." American Sociological Review 23 (December): 652-660.
DENZIN, N. K. (1970) *The Research Act: A Theoretical Introduction to Sociological Methods.* Chicago: Aldine.
FILSTEAD, W. (ed.) (1970) *Qualitative Methodology: Firsthand Involvement with the Social World.* Chicago: Markham.
GARFINKEL, H. (1972) "Common sense knowledge of social structures: The documentary method of interpretation," pp. 356-378 in J. Manis and B. Meltzer (eds.) *Symbolic Interaction: A Reader in Social Psychology.* Boston: Allyn & Bacon.
GLASER, B. and A. STRAUSS (1965) "Discovery of substantive theory: A basic strategy underlying qualitative research." American Behavioral Scientist 3 (February): 5-12.
GOLDEN, P. M. (ed.) (1976) *The Research Experience.* Itasca, Ill.: F. E. Peacock.
LEWIS, G. (ed.) (1975) *Fist-fights in the Kitchen: Manners and Methods in Social Research.* Pacific Palisades, Calif.: Goodyear.
LOFLAND, J. (1971) *Analyzing Social Settings.* Belmont, Calif.: Wadsworth.
O'NEILL, J. (1972) *Sociology as a Skin Trade.* New York: Harper & Row.
PSATHAS, G. (1968) "Ethomethods and phenomenology." Social Research 35 (September): 500-520.
SCHATZMAN, L. and A. L. STRAUSS (1973) *Field Research: Strategies for a Natural Sociology.* Englewood Cliffs, N.J.: Prentice-Hall.
SPEIER, M. (1973) *How To Observe Face-to-Face Communication: A Sociological*

Introduction. Pacific Palisades, Calif.: Goodyear.

TRUZZI, M. (ed.) (1974) *Verstehen: Subjective Understanding in the Social Sciences.* Reading, Mass.: Addison-Wesley.

TURNER, R. (ed.) (1974) *Ethonomethodology: Selected Readings.* Baltimore: Penguin.

About the Author

JON WAGNER is presently Lecturer and Academic Coordinator in the Field Studies Program, an undergraduate teaching program in field-based, experiential education, at the University of California, Berkeley. In addition, he is a member of the Anthropology-Sociology Department at Trenton State College, from which he is currently on leave. In his varied professional career, he has been an instructor at Columbia College (Chicago, Illinois) and at the school called "Mission Academy" in this book, an urban research intern with the Model Cities Program (Washington, D.C.), an engineering aide at the Stanford Linear Accelerator Center, and a play supervisor at the Peninsula Children's Center (Menlo Park, California). He received his Ph.D. in sociology from the University of Chicago in 1971. His current research and writing focus on experiential education, patterns of personal troubles and social structure, and environmental design. These areas reflect his general interest in the sociology of service and social reform. His recent field work and teaching have emphasized the use of photography in social research.

Date Due